While many books have simply focused [...] *People of God* also explores other issues [...] including modern cultural and theological developments [...] read ancient texts and think about God and gender. This book is certain to help many Christians wrestling with gender issues.

ROY E. CIAMPA, manager for biblical scholarship and integrated training, Nida Institute for Biblical Scholarship

It is a pleasure to endorse Dr. Alice Mathews's book. It is a tender, compassionate explanation of the teaching of Scripture on this delicate subject. Her desire is to be fair to what our Lord has taught in his Word, not to win an argument. I urge Christ's church to center its thinking on this topic with Alice's firm base on Scripture rather than numerous alternative routes that are often used to discuss this topic.

WALTER C. KAISER JR., president emeritus, Gordon-Conwell Theological Seminary

In this book, Dr. Alice Mathews harvests a lifetime of serious scholarship and practical ministry experience in the church and academy to make a cogent case— biblical, historical, theological, and practical—for the liberation and employment of the spiritual gifts of all God's gifted and called people, both women and men. I recommend her work with enthusiasm and confidence and would like to see it in the hands of every seminary student in the country.

DR. JOHN JEFFERSON DAVIS, professor of systematic theology, Gordon-Conwell Theological Seminary

A concise, cogent, and convincing treatment of gender roles for God's people. Alice Mathews has confidently walked onto the historical turf of biblical theology, looked her opposition straight in the eye, and with grace-filled clarity of heart and mind boldly challenged outdated presuppositions, defended a God-honoring position of gender roles, and walked off the playing field victoriously. I delight in this incredible *ezer-kenegdo* woman of God.

STEPHEN A. MACCHIA, founder and president of Leadership Transformations, director of the Pierce Center for Disciple-Building at Gordon-Conwell Theological Seminary, and author of *Broken and Whole*

Regardless of your position on the gender roles issue, this book will challenge your thinking and provide fresh perspectives on this important issue in the church. Dr. Mathews has inspired countless women to live out their spiritual gifts over the years. For the kingdom's sake, we should read and examine what she so carefully offers in this important book.

EVAN MORGAN, senior vice president of global ministry efforts, Our Daily Bread Ministries

Alice Mathews helps the entire church rethink the concept of gender and gender roles with fresh biblical, historical, theological, and cultural insights. She releases us from our natural binary impulses to reconsider our God-given human responsibilities as people loved and created by God. This is a timely book for those battling in traditional gender wars.

MATTHEW D. KIM, assistant professor of preaching and ministry, Gordon-Conwell Theological Seminary, and author of *Preaching with Cultural Intelligence*

Readers of this important book by Dr. Mathews will find it helpful and hopeful. Helpful because in this one volume we have a clear interaction with and integration of the hermeneutical, theological, historical, and sociological issues that have impacted the current debates in some of our Christian communities. Hopeful because we see afresh God's creation of and call to women and men together to be full participants in the life and mission of God for the sake of the world.

WYNDY CORBIN REUSCHLING, professor of ethics and theology, Ashland Theological Seminary

Alice Mathews provides readers with a thorough rethink about gender roles. Her compelling claims help to enhance and enrich the discussion about the practice of men and women in the home and in the ministries of the church.

SCOTT M. GIBSON, DPhil, Haddon W. Robinson professor of preaching and ministry, Gordon-Conwell Theological Seminary

Dr. Mathews's book is an eye-opening journey from creation, through biblical narratives and debated texts, on to a revealing discussion of church history right up to the present. Gender issues raised in this book (much of them alarming) impact every man and woman in the church and threaten future generations of believers. They tarnish our witness, weaken our relationships, and hinder our mission in the world. This is a vitally important read!

CAROLYN CUSTIS JAMES, author of *Half the Church* and *Malestrom*, and FRANK A. JAMES III, DPhil, PhD, president, Biblical Theological Seminary, and professor of historical theology

Overcoming the sin of sexism—what we call in my culture "machismo"—is an ongoing struggle in our churches, homes, and communities. Alice Mathews has gifted the church with a biblically sound, theologically sophisticated, historically relevant, and pastorally sensitive book. This is required reading for all who would advance the gospel of Jesus Christ and his reign.

REV. ELDIN VILLAFAÑE, PhD, distinguished professor of Christian
social ethics, emeritus, Gordon-Conwell Theological Seminary

Clear and fair, this is a helpful hard-hitting introduction to questions about gender roles. Alice Mathews draws on her familiarity with the breadth and depth of biblical, theological, and historical scholarship related to these controversial issues to provide an instructive summary, regardless of whether your position is still in process or seemingly settled.

DAVID A. CURRIE, associate professor of pastoral theology,
Gordon-Conwell Theological Seminary

Discussions on gender dominate much of our present culture, and not just in the academy or on the extreme fringes of social media. This book refutes simple gender-based hierarchical approaches that have emerged from some parts of the church and provides a richer and more holistic understanding that is faithful to both Scripture and tradition. This model of informed discourse will serve the church for years to come.

GRAYSON CARTER, associate professor of church history,
Fuller Theological Seminary

Alice Mathews's combination of laser-like clarity and loving charity toward the hierarchicalists she disagrees with is enlightening and refreshing. Spanning Scripture, theology, tradition, ecclesiology, and ministry, with a touch of sociology, this is one of the most succinct and yet comprehensive syntheses of the best scholarship you'll find on the subject. It is truly a liberating book.

GORDON PREECE, Rev'd Dr, director of the Center for Research in
Religion and Social Policy, University of Divinity, Melbourne

Don't miss this engaging and well-written book. Read it for its timely and important insights. And read it for its exceptional model of how to study and interpret Scripture. This is a valuable resource for the church, and I will be recommending it often.

MERI MACLEOD, PhD, theological educator

Alice Mathews has spent decades assisting Christians to rethink what they have been taught about gender roles. Very few people have thought as long or as carefully about these issues from a biblical perspective. She provides us with a worthwhile and lively summary of a lifetime of experience and teaching from a woman who has walked the talk.

ALISTAIR MACKENZIE, teaching fellow,
Laidlaw College, Christchurch, New Zealand

Engaging, respectful, honest, and biblical, Dr. Mathews avoids strident tones and, as a friend, helps us reread familiar passages and rethink old ideas. If you believe that only Scripture should limit a person's ministry, you should read this book.

J. KENT EDWARDS, professor of preaching and leadership, Talbot School of Theology, and founder, CrossTalk Global

Alice Mathews has made a major contribution to the ongoing dialogue regarding women in the church. Both the tone and content of this book reflect a teacher's desire to encourage careful thinking rather than to push a particular point of view. She demonstrates a refreshing optimism—believing that rethinking gender roles can lead to renewed effectiveness of men and women working together in building God's kingdom on earth. What a possibility!

M. GAY HUBBARD, PhD, counselor, Life Management Services

Alice Mathews has written a thoughtful, reflective, and carefully crafted work. The examination of both historical and contemporary factors in determining the roles of men and women is informative and convincing. This book is an excellent resource for both educational and personal study. An important read for anyone who has the courage and wisdom to reexamine this often controversial issue.

RAYMOND F. PENDLETON, professor of pastoral care and counseling, Gordon-Conwell Theological Seminary

Over my forty-five-plus years as a Christ follower, I have grieved that so many Christians, especially leaders, refuse to do the hard work of sorting out key issues related to gender roles in the church and home. *Gender Roles and the People of God* should be included on every Christian's must-read list.

DR. SUE EDWARDS, associate professor of educational ministries and leadership, Dallas Theological Seminary

Dr. Mathews has written an urgently needed book on gender roles that is thoroughly biblical, both theologically and culturally sensitive, and pastorally prophetic. Above all, her vision of homes and churches led by a "Blessed Alliance" of men and women under the authority of Jesus is deeply hopeful.

CHRIS SCHUTTE, pastor, Christ Church Anglican, Phoenix, Arizona

GENDER ROLES

AND THE
PEOPLE OF GOD

RETHINKING WHAT WE
WERE TAUGHT ABOUT MEN
AND WOMEN IN THE CHURCH

ALICE MATHEWS

ZONDERVAN

Gender Roles and the People of God
Copyright © 2017 by Alice P. Mathews

This title is also available as a Zondervan ebook.

Requests for information should be addressed to:
Zondervan, *3900 Sparks Dr. SE, Grand Rapids, Michigan 49546*

ISBN 978-0-310-52939-2

Cover design: John Hamilton Design
Cover photo: Lucas Cranach the Elder (public domain)
Interior imagery: © blue pencil/Shutterstock
Interior design: Kait Lamphere

Printed in the United States of America

17 18 19 20 21 22 23 24 /DHV/ 20 19 18 17 16 15 14 13 12 11 10 9 8 7 6 5 4 3 2 1

For my three amazing daughters —
Drs. Susan, Karen, and Cheryl.
And for my five splendid granddaughters-in-law —
Amy, Angela, Joy, Kaitlyn, and Maddie.
And for all the women
who have encouraged me
when my own spirits flagged.

CONTENTS

ACKNOWLEDGMENTS

Some books start out as books in their authors' minds. Other books emerge over time from learning gathered on long journeys in other forms. This book took that delayed route. Eighteen years ago as a classroom professor at Gordon-Conwell Theological Seminary, I realized that my personal questions about my role as a female follower of Jesus Christ were questions that many of my students shared. The chapters of this book began as classroom lectures in a course I called "Women and Church Leadership." For several decades, I had been rethinking what I had been taught about men and women in the church. Throughout those years, God's Word was and remains the first and last word beyond which I could not step, and so Scripture has bounded both the classroom course and this book.

Two years ago, a woman student who completed the course was certain that I needed to put those lectures and class discussions into a book. She was so insistent that she actually found a donor who would finance self-publication so she could send the book to her friends. In the course, I had pointed her to the myriad biblical scholars on whose shoulders I stood in the classroom, and she could do the same. But she wanted one volume that gathered up into one place my decades of reading and research. At that point, I realized I could not ignore her, but I did not want the hassle of self-publication. When I contacted Zondervan, I was pleased beyond words by their positive response, and, as they say, "the rest is history."

So first I want to acknowledge Madison Trammel and his crew at Zondervan, who had enough faith in this book to guide me in its creation. Beyond their support, however, I must be clear that without all of the spadework done by scores of biblical and theological scholars over the centuries, as well as in recent decades, I would have had no basis for writing this book. Through their diligent exegetical work and theological reflection, I have a clearer sense of God's intention in Genesis 1:26–28 for a "Blessed Alliance" of men and women working together shoulder to shoulder for Christ and his kingdom.[1]

Then I want to acknowledge my debt to my student Tammy, who pushed me into this project, and to all of the women over the years whose questions, tears, fears, and anguish have given urgency to my work. Alongside them also stand other women like Cathie Kroeger and Carolyn Custis James, whose own journeys have been painful but whose writings have seeded some of my own.

And of course, I want to acknowledge the ongoing role of my husband, Randall, who has patiently read chapters as I've written them and washed dishes and put up with my work hours with love and without murmuring. I have been blessed with the best of all spouses. Thank you, Lord, for this gift!

---

1. I owe a debt of gratitude to Carolyn Custis James for this phrase ("Blessed Alliance"); see her *Half the Church: Recapturing God's Global Vision for Women* (Grand Rapids: Zondervan, 2011), 135.

INTRODUCTION

Gender.
Roles.
The people of God.

When these words appear together in the same sentence, they send shudders through some segments of the Christian church. What are we in for when these words are joined together in a book title? What will this author say that we haven't already heard many times before? And what is this about *rethinking* what we've been taught? Do we really have to go there?

GENDER

The first thing to say about gender is that it was God's idea. In Genesis 1:27, we read, "So God created mankind in his own image, in the image of God he created them; male and female he created them." Note two things about God's gender initiative. First, male and female were both created in God's image and likeness, and in some way both of them reflect something about their source, God. Second, God's mandate to the new pair was twofold: they were to populate the earth, and they were to subdue creation and steward it. While theoretically God could have come up with another idea for population growth, he chose a method that would involve both sexes intimately, together. They were also to serve as God's stewards of his creation, together.

The second thing to say about gender is that in short order, humanity decided that men were more important than women. The Greek philosopher Aristotle described women as "deformed males," and in his work *Politics*, he declared that "the male is by nature superior and the female inferior, the male ruler and the female subject."[1] His influence on other philosophers and on the church fathers prevailed and is still with us today.

The third thing about gender is that the word is used in at least two different ways in today's Western world. A lot of people prefer the word *gender* as a nicer word than *sex* to describe males or females physically. But social scientists insist on using *sex* to describe all of the physiological differences between men and women, and they use *gender* for those differences between the sexes that are socially learned. For them, *sex* is biological: male and female; *gender* is learned behavior: masculine and feminine. When Christian writers talk about masculinity and femininity, they are using social science terminology for what is socially learned about roles.

This book talks quite a bit about "gender-based hierarchy." In that case, the word *gender* is being used comprehensively to refer to men and women in every dimension of life.

ROLES

The first thing to say about roles is that they come and go. For years, one of my roles was as "daughter," but when my parents died, I no longer had that daughter role. Roles change frequently throughout the life cycle. We gain some roles and lose others over time. And if we take on too many roles at once, it can cause a physical and emotional overload that is hard to cope with.

At the same time, roles fill useful functions. They provide us with our individual identity. They tend to organize our lives for us. And they

---

1. Quoted in Nicholas D. Smith, "Plato and Aristotle on the Nature of Women," *Journal of the History of Philosophy* 21.4 (October 1983): 467–78.

lend predictability to life. Because roles do these things, we can become overly attached to them.

Roles always carry two sets of expectations: those expectations I place on myself, and those expectations that other people place on me. Sometimes those two sets of expectations collide. This can happen to women trying to deal with external expectations that conflict with their own inner sense of personhood. So roles can be tricky things. Necessary, but tricky.

THE PEOPLE OF GOD

This book is about a particular group of people—the people of God. It's not about humanity in general, but about those who are serious followers of Jesus Christ. This assumes that we want to obey God's Word as we "walk in the way of love just as Christ loved us and gave himself up for us" (Ephesians 5:2).

It happens that the people of God are divided on the roles that gendered people (men and women) are to play in the church and in the home. Some use the Bible to support gender-based hierarchy in the church and home, and others use the Bible to tear down that teaching. Concerned about the people of God, this book examines most of the ways the Bible is used by both sides of the gender debates.

But this book doesn't stop there. Once we've seen the rationales used from Scripture, we must also look at the way Christians used those rationales throughout two thousand years of church history.

RETHINKING WHAT WE WERE TAUGHT

In September 1945 as a high school junior, I signed up for a course in chemistry. Our chemistry textbook at the time insisted that the atom was the smallest possible particle and could not be split. However, just a month earlier in August 1945, World War II ended with the bombing of Hiroshima and Nagasaki—with an "atomic bomb" based on split atoms. In one short stroke, our chemistry textbook had become obsolete. Our teacher had to rethink a fundamental precept in her field. It was time for new learning.

Remember those two astronomers, Copernicus (1473–1543) and Galileo (1564–1642)? Their scientific study had convinced them that the earth revolves around the sun (and not the reverse). But the church could not tolerate that notion and used the Inquisition to punish Galileo severely. (Copernicus escaped that punishment by refusing to publish his work until he was on his deathbed.) The church then put both men's books on the Index of Prohibited Books, where they remained for the next two hundred years. Sometimes unlearning takes a long time.

For that reason, the first two parts of this book will explore both familiar and unfamiliar biblical texts touching our lives as men and women, gendered beings, as we attempt to rethink what we've been taught. Part 3 will take us on a journey through two thousand years of men's and women's experience in church history. We'll watch stumbling humanity embrace one idea, then another, constantly having to rethink old teachings and see what had earlier been missed.

Join me as we revisit what it means to be male or female as part of the people of God. What can we learn from Scripture and from history that will help us reach the clearest understanding of gender difference in God's purposes for us? The journey may drive us to rethink what we've been taught. It may help us see what we might otherwise have missed.

Chapter One

THE DANGERS OF A MISLEADING READING

*Do your best to present yourself to God as one
approved, a worker who does not need to be ashamed
and who correctly handles the word of truth.*
2 TIMOTHY 2:15

Most major cities around the world have electrified light-rail systems—trains that transport city dwellers quickly and safely throughout their urban areas. Many of these systems are underground. Virtually all of them depend on electrical current to power the trains. This power is transmitted by a third rail running parallel to the tracks. The third rail makes it hazardous for anyone who falls onto the tracks because most third rails carry currents starting as high as 1,200 to 1,500 volts, enough to kill a person.

In politics, "the third rail" is any issue so controversial that it can't be addressed with much hope of success. Politicians like to say, "Touch that issue, and you die!" Accomplishing legislation around third-rail issues in government becomes impossible unless opposed political parties are willing to work together for "the common good."

...any churches and denominations around the world, the subject
...w men and women relate in the church has become a third-rail issue.
...hen that issue also reaches into the home, it further complicates the
conversation. One part of the complication is that our final authority
is always the Bible, and verses in the Bible can sometimes be twisted in
odd ways to support a point. To avoid that, we must begin with some
understanding of the hermeneutics or the interpretive grid that we bring
to any part of this third-rail subject. Every book or sermon on this subject
is inherently based on a hermeneutic, a way of interpreting all of the texts
relevant to leadership in Christian homes and churches.

THINKING ABOUT YOUR HERMENEUTIC FOR INTERPRETING THE BIBLE

While readers of the Bible have always brought some kind of interpretive grid to the way they understand biblical teachings, only in recent centuries have theologians taken a closer look at what these interpretive grids look like, how they are formed, and what their strengths and weaknesses are.

A hermeneutic is a kind of lens through which we look at Scripture, allowing us to see certain things. But our hermeneutic can also cause us to miss other things that our chosen lens may make opaque. Anyone who wears bifocal glasses understands how this works. If you try to read street signs through the lower half of the lens, everything is blurred. If you try to read a book through the upper half, the result is the same: blurred. We must recognize this fact about whatever interpretive grid we use.

Some people choose to read the Bible through a "dispensational" lens; others choose to read it through a "covenantal" lens. Still others use a "Christocentric" lens or a "first-mention" lens or an "allegorical" lens. The hermeneutical lens used in this book is the historical-grammatical method based on the interplay of linguistic, grammatical, historical, sociopolitical, geographical, and cultural factors that we must discover about the text.[1]

All this to say that the task of hermeneutics is multifaceted if we want to get at the core meaning of any biblical text. But even as we do that, we always face three obstacles as we interpret Scripture:

First, most of us do not speak the languages of the ancient Near East. Language reflects culture, and as people living more than two thousand years after the periods recorded in the Bible, most of us don't have daily experience in first-century Hebrew, Aramaic, or Koine Greek languages. This may impact finding the correct meaning of many words.

Second, although we live nearly two millennia after the close of the biblical canon, we tend to impose our own cultural standards on Bible times. But the first-century cultures in both Palestine and in the Mediterranean Roman world were radically different from our own. Even more different were the Old Testament cultures from Abraham (around 2000 BC) onward.

Third, we may bring our twenty-first-century religious, moral, and cultural expectations to the biblical text.[2]

Any hermeneutic that ignores these obstacles can mislead sincere Christians who assume that what is true for us now was also true for the writers two thousand years ago.

THE DANGER OF A MISLEADING READING OF THE BIBLE

Before we touch the third-rail issue of gender difference in the church and home, it can help us to step back into history and look at a fierce debate that raged in the United States for fifty years in the nineteenth century.

---

1. Henry A. Virkler discusses this hermeneutic in detail in *Hermeneutics: Principles and Processes of Biblical Interpretation*, 2nd ed. (Grand Rapids: Baker Academic, 1981, 2007).
2. David L. Barr explores the significance of these three obstacles in his book *New Testament Story* (Belmont, CA: Wadsworth, 1995).

It was the debate over slavery. Christians lined up Scripture verses to support their approval of slavery even as other Christians used the Bible to oppose the practice. I am indebted to Willard Swartley's book *Slavery, Sabbath, War, and Women* for details of this debate.[3]

How do you feel about tearing another human being by force from his or her homeland, putting that person in chains, and then selling him or her in a slave market, knowing that person will never again have the freedom to come and go, to rest or work at will, or to have a normal home and family life? Most of us have a hard job imagining how the church could vigorously defend something as evil as enslaving human beings created in God's image. Yet in the mid-nineteenth century, a majority of evangelical churches in the U.S. were aligned *against* the abolition movement, and they used the Bible to support their pro-slavery position. In fact, Charles Hodge, the renowned Princeton theologian, stated that "if the present course of abolitionists is right, then the course of Christ and the apostles were wrong."[4]

Did you hear that? If the effort to abolish slavery was right, then Jesus Christ and the apostles were wrong. How could Bible-believing preachers and theologians defend slavery on the basis of the Bible?

Pro-slavery Christians used four major arguments to support their position.[5] The *first* argument was that slavery was divinely sanctioned by the Old Testament patriarchs. It began with Genesis 9:24–27,[6] Noah's

---

3. Willard Swartley, *Slavery, Sabbath, War, and Women: Case Issues in Biblical Interpretation* (Harrisonburg, VA: Herald, 1983). If you want to look at other extended case studies in hermeneutics, Swartley's book is a good resource.

4. Charles B. Hodge, "The Bible Argument on Slavery," in *Cotton Is King and Pro-Slavery Arguments Comprising the Writings of Hammond, Harper, Christy, Stringfellow, Hodge, Bledsoe, and Cartwright on This Important Subject*, ed. E. M. Elliot (1860; repr., New York: Negro Universities Press, 1969), 849.

5. These were published by Dr. Thomas Stringfellow, a pastor in Richmond, Virginia, in an essay titled "The Bible Argument or Slavery in the Light of Divine Revelation."

6. "When Noah awoke from his wine and found out what his youngest son had done to him, he said, 'Cursed be Canaan! The lowest of slaves will he be to his brothers.' He also said, 'Praise be to the LORD, the God of Shem! May Canaan be the slave of Shem. May God extend Japheth's territory; may Japheth live in the tents of Shem, and may Canaan be the slave of Japheth.'"

curse on Canaan, and was called "the first appearance of slavery in the Bible." Episcopal bishop John Henry Hopkins called it "the wonderful prediction of the patriarch Noah." Pastor Thomas Stringfellow agreed that Noah's curse on Canaan was a prediction and wrote, "God decreed this institution before it existed." For these writers, Noah's curse on Canaan prophesied the black Africans' destiny.[7]

Pro-slavery proponents also used Abraham as an example of divine sanction for slavery among the patriarchs. The New Testament holds up Abraham as a champion of faith for all Christians (Hebrews 11:17–19). Yet he was also a slaveholder.[8]

To carry the argument further, pro-slavery preachers also pointed to Joseph, who was commanded by God to buy up the land and the people, making them slaves of Pharaoh (Genesis 47:15–25). So the first argument used by pro-slavery Christians in the nineteenth century, taken from the Bible, was that slavery was sanctioned by the patriarchs.

The *second* argument was that slavery was incorporated into Israel's national constitution.[9] Pro-slavery ministers and theologians also argued that God authorized two types of slavery for Israel's national life. First, Israel could take foreigners as slaves (Leviticus 25:44–46). Israelites could buy slaves, hold them as property, and will them to their descendants. From this text, Stringfellow argued that "God ingrafted hereditary slavery upon the constitution of government." Second, the law allowed Israelites to sell themselves and their families into slavery for limited periods of time (Exodus 21; Leviticus 25). So not only was slavery sanctioned

---

7. Swartley (*Slavery*, 33) cites S. A. Cartwright's 1843 essay stating that when Japheth became enlarged by the discovery of America [foretold 3,800 years earlier?!], Canaan appeared on the African beach to get passage to America, "drawn thither by an impulse of his nature to fulfill his destiny of becoming Japheth's servant."

8. Abraham brought slaves from Haran (Genesis 12:5); he armed 318 slaves born in his house (Genesis 14:14); he included these slaves in his property list (Genesis 12:16; 14:35–36); he received slaves as a gift from Abimelech (Genesis 20:14); he willed his slaves as part of his estate to his son Isaac (Genesis 26:13–14); and the Bible says that the Lord blessed Abraham by multiplying his slaves (Genesis 24:35).

9. Swartley, *Slavery*, 33–34.

by the Old Testament patriarchs; it was also incorporated into the Old Testament law governing God's people.

The *third* argument was that both Jesus Christ and the apostles recognized and approved of slavery.[10] To support this assertion, slavery's proponents made seven different arguments:

1. Jesus and the apostles saw the cruel slavery practices in the Roman Empire but never said a word against them. Nineteenth-century preachers used 1 Timothy 6:1–6 to show that slaves should be content in their situation.[11]

2. Christians must distinguish between the institution of slavery and its abuses. They should work to correct the abuses, but they cannot tamper with the institution.

3. The church has no authority to interfere with slavery as a political system. The church should not interfere with the political and economic systems in force.

4. Distinctions between master and slave are not an impediment to faith and are thus insignificant. Whether a person is a slave or a master, he or she can be equally good as a Christian.[12]

5. Paul allowed slaveholders not only to be members of the church but to serve as leaders in the church.[13]

---

10. Ibid., 34–37.

11. On the basis of this text, Governor James Henry Hammond of South Carolina wrote, "It is impossible, therefore, to suppose that Slavery is contrary to the will of God. It is equally absurd to say that American Slavery differs in form or principle from that of the chosen people. We accept the Bible terms as the definition of our Slavery, and its precepts as the guide for our conduct" (quoted in ibid., 34–35).

12. Charles Hodge wrote, "These external relations . . . are of little importance, for every Christian is a freeman in the highest and best sense of the word, and at the same time is under the strongest bonds to Christ (1 Corinthians 7:20–22) . . . Paul treats the distinctions which slavery creates as matters of very little importance in so far as the interests of the Christian life are concerned" (quoted in ibid., 35–36).

13. Albert Taylor Bledsoe stated, "As nothing can be plainer than that slaveholders are admitted to the Christian church by the inspired apostles, the advocates of [the antislavery] doctrine are brought into direct collision with the Scriptures. This leads to one of the most dangerous evils connected with the whole system, that is, a disregard for the authority of the Word of God, a setting

6. The apostles gave no directives that Christian masters should free their slaves but said that slaves should remain in their existing state because masters have a right to their slaves' labor (1 Corinthians 7:20–24). Thus Paul ordained the pattern for the church that slaves should be content with their state unless they could be freed lawfully.

7. Most importantly, Paul sent the converted slave Onesimus back to his owner, Philemon, and gave his reason for doing so that the master had a right to his slave's services.[14]

The *fourth and final* argument given was that slavery was a merciful institution.[15] This astonishing argument noted that by enslaving them, prisoners taken in war were spared being put to death. Also, through slavery "millions of Ham's descendants" who otherwise "would have sunk down to eternal ruin" have been "brought within the range of the gospel influence."[16]

Summary arguments for slavery included the assertion that political, economic and social institutions function for the common good when, as Charles Hodge wrote, "the rights of the individual are subordinate to those of the community." As a parallel to this, he noted that "in this country we believe that the general good requires us to deprive the whole female sex of the right of self-government. They have no voice in the formation of the laws which dispose of their persons and property."[17]

These are the chief arguments (based on the Bible) used in the nineteenth century to support slavery. Regardless of this use of Scripture,

---

up of a different and higher standard of truth and duty, and a proud and confident wrestling of Scripture to suit their own purposes" (quoted in ibid., 36).

14. So pro-slavery writers asked, "If Paul thought slavery was wrong, why didn't he counsel the fugitive Onesimus to claim his right to freedom? The answer is very plain. St. Paul was inspired and knew the will of the Lord Jesus Christ, and was only intent on obeying it. Who are we that in our modern wisdom presume to set aside the Word of God?" (quoted in ibid., 37).

15. See ibid., 38.

16. Ibid., 37.

17. Quoted in ibid., 49.

however, history has judged slavery to be a horrific evil, and one by one, Western nations abolished it. The facts that slavery had a long history and broad cultural support, and that such a "persuasive" biblical defense of it could be made by some of the best theologians of their day, ultimately lost to the larger biblical issues of God's justice and righteousness.

WHAT MIGHT SUPPORTERS OF SLAVERY HAVE MISSED SEEING IN THE BIBLE?

Clearly, supporters of slavery in the mid-nineteenth century found almost every verse in the Bible that could validate their slave-owning practices. But in several cases, their hermeneutic ignored the contextual, historical, and cultural settings of the verses they quoted. For example:

- Abraham *did* hold slaves of some kind, as the pro-slavery advocates argued. He also practiced concubinage with Hagar and lied about his wife, Sarah, on at least two occasions. We cannot copy his morality across the board and assume that because Abraham did something, it was morally justifiable.
- It's true that God regulated slavery in the Mosaic Law, but neither God nor Israel originated slavery. Pagan cultures practiced slavery at that time, and God used the Sabbath, the seventh year, and the year of Jubilee to modify the practice in the direction of justice and mercy.
- Some scholars have estimated that fully a third of all people in the first-century Roman Empire were slaves. While Jesus and Paul did not make the *abolition* of slavery a central focus of their work, for Jesus, setting the oppressed free was an integral part of his kingdom work calling (Luke 4:18). In 1 Timothy 1:10, the apostle Paul lists crimes committed by "slave traders and liars and perjurers," specifically including slave traders in his list of

"lawbreakers and rebels, the ungodly and sinful, the unholy and irreligious" (1 Timothy 1:9). Slavery proponents ignored the fact that for the apostle Paul, "man-stealing" was a mortal offense.

Thus, making an appeal to the Bible does not guarantee a correct interpretation.[18] It's not enough to look for words that say what we want them to say. We must be sure of the textual, historical, and cultural context of those words.

Recall that our hermeneutic is a lens that allows us to see some things clearly while making other things opaque. Historian Anne Firor Scott reminds us:

> It is a truism, yet one easy to forget, that people see most easily things they are prepared to see and overlook those they do not expect to encounter . . . Because our minds are clouded, we do not see things that are before our eyes. What clouds our minds is, of course, the culture that at any time teaches us what to see and what not to see.[19]

THE CASE FOR GENDER-BASED HIERARCHY

Proponents of gender-based hierarchy base their case on the presupposition that it is the will of God for men and women in both marriage and in the church. Like the anti-abolitionists in the nineteenth century, they support this presupposition with a wide range of biblical citations. They use Scripture to back up the affirmations found in the Danvers Statement.[20] The Statement's basic ideas include the following:

---

18. See ibid., 58.

19. Anne Firor Scott, "On Seeing and Not Seeing: A Case of Invisibility," *The Journal of American History* 71:1 (June 1984): 7–21.

20. This document was issued by the Council on Biblical Manhood and Womanhood in 1987 as a response to egalitarian scholarly papers read at the 1986 annual meeting of the Evangelical

- "Distinctions in masculine and feminine roles are ordained by God as part of the created order, and should find an echo in every human heart."

- "Adam's headship in marriage was established by God before the Fall, and was not a result of sin."

- "The Fall introduced distortions into the relationships between men and women. In the home, the husband's loving, humble headship tends to be replaced by domination or passivity; the wife's intelligent, willing submission tends to be replaced by usurpation or servility. In the church, sin inclines men toward a worldly love of power or an abdication of spiritual responsibility, and inclines women to resist limitations on their roles or to neglect the use of their gifts in appropriate ministries."

- "Redemption in Christ aims at removing the distortions introduced by the curse. In the family, husbands should forsake harsh or selfish leadership and grow in love and care for their wives; wives should forsake resistance to their husbands' authority and grow in willing, joyful submission to their husbands' leadership. In the church, redemption in Christ gives men and women an equal share in the blessings of salvation; nevertheless, some governing and teaching roles within the church are restricted to men."

In 1991, John Piper and Wayne Grudem edited *Recovering Biblical Manhood and Womanhood: A Response to Evangelical Feminism* in which multiple authors laid out the biblical case for the above assertions. They cover all of the major texts in the Bible that might lend support to the basic tenets of gender-based hierarchy. Chapters 2 through 9 in

Theological Society. It continues to be the primary statement of beliefs supporting gender-based hierarchy. The statement can be found in appendix 2 in John Piper and Wayne Grudem, eds., *Recovering Biblical Manhood and Womanhood*, 2nd ed. (1991; repr., Wheaton, IL: Crossway, 2006), 469–71.

this book explore each of the major texts used to support gender-based hierarchy.

How can we evaluate this or any other case? Most textbooks on hermeneutics would insist on the following principles:

First, the context of any text controls its interpretation. Someone has said, "A text without its context is merely a pretext" for just about anything we might want to say. Others have noted that it's possible to prove almost anything by the Bible by taking texts out of their context.

Well-intentioned Christians have walked away from God and faith when what they thought the Bible promised them did not materialize. Others have been bound in misery by ideas presented to them from verses of Scripture taken out of context. This first rule for accurate interpretation of biblical texts is a safety net to keep us from tumbling into harmful notions about God and the Christian life that might otherwise harm us. The context of any Bible verse is king.

Second, we must listen to the full testimony of Scripture.[21] We have to consider *all* the texts on a given topic. When God gave Moses the Ten Commandments on Mount Sinai, the eighth commandment was "you shall not steal" (Exodus 20:15). What the pro-slavery advocates missed was the context of this command in Exodus 21:16: "Anyone who kidnaps someone is to be put to death, whether the victim has been sold or is still in the kidnapper's possession." So the eighth commandment includes "man-stealing" and calls it a capital offense. As noted earlier, while Paul did not advise Onesimus to remain a runaway slave, he considered anyone in the business of enslaving others to be "lawbreakers and rebels, the ungodly and sinful, the unholy and irreligious" (1 Timothy 1:9). Hearing the full testimony of Scripture includes both specific examples and general principles. The overriding biblical principle of impartial love for all and mutual service to any in need must also be part of the debate.

---

21. See Swartley, *Slavery*, 60.

Third, texts should be used for their main emphasis, not for some attendant feature.[22] Hebrews 11 holds up Abraham as a model of faith in God's promises, but he was not a model as a liar or as a slaveholder. First Timothy 6:1–6 does contain specific directives on the subject of slavery. But Jesus' command to love our neighbor also has direct bearing on any evaluation of the morality of slavery. So not only do we look for specific words that say what we want them to say, but we also include broad moral imperatives found in Scripture. We might want to ponder questions like these: What did Jesus emphasize in his teaching? What was the stated purpose of his ministry on earth? What was the purpose of the gospel, the new order he came to inaugurate? How do Jesus' words and deeds fit into the larger plan of God laid out in the Old Testament?

Distinguishing between Descriptive and Prescriptive Texts

From where do we derive our moral guidance? How do we distinguish between texts that are only *descriptive* and those that are *prescriptive*? Sometimes the grammar of a verse can help us, but not always. For example, the case laws in Exodus 21–23 are concrete and explicit: this is how Israelites were to treat slaves in Israel. But today most Christians regard those teachings on the treatment of ancient slaves as irrelevant to faith. On the other hand, Jesus' teaching about our attitudes (while appearing in descriptive passages like parables) are most certainly authoritative.

A number of years ago, the Christian magazine *The Other Side* carried a short self-exercise called "The Temporary Gospel?" The exercise listed fifty different commands from the New Testament. Readers were asked to put a P in front of those they thought were "permanent"

---

22. Ibid.

(applying the command to all Christians at all times in all places) and a T in front of those they thought were "temporary" (applicable in some circumstances but not binding on all people all the time).

It turns out you can approach the commands in the Bible from one of three positions: (1) If you place a P in front of every statement, you're implying that all commands in the Bible are literal and binding on all Christians at all times in all places. (2) If you place a T in front of every command, you're implying that all commands are cultural and must be reinterpreted in the light of our circumstances today. (3) But if you place a P in front of some statements and a T in front of others, you're noting that some commands in the Bible are binding and others are cultural, and you have to decide to which category a command belongs before you apply it today. That third category (obviously the right choice) is the toughest one because you have to weigh each command, not only in its immediate context in the Bible, but also within the overall teachings of the Bible.

Our hermeneutic matters because a wrong hermeneutic—the hermeneutic of the Pharisees—can lead us to be letter-of-the-law perfect, and yet be dead wrong. These religious leaders observed every specific command concerning the Sabbath, etc., but they directly opposed God's Messiah.[23] Jesus denounced their approach in Matthew 23:23–24:

> "Woe to you, teachers of the law and Pharisees, you hypocrites! You give a tenth of your spices—mint, dill and cumin. But you have neglected the more important matters of the law—justice, mercy and faithfulness. You should have practiced the latter without neglecting the former. You blind guides! You strain out a gnat but swallow a camel."

---

23. In no way am I implying that someone holding a position different from my own is thereby a "Pharisee." What I am writing here applies to every Christian reading and interpreting Scripture.

Jesus teaches us to go beyond the letter to the spirit behind the letter. We are to hear the main intentions of the biblical writers. The slavery debate alerts us to self-justifying tendencies at work in how we use the Bible. Whenever our interpretation leads to injustice, oppression, or structural violence, then the very heart of the Bible is repudiated. Such views are anti-biblical, no matter what texts they cite.[24]

What happened in approaches to the issue of slavery has also happened to approaches to the issue of men and women in the church and home. If you pick up a book written by a traditionalist, the focus is likely to be on texts that support the subordination of women. On the other hand, if you pick up a book written by an egalitarian, the focus is probably on texts that proponents of gender-based hierarchy consider irrelevant. For example, when theologian Stephen Clark wrote about Genesis 2, he saw the man as central to the narrative and therefore the head. But when theologian Perry Yoder wrote about Genesis 2, he saw the woman as the climax of the narrative, giving her an equal or even more important role.[25]

It's not easy to step back and put on a different pair of hermeneutical glasses in order to see what we might have missed in the past. But if we want to be obedient to the whole counsel of God, we must make the effort to do so. So now we begin our journey through Scripture and through church history, seeing some things we always knew were there, and perhaps seeing other things we hadn't thought about before.

---

24. Our life situation and experience shape our perception and understanding. In the nineteenth century, whether Americans grew up in the North or the South, or were black or white, would influence their view of slavery—and would influence what they understood the Bible to say. As we approach the Bible, we must keep in view the fact that we can "see" some things more clearly than others simply because we reflect the culture of the home and church in which we grew up.

25. See Swartley, *Slavery*, 154.

Questions for Personal Reflection or Group Discussion

1. As you think about your own ways of interpreting what you read in the Bible, how would you describe your "hermeneutic"?
2. How does a knowledge of the cultural and historical background of any part of the Bible help us understand a text's meaning?
3. How do you deal with things in the Bible that seem to contradict or collide with other things you've already read there?
4. As you begin this study, what are the most important questions you have?

PART ONE

Stand-out Women in their Patriarchal Worlds

Patriarchy has been around almost from the beginning of time. We spot it in some of the earliest recorded histories; we bump into it at every turn in more recent histories; and now in newscasts we hear of it alive and well somewhere in the world. Some regard it as a blessing; others think of it as a curse. Because it touches our lives in one way or another, we can't ignore it. For followers of Jesus Christ, the question is whether there is a biblical justification for patriarchy.

Is the Bible "patriarchal"? If we mean by that question, does the Bible accurately describe the patriarchal societies, beliefs, and actions recorded in Scripture, the answer is yes. The Bible shows us the many faces of patriarchy. But if we mean, does the Bible endorse the patriarchal culture in which its history and teachings are displayed, the answer is no. This is the difference between what is *de*scriptive and what is *pre*scriptive in the Bible.

Throughout the Bible, we see women in situations that call them to actions not normally permitted in a patriarchal setting. Sometimes they had to negotiate the claims of the helpless over against the claims of those who ruled them. Other times they had to take leadership into their hands when the situation urgently demanded it. In the process, the situation often changed them even as they became agents of change. These are *ezer* women, women of strength.

In chapter 2, we'll learn about *ezer* women when God created Eve to partner with Adam (Genesis 2:18). Then in chapters 3–5, we'll see the many faces of an *ezer* woman: the courage to risk their lives by disobeying the king, seen in Shiphrah and Puah; the initiative of Abigail in saving her household; the driving concern of Ruth for a disheartened mother-in-law; the determination of the daughters of Zelophehad; the powerful gift used by Deborah and Huldah; the countercultural women who dared to be part of the Jesus band; and the many named women serving shoulder to shoulder with the apostle Paul in the New Testament churches.

Join me in part 1 for a quick trip through the Bible as we see a handful of courageous women who were willing to stand up against their culture. But beware: these examples may shatter some of our notions about God's purpose in creating women as *ezer kenegdo.*

Chapter Two

THE BIRTH OF PATRIARCHY

The LORD God said, "It is not good for the man to be alone. I will make a helper suitable for him."
GENESIS 2:18

John Piper, a leading complementarian, explains this verse: "God teaches us that the woman is a man's 'helper' in the sense of a loyal and suitable assistant in the life of the garden."[1]

Wherever we find any arrangement (as here in Genesis 2) in which one person is "under" the other person, we have some kind of hierarchy. When that hierarchy has a woman under a man's direction or rule, it's called *patriarchy* (literally, "the rule of the father," from the Greek *patri-arkhēs*). Patriarchy has been with us almost from the beginning of the human race. In a patriarchal society, men hold power over women and children, sometimes with good outcomes, often with more destructive outcomes.

Historically the term *patriarchy* referred to the male heads of households who possessed complete authority over everyone in the family. In Roman times, when a baby was born into a family, its father determined

---

1. John Piper and Wayne Grudem, eds., *Recovering Biblical Manhood and Womanhood: A Response to Evangelical Feminism*, 2nd ed. (Wheaton, IL: Crossway, 2006), 87.

whether that baby would remain in the family or would be "exposed," that is, dropped in a public place where the infant could be taken by anyone for any purpose or left to die.[2] Today, while that practice for most of us is unthinkable, patriarchy remains a widespread reality in the many cultures in which men hold power over women.

How are we to think about the role or place of a woman in a patriarchal system? What is this woman, created as the man's helper, according to Genesis 2:18? Is she, as noted above, merely "a loyal and suitable assistant" to a man? Is this what God intended us to learn from that text? Or is there more to the story? If so, what is that story?

God's Human A-Team for His New World

The first chapter of the Bible provides an overview of the entire process of creation. Gilbert Bilezikian reminds us that God assigned limits to the firmament, to water, and to the earth. He set boundaries to the process of reproduction to preserve the integrity of each species (they produce "according to their kinds"). He gave celestial bodies "to mark sacred times, and days and years" and he established the sun "to govern the day" and the moon "to govern the night" (Genesis 1:14–16). He prescribed in detail the human rulership over every living thing that moves over the earth (1:28). In sum, the whole created universe (from stars in space to fish in the sea) is carefully organized into a hierarchy of order.[3] But God's next move did not follow that pattern.

In a dramatic climax, God crowned this new work with the creation of man—humankind in two forms, male and female, created in God's image and likeness. Then he gave this new pair of human beings two commands: (1) fill the earth with offspring and (2) subdue the earth as

---

2. Frequently, an infant would be retrieved only to be reared as a slave or as a temple prostitute, i.e., to benefit financially the person taking the child.

3. See Gilbert Bilezikian, *Beyond Sex Roles: What the Bible Says about a Woman's Place in Church and Family*, 3rd ed. (Grand Rapids: Baker, 2006), 19–20.

stewards over all creation (Genesis 1:26–28). No hint of any hierarchy at this point.

Three times the text tells us that humanity was created in God's image. It is on the basis of this image, this likeness, that Eve and Adam were given dominion over God's creation.[4] It wasn't that the man and woman were stronger than the lions, tigers, or hippopotami around them. It was that they stood between God and his creation as his representatives. Imaging God in the new world, they had a responsibility to care for everything God put under them. And in addition to ruling God's creation, Adam and Eve were told to be fruitful and increase in number by having children.

Everything in this text points to equal sharing in family building and in exercising dominion. God did not say to Adam, "You are to exercise dominion," and to Eve, "You are to build the family." Both the man and the woman were given both commands, pointing to shared parenting and shared dominion. In a world already carefully organized into a hierarchy of order, God placed a man and a woman without hierarchy. They are a team working together as parents and as caretakers of God's new world. From Genesis 1:26–28, it appears that the ontological equality the first man and woman shared is also a functional equality.

Is ONTOLOGICAL EQUALITY ALSO FUNCTIONAL EQUALITY?

Immediately proponents of a gender-based hierarchy step in and say no: "Adam's headship in marriage was established by God before the Fall, and was not a result of sin."[5] Most commentators who deal responsibly with Genesis 1 agree that it underscores the *ontological* equality of the

4. See Francis Schaeffer, *Genesis in Space and Time* (Downers Grove, IL: InterVarsity, 1972), 48.

5. The Danvers Statement, affirmation 3, quoted in Piper and Grudem, eds., *Recovering Biblical Manhood and Womanhood*, 470.

man and woman.[6] But as we move into Genesis 2, we are told that from the beginning, the relationship of the woman to the man is functionally subordinate.

In Genesis 1, it appeared that the man and woman were created in a single event, but now in Genesis 2, we learn that the man was created before the woman, and that a crisis—the man's aloneness—played a part in the woman's creation. The key verse is Genesis 2:18: "The LORD God said, 'It is not good for the man to be alone. I will make a helper suitable for him.'" On the basis of this verse, proponents of gender-based hierarchy put forward four main points that they believe teach the woman's subordination to the man from the beginning.

The first argument for a male/female hierarchy is that Eve was created as Adam's "helper." This is the most widely used argument of the four. George W. Knight III put it this way: "It is simply the proper application of concepts and realities to affirm that if one human being is created to be the helper for another human being, the one who receives such help has a certain authority over the one who is his helper."[7] The church father Augustine (354–430) held that the woman was a helper only in childbearing, but in every other case, another man is a better help.[8] It was obvious to many that the woman's task was subordinate to the man's task.

But is that what the text actually tells us?

Genesis 1 ends by telling us that God "saw all that he had made, and it was very good." But then in Genesis 2:18, God says, "It is *not* good for the man to be alone. I will make a helper suitable for him" (emphasis added). What is this "helper suitable for him"? In our day, the idea of "helper" usually suggests a less-qualified subordinate, like a plumber's apprentice who hands the plumber the proper wrench. But

---

6. *Ontology* means "the nature of being," our essence (who we are essentially).

7. George W. Knight, III, *The New Testament Teaching on the Role Relationship of Men and Women* (Grand Rapids: Baker, 1977), 43.

8. Augustine, *De Genesi ad litteram* IX.5.

two Hebrew words in the text give us a very different sense of God's intention for women.

The first Hebrew word, transliterated *ezer*, appears twenty-one times in the Old Testament. When we look at all of these occurrences together, we get a sense of its meaning. In two cases, it is used to describe the woman Eve (Genesis 2:18, 20), and three times, it refers to nations to whom Israel appealed for military help when faced with a powerful enemy (Isaiah 30:5; Ezekiel 12:14; Daniel 11:34). In the remaining sixteen cases, it refers to *God* as our help.[9] God is the one who comes alongside us in our helplessness. Any idea here of inferiority is untenable. God is not subordinate to his creatures. Philip Payne put it this way: "The noun used here [*ezer*] throughout the Old Testament does not suggest 'helper' as in 'servant,' but 'help, savior, rescuer, protector' as in 'God is our help.' In no other occurrence in the Old Testament does this refer to an inferior, but always to a superior or an equal . . . 'help' expresses that woman is a help/strength who rescues or saves man."[10]

While many Christians see Eve's function as a subordinate, the word *ezer* does not support that idea. Eve was not created to serve Adam but to serve *with* him. Furthermore, the Hebrew language has other words translated "helper" that do have the idea of subordination, but none of them are used in Genesis 2:18.[11]

The other Hebrew word in Genesis 2:18 is *kenegdo*, translated "comparable to him" or "suitable to him." It also carries no idea of a subordinate; this person is an equal in every way and comes alongside the man to complete him.

Watch what happens next in Genesis 2: God parades all the animals

---

9. The sixteen references to God as our help are in Exodus 18:4; Deuteronomy 33:7, 26, 29; Psalms 20:2; 33:20; 70:5; 89:19; 115:9, 10, 11; 121:1, 2; 124:8; 146:5; Hosea 13:9. For an excellent discussion of *ezer*, see Carolyn Custis James, *Half the Church: Recapturing God's Global Vision for Women* (Grand Rapids: Zondervan, 2011), 111–15.

10. Philip Payne, *Man and Woman, One in Christ: An Exegetical and Theological Study of Paul's Letters* (Grand Rapids: Zondervan, 2009), 44.

11. Bilezikian, *Beyond Sex Roles*, 3rd ed., 206, note 9.

in front of Adam to be named. Then God observes that among all the animals "there was not found a helper suitable to him" (*ezer kenegdo*). This was an object lesson for Adam, reinforcing the lesson that his need would not be filled by any but Eve. While he was alone, he was only half the story without a female counterpart. God had created humanity in the divine image as male and female, and it takes both together to image God in the world.

Also from this text we see that being male doesn't automatically imply completeness. Woman isn't an afterthought or an optional adjunct to an independent, self-sufficient man. Without her, Adam's condition was "not good." He needed an *ezer kenegdo*, one who would complement him as his equal, one who could do for him what he could not do himself.

Only then was the stage set for the woman's creation. Note that in Genesis 2:7 God created the man "from the dust of the ground." In Genesis 2:9 "the LORD God made all kinds of trees grow out of the ground." Then in Genesis 2:19 we read, "Now the LORD God had formed out of the ground all the wild animals and all the birds in the sky." In contrast, God formed Eve, not out of the ground, but from one of the man's ribs. There is no possible confusion about her identification with him in his humanity. From one being has come two persons (Genesis 2:21–24).

The text ends with the statement, "That is why a man leaves his father and mother and is united to his wife, and they become one flesh." This is God's basis for marriage. It is the only statement about marriage repeated four times in the Bible.

The second argument for a male/female hierarchy is that the woman was created after the man and is therefore secondary to him. Does being created prior to something else in itself imply superiority of function or being? In Genesis 1:24–25, the animals were created before humanity. Does that make them superior over humanity? No, God gave the human pair dominion over the animals (Genesis 1:28).

Those who hold that Adam's prior creation made Eve his subordinate base it on Paul's statement in 1 Timothy 2:13–14: "For Adam was formed first, then Eve. And Adam was not the one deceived; it was the woman who was deceived and became a sinner." It was on this basis that Paul had just written that a woman was not to teach or exercise authority over a man, but to be in silence (1 Timothy 2:12).

Old Testament scholar Walter Kaiser observes that the verb in 1 Timothy 2:13 is not *ktizō*, translated "create"; it is *plassō*, translated "form." Kaiser sees this as educational formation, not creation, reflecting the need for women to learn (2:11). A more broadly accepted understanding of 1 Timothy 2:13, however, notes that *plassō* is the Greek word used to translate "create" in the Septuagint version of the Old Testament Scriptures. First Timothy 2:13, in any case, cannot be used as proof that Adam's prior creation gave him authority over Eve. This text will be examined in greater detail in chapter 6.

In a different vein, James Hurley used the Old Testament law of primogeniture to prove that Adam's prior creation to Eve gave Adam superiority. This law entitled the eldest son in a family to inherit twice the amount of the estate received by his brothers. Hurley states that "Adam's status as the oldest carried with it the leadership appropriate to the first-born son."[12] Two things must be said in response to that. First, the primogeniture law came much later in Genesis and we are not justified in projecting this law retroactively back into the creation story where the practice receives no sanction. Furthermore, note that God overrode the law in choosing Abel over Cain (Genesis 4), Jacob over Esau, then Joseph over his brothers (Genesis 48:21–49:28), David over his older brothers (1 Samuel 16:1–13), and Solomon over Adonijah (1 Kings 1–2). Second, the law refers to how brothers inherit from their father. At no time in Scripture was it applied to the relationship

---

12. James B. Hurley, *Man and Woman in Theological Perspective* (Grand Rapids: Zondervan, 1981), 207.

of husbands and wives. To apply it here strains the definition of primogeniture.

The third argument for a male/female hierarchy is that the woman was "taken from the man" and is therefore secondary to him. Samuele Bacchiocchi argued that "in Biblical thought origin and authority are interrelated . . . A child must respect the authority of his parents because he derives from them. In Adam's historical situation Eve derived from him in the sense that God formed her from his body. Thus, Adam was her 'source,' and to him was due appropriate respect."[13] Bacchiocchi may be building on Edmond Jacob's statement that "man by himself is a complete being; the woman who is given to him adds nothing to his nature whilst the woman drawn forth from man owes all her existence to him."[14]

Gail Taylor responded to this reasoning, stating that Eve's "first and primal contact is with her Maker! Woman herself knew God before she knew her counterpart, the man."[15] And Phyllis Trible commented, "Man had no part in making woman . . . he is neither participant nor spectator, nor consultant at her birth. Like man, woman owes her life solely to God. For both of them, the origin of life is a divine mystery."[16]

It is as wrong to say that woman owes all her existence to man as it would be to say that man owes all his existence to dust and is therefore subordinate to it. Both the man and the woman are direct, individual, and purposeful acts of the creator God. The whole emphasis of Genesis 2 is not on the difference between male and female but on their relatedness: "That is why a man leaves his father and mother and is united to his wife,

---

13. Samuele Bacchiocchi, *Women in the Church: A Biblical Study on the Role of Women in the Church* (Berrien Springs, MI: Biblical Perspectives, 1987), 70. Bacchiocchi does acknowledge that this line of reasoning is not explicit in Genesis 2.

14. Edmond Jacob, *Theology of the Old Testament* (London: Hodder & Stoughton, 1958), 172–73.

15. Gail Taylor, "Woman in Creation and Redemption," *Christian Brethren Research Fellowship Journal* 26 (1974): 18.

16. Phyllis Trible, *God and the Rhetoric of Sexuality* (Philadelphia: Fortress, 1978), 102.

and they become one flesh" (Genesis 2:24). The chapter emphasizes that the whole human race came from one ancestor, establishing the absolute unity of humanity.[17]

We noted that in Genesis 2, God created the beasts and birds, as well as Adam, from the ground. Had Eve been created from the ground as Adam was, what was to connect her to him rather than to the beasts and birds? God chose a method of creation that underscored the absolute unity of the man and woman.

The fourth argument establishing a male/female hierarchy is that Adam named the woman, making her subordinate to him (Genesis 2:23). James Hurley explains this argument: "'Name' was associated with function and the power to assign or to change a name was connected with control . . . Within this context we can begin to see the importance of God's bringing of the animals to the man whom he had appointed to rule the earth in order to see what the man would call them."[18] Hurley argues that assigning names reflects control. This argument is based on the idea that in the Old Testament, naming implied dominion, and that in Genesis 2:23, Adam is exercising dominion over Eve. But that argument is overturned by two factors we must consider here.

First, in the Old Testament, the standard naming formula includes both the verb "to call" and the noun "name" (for example, see Genesis 4:25). In this chapter, this naming formula appears only in Genesis 2:19 (in the naming of the animals). In verse 23, the noun *name* does not appear. Second, in verse 23, the word *woman* is never used as a proper name. It is a common noun designating gender. It is in Genesis 3:20, *after* the fall, that Adam "named his wife Eve." What we have in Genesis 2:23 is only excited recognition that, after that long circus parade

---

17. This is corroborated by the Human Genome Project, which noted that there is only one race of human beings.

18. Hurley, *Man and Woman*, 211.

of animals, at last here is "bone of my bones, and flesh of my flesh"—someone like me!

It turns out that each of the four arguments in support of gender-based hierarchy is based on flawed reasoning or on an inaccurate reading of the texts.

As we come to the end of the first two chapters in the Bible, we learn two things. Both the man and woman are created in the image of God, and humanity exists in two parts: male and female. We also learn that each is a complete individual, but what is stressed here is not their individuality or the difference between them. It is their unity and the fact that they are indissolubly bound together.

On the strength of these two chapters, the passage concludes: "That is why a man leaves his father and mother and is united to his wife, and they become one flesh" (Genesis 2:24). Far from teaching any kind of hierarchy, Genesis 2 stresses the reciprocal dependency and mutuality of the man and woman. It is in Genesis 3:16 (God speaking to the woman) where we first see hierarchy in human relationships: "I will make your pains in childbearing very severe; with painful labor you will give birth to children. Your desire will be for your husband, and he will rule over you."

Unequal in Eden!

Complementarians and egalitarians pretty much agree that Genesis 3 describes a hierarchical relationship between the man and the woman. But in contrast to the belief that the fall led inevitably to hierarchy, Raymond Ortlund states, "We have seen . . . that God built male headship (not male domination) into the glorious, pre-fall order of creation."[19] Though complementarians and egalitarians agree on the result (hierarchy), they do not agree on the prior condition of complementary equality in Eden.

---

19. Raymond C. Ortlund Jr. "Male-Female Equality and Male Headship," in *Recovering Biblical Manhood and Womanhood*, 106.

At the beginning of Genesis 3, Adam was present: "When the woman saw that the fruit of the tree was good for food and pleasing to the eye, and also desirable for gaining wisdom, she took some and ate it. She also gave some to her husband, who was with her, and he ate it" (Genesis 3:6). Watch him remain silent while Satan tempted Eve. Various scholars throughout the ages have held Eve responsible for the entrance of sin into the world and some have puzzled over the fact that God held Adam, not Eve, responsible for that result (Romans 5:12–14; 1 Corinthians 15:22). Eve's sin lay in her vulnerability to deception (2 Corinthians 11:3; 1 Timothy 2:14). The chronology in Genesis 2 makes clear that Eve had a relatively limited knowledge of God, compared to Adam. She was more vulnerable to error than Adam because she did not have as much experience with God and his desire for the best for humanity. Adam knew better, but he stood by as Satan challenged Eve to eat the fruit because "God knows that when you eat from it your eyes will be opened, and you will be like God, knowing good and evil" (Genesis 3:5).

It is noteworthy that while Eve was the first to eat the fruit, God challenged Adam first, not Eve, about their disobedience (Genesis 3:9). Some take this as an indication that Adam had been in charge of Eve (the male headship mentioned by Ortlund). Note that in verses 9 through 12, God addressed only Adam, using singular second-person pronouns. He asked Adam, "Have you [singular] eaten from the tree that I commanded you [singular] not to eat from?" (3:11). Adam had received that command directly from God (2:17) before Eve was created and formed, putting Adam first in line to account for his disobedience.

In that account, Gilbert Bilezikian notes that "instead of owning up to personal guilt, [Adam] recited a history of the temptation that tended to hold others, both God and Eve, responsible for his fault . . . Obviously, this cowardly subterfuge was not acceptable to God. When the promised sentence of death fell upon Adam and Eve, it was pronounced not on Eve but on Adam (3:19)."[20]

In Adam's response to God (Genesis 3:12), we see the relationship between husband and wife rapidly deteriorating as he blamed her. By the end of the chapter, the consequences of the fall are already at work: alienation from God their creator, alienation from each other, and alienation from their natural environment—the earth Adam would then have to till by the sweat of his brow.

Note that when God turned to Eve (Genesis 3:13), he asked her a different question from the one he asked Adam. He asked her to describe what she had done. When she admitted she had been deceived by the serpent and had eaten the fruit, God laid out the consequences in Genesis 3:16: "I will make your pains in childbearing very severe; with painful labor you will give birth to children. Your desire will be for your husband, and he will rule over you."

Francis Schaeffer observed that sin inevitably leads to hierarchy. "This one sentence puts an end to any pure democracy. In a fallen world pure democracy is not possible. Rather, God brings structure into the primary relationship of man—the man-woman relationship. In a fallen world (in every kind of society—big and small—and in every relationship) structure is needed for order."[21] In short, sin requires some form of hierarchy.

Hierarchy was not God's will for the first pair, but it was imposed when they chose to disregard his command and eat the forbidden fruit. As for Adam, "cursed is the ground because of you: through painful toil you will eat food from it all the days of your life. It will produce thorns and thistles for you, and you will eat the plants of the field. By the sweat of your brow you will eat your food until you return to the ground, since from it you were taken; for dust you are and to dust you will return" (Genesis 3:17–19).

Adam would now be subject to his source (the ground), even as Eve was now subject to her source (Adam). This was the moment of the birth

---

20. Bilezikian, *Beyond Sex Roles*, 3rd ed., 42.
21. Schaeffer, *Genesis in Space and Time*, 93–94.

of patriarchy. As a result of their sin, the man was now the master over the woman, and the ground was now master over the man, contrary to God's original intention in creation.

Hope in the Middle of a Hopeless Situation

In the midst of this horror, note that God cursed the serpent (Genesis 3:14–15) and the ground (3:17), but he did not curse Adam and Eve. Many people think that the human pair was cursed, but this is not so. They would suffer greatly for their sin. But even in the litany of their woes, they were still promised the hope of redemption (3:15). Speaking to the serpent, God had said, "I will put enmity between you and the woman, and between your offspring and hers; he will crush your head, and you will strike his heel." We know this passage as the first announcement of God's redemption, alluded to by Paul in 1 Timothy 2:15. Death now permeated all realms of life, and suffering would attend the process of life from its beginning. The woman would have pain in childbirth, and the man would suffer in tilling a resistant soil. Life would go on after the fall, but it would be a struggle from beginning to end.

Eve was created to be Adam's *ezer* in his time of need, but she succumbed to the serpent's temptation. She had known "the perfect life," but it wasn't "enough." She wanted "the knowledge of good and evil." By her action, she gained that. No woman since then has endured a comparable pain in moving from a flawless situation to the misery of a hard life outside the garden. And in the midst of her new and harsh life, she watched one son murder another son.

Eve's story is tragic, not only for her, but for the whole human race. Once she made the decision about eating a piece of appealing fruit, she could not change the ending for herself or for Adam. She could not undo what she had done, nor could Adam undo his deed. But the Author of the story could step in and change the ending.[22] And he did, in the incarnation.

God's first human team had failed. But in the following chapters, we watch God step back into his story and call out other men and women to be his agents of change in a brutal world. These men and *ezer* women were bold and courageous, sometimes risking their lives to further God's redemptive work in this broken world. They led as they again and again reversed the course of history through their intrepid actions. Their stories overturn some of our ideas about the nature of "manhood and womanhood."

Questions for Personal Reflection or Group Discussion

1. Read through Genesis 1–3. What is your most important takeaway from this story?
2. As scholars have wrestled with the implications of the first three chapters of the Bible, where do you come out on the question of gender equality or subordination?
3. As you think about women being created as *ezer* "helpers," how does this change your idea of what a woman can or cannot do in every part of her life?
4. What difference does it make for a woman whether she is "equal" with men or is in a subordinate position to men?

---

22. See Alice Mathews, *A Woman God Can Use: Lessons from Old Testament Women Help You Make Today's Choices* (Grand Rapids: Discovery House, 1990), 28.

Chapter Three

EZER WOMEN IN A PATRIARCHAL WORLD

Chapter 2 ended with the first man and woman being driven out of Eden into a harsh new world in which survival would be a daily struggle. The alienation[1] that emerged in Eden spread through the generations of men and women that followed, with devastating consequences for the whole human race. So in Genesis 6:5 we read, "The LORD saw how great the wickedness of the human race had become on the earth, and that every inclination of the thoughts of the human heart was only evil all the time." In short order, the whole human race had become so evil, so murderous, so oppressive, that God saw no solution other than to begin again with a new human A-team in a world washed clean by a great flood.

Even some of the family of the godly man Noah soon abandoned God, and eventually another new A-team was formed around the man Abraham. With him, God established a new covenant, which passed through his son Isaac, then through his grandson Jacob. Some of their stories are not pretty, but by and large, they hewed to the covenant God had made with their ancestor Abraham. By then, Abraham's single family had swelled into a tribe living in Palestine, headed by Jacob's many sons.[2]

---

1. This is a threefold alienation: between the man and woman, between them and God, and between them and their newly hostile environment.

2. While women like Sarah, Rebekah, Leah, and Rachel played important roles in their families, in a patriarchal society, the story generally highlights the men who headed the clans.

Eventually, a famine in Palestine drove that tribe to relocate to Egypt, where food was available, and for a time, Jacob's descendants thrived in the new land. But over time, a new pharaoh, fearing their growing numbers and power, enslaved them, forcing them to build some of Egypt's great cities and monuments. It is at this point that we will pick up the story of some outstanding A-team women in the Bible.

While complementarians have assigned women a subordinate "helping" role, like a plumber's assistant handing the man the right wrench, the Old Testament reveals true *ezer* women bringing their unique strengths to rescue God's people in times of crisis.[3]

When God created the woman in Genesis 2:18, he called her an *ezer kenegdo*, a particular kind of helper to the man, in a vein similar to God's help to his people. An *ezer* helper is not a subordinate to the one being helped. Instead, an *ezer* helper brings aid that the recipient badly needs but cannot provide for himself. In eight of the twenty-one times the word is used in the Old Testament, this "helper" is a "savior"; in the remaining occurrences, this help is a "strength."

So the woman as *ezer kenegdo* is a strong counterpart, brought to the man as fully his equal. God made for the man a power or a strength that would in every way "correspond to him" as his equal.

SOME REPRESENTATIVE *EZER* WOMEN IN THE PATRIARCHAL WORLD OF THE OLD TESTAMENT

In Exodus 1:8–21, we meet Shiphrah and Puah, *ezer* women, who began the rescue of God's people enslaved in Egypt. The Egyptian pharaoh (king) had forced the Israelites to build great cities and monuments with poor materials and hard labor. But these sturdy people were growing

---

3. Someone may argue that God appears to work generally through men and occasionally through women in times of crisis, and from that they may infer female subordination. That, however, mistakes the nature of the "Blessed Alliance" (see Genesis 1:26–28).

too numerous for the pharaoh's comfort. The more the Israelites were oppressed, the more they multiplied. So the pharaoh sent for Shiphrah and Puah and gave them a harsh assignment: "When you are helping the Hebrew women during childbirth on the delivery stool, if you see that the baby is a boy, kill him; but if it is a girl, let her live" (Exodus 1:16).

But the midwives refused to do that. When the pharaoh demanded the reason that boy babies were still allowed to live, the two women told him that Hebrew women are vigorous and give birth before the midwives arrive. The text then tells us that "God was kind to the midwives and the people increased and became even more numerous. And because the midwives feared God, he gave them families of their own" (Exodus 1:20–21).

Put yourself in the place of the two midwives. An autocratic dictator has given them orders that, if followed, would eventually lead to the extinction of the Hebrew race. In one generation, with no Hebrew men to inseminate the women, sooner or later the Israelites would cease to exist as a people. Children born to the Hebrew women would have had Egyptian fathers and would be assimilated into Egyptian life. In that patriarchal Egyptian culture, God's team for changing the world would be gone.

But Shiphrah and Puah were made of sterner stuff. They were *ezer* women, women of strength. Putting their own lives on the line, they refused to comply with the king's command. Jonathan Magonet has called them "the earliest and in some ways the most powerful examples of resistance to an evil regime."[4] Because they believed in the Lord God, they could defy a powerful potentate as helpers of those who needed the help that only they could give. They used their professional expertise to come to the aid of Hebrew babies in a time of crisis. They were *ezer* women, and God honored their faith and courage by giving them families of their own.

---

4. Jonathan Magonet, *Bible Lives* (London: SCM, 1992), 8.

Exodus 1 ends with these words: "Then Pharaoh gave this order to all his people: "Every Hebrew boy that is born you must throw into the Nile, but let every girl live." We then read about the birth of a particular boy later named Moses.

Had Shiphrah and Puah followed the king's command, this boy who became God's leader would not have survived. The courage and resulting initiative of the midwives made possible a leader who would eventually defy the pharaoh and enable the Hebrew people to escape from slavery in Egypt.[5]

The midwives went up against a foreign king. In 1 Samuel 25, we meet Abigail, who risked going up against her evil husband. Created by God to partner with her husband as equals (Genesis 2:18), but living in a fallen world now dominated by patriarchy (Genesis 3:16), she knew she could not go on living quietly under Nabal's harsh rule when his stupidity was leading to the annihilation of her household. Everyone under her roof was in imminent danger unless she became their "help" as the *ezer* woman God created her to be.

This is the story: Nabal, a wealthy rancher in southern Palestine, was a nasty man, "surly and mean in his dealings" (1 Samuel 25:3). His three thousand sheep and one thousand goats were tended in unfenced land by shepherds who relied on a nearby militia to protect them from brigands and wild animals. That militia was led by David, on the run from jealous King Saul, who wanted to kill him. It was customary at sheep-shearing time each year that the owner of the ranch would reward such men with quantities of food. But when David sent a delegation to Nabal for that purpose, Nabal sneered. "Who is this David? . . . Why should I take my bread and water and the meat I have slaughtered for my shearers, and give it to men coming from who knows where?" (1 Samuel 25:10–11). When

---

5. In this story of the courageous midwives, someone may conclude they really did not challenge patriarchy. But when the Hebrew women risked their lives to defy the Egyptian pharaoh, they went up against the most powerful ruler in their patriarchal world.

David's men returned empty-handed with Nabal's response, David said, "Each of you strap on your sword!" and taking four hundred men with him, David set out for Nabal's ranch (25:13).

When Abigail heard what had happened and the imminent danger Nabal's meanness meant for everyone in that large household, she gathered up a huge amount of food, loaded it on donkeys, and set out to find David's men. Riding her donkey and leading the other animals loaded with food, she entered a mountain ravine and saw David and his men coming toward her. David had just finished telling his four hundred armed men that all they had done for Nabal had been useless: "He has paid me back evil for good. May God deal with David, be it ever so severely, if by morning I leave alive one male of all who belong to him!" (1 Samuel 25:21–22).

As an *ezer* woman, Abigail had taken two risks: she disobeyed the clear intention of her lord and master, Nabal, and she was now face-to-face with someone intent on killing him and his household. Quickly dismounting from her donkey and bowing down before David, she could not know whether he would immediately kill her or would allow her to speak. Seizing the moment of silence between them, she spoke first, making four points:

1. Ignore Nabal, David, because he's not only wicked but also stupid.
2. I didn't see your delegation, or I would have acted sooner.
3. Her third point brought God into the picture: God has used my coming here with food to keep you from avenging yourself by murdering my household.
4. Accept this gift of food and drink for you and your men.

In that patriarchal society, Nabal was her lord, a fact she could never forget. But she also called David "lord," acknowledging the reality of male power in that culture. However, she then brought in the true Lord, the God of Israel, who was using her to keep David from bloodshed that day.

David got that last use of *lord* immediately and grasped that the hand of God was at work through this woman. His response to Abigail's plea was immediate. It also had four parts:

1. Abigail, you were sent to me by God to keep me from harming you and your household.
2. God bless you for your good judgment and for keeping me from a rash act of vengeance.
3. If you hadn't done this, every male in Nabal's house would have been dead before daybreak.
4. I accept your gift of food and grant your request so you can go home in peace.

After that encounter, Abigail still had to return home and tell Nabal what she had done. In overturning his ruling, she had taken a great risk. But when she told him what had happened, he was so stunned by the reality of the near-consequence of his stupidity that "his heart failed him and he became like a stone. About ten days later, the LORD struck Nabal and he died" (1 Samuel 25:37–38).

When David heard that Nabal was dead, he proposed marriage to Abigail. On his first encounter with her in that mountain pass, he had praised her for her good judgment and quick action. Now he wanted her as his wife. The text tells us that "she bowed down with her face to the ground and said, 'I am your servant and am ready to serve you and wash the feet of my lord's servants.' Abigail quickly got on a donkey and . . . went with David's messengers and became his wife" (1 Samuel 25:41–42).

Note the glimpses of women's roles in a patriarchal society. She identified herself as David's "servant," ready to "wash the feet of my lord's servants." In that society, a woman needed a man to provide for her, but that arrangement came within a clearly hierarchical relationship. Marriage to David was her best option.

David already had two other wives—Michal and Ahinoam—and later would marry five other women.[6] In that patriarchal culture, having multiple wives was a sign of a man's wealth, power, and prestige. Even though David was a fugitive from King Saul at the time he met Abigail, he was part of a cultural assumption that wives were "collectible." This piece of patriarchy ignored God's intention for marriage, stated in Genesis 2:24.

In short order after Adam's expulsion from Eden, the next biblical snapshot of this curvature of the soul without God shows us polygamy now in human practice. There we meet Lamech boasting to his two wives: "Adah and Zillah, listen to me; wives of Lamech, hear my words. I have killed a man for wounding me, a young man for injuring me" (Genesis 4:23). A drive toward excess now ruled. The patriarchy that allowed him to take more than one wife was matched with an excess in violence: it was not enough to wound an adversary; kill him!

As we move through the Old Testament, we see one of the consequences of Genesis 3:16: male rule with its one-sided power in a broken and sin-soaked world. The power of one man over one woman now extended to clans and ultimately to nations. By the time we meet Nabal, Abigail, and David in 1 Samuel 25, we see that the end result of Genesis 3:16 was so ingrained in people's thinking that neither Abigail nor David wondered at her use of the title "lord." Any male—husband or enemy—was a "lord" over a woman in those days. But Abigail was still an *ezer* woman. She could defy patriarchal power when necessary in order to save the lives of those in her household.

---

6. David's eight wives were Michal (1 Samuel 18:20–27), Ahinoam (1 Samuel 25:43), Abigail (1 Samuel 25:42), Maachah, Haggith, Abital, Eglah (2 Samuel 3:3–5), and Bathsheba (2 Samuel 11:27).

What about those times when the problem isn't caused by a specific oppressor but by an ingrained system that is universally accepted? What about cultural settings that work against God's original intention for men and women to serve together as complementary equals?

In the ancient Near East, a woman's world was bounded by her need to have a man as her provider and protector. It could be her father, her husband, or her son, but it must be a male. Wealth passed down through the generations from father to son, not to daughters.

We do have one example in the Bible (Numbers 26:33) of women who protested that system. Zelophehad had no sons, but had five daughters. When he died, his five daughters went to Moses with this request: "Why should our father's name disappear from his clan because he had no son? Give us property among our father's relatives" (Numbers 27:4).

When Moses took the issue up with the Lord, God told him that the women were right and should have their father's property as an inheritance. The daughters' request became the basis for a new law: "If a man dies and leaves no son, give his inheritance to his daughter . . . This is to have the force of law for the Israelites, as the LORD commanded Moses" (Numbers 27:8, 11).

That law was later narrowed when male members of Zelophehad's clan raised the issue, "Suppose [his daughters] marry men from other Israelite tribes; then their inheritance will be taken from our ancestral inheritance and added to that of the tribe they marry into" (Numbers 36:3–4). So Zelophehad's daughters married their cousins on their father's side so their inheritance would remain in their clan. As complicated as the inheritance laws may appear, for the most part, wealth always passed from male to male.

We meet these laws in the book of Ruth. Elimelech had inherited a piece of ground in the town of Bethlehem. He married Naomi, who later presented him with two sons, Mahlon and Kilion. A prolonged famine in Bethlehem drove this family of four to resettle in neighboring Moab, where food was available. There the two sons married local women—Moabites. In time, both the father and the two sons died, leaving three widows: Naomi from Bethlehem and two daughters-in-law (Ruth and Orpah) from Moab.

Now with all three women widowed, who would care for them? Naomi decided to return to Bethlehem after telling both daughters-in-law to return to their fathers' house so new marriages could be arranged. Orpah did so, but Ruth would not leave her destitute mother-in-law, but would instead go to Bethlehem with her and somehow figure out how to meet their daily needs. What could two widows do in Bethlehem except to rely on the generosity of neighbors?

That was one problem. But Ruth's ethnicity also worked against her move to Bethlehem: the Hebrew people hated Moabites (and vice versa). But in the face of these realities, Ruth—the *ezer* woman—immediately set out to resolve their dilemma. Watch this young Moabite woman crawl along the ground behind reapers to pick up any grains of barley or wheat that had been left behind. See the owner's interest in this determined woman and his decision to add to her pickings and load her down with reaped grain. Think about her mother-in-law's scheme to have Ruth propose marriage to that owner! The owner liked that idea—but it then raised the issue of Elimelech's property and inheritance issues. One of Naomi's relatives wanted that property. But when the relative realized Ruth went with the bargain, he backed out because—inheritance laws again!—if he married Ruth and she gave birth to a male child and gave that child to Naomi, the property would go to that son and not to the greedy relative.

This story has a fairy-tale ending. Not only did the foreign woman from Moab marry the rich owner, but they ultimately became the great-grandparents of Israel's greatest king, David.

Ruth has taken up the cause of an older woman who needed her help, bringing the help that the older woman had no resources of her own to meet. In that midnight proposal scene, Boaz's response to Ruth's marriage proposal was essentially, "WOW! All the people of my town know you are a woman of noble character" (Ruth 3:11). We can miss the force of his exclamation because most translators don't give this text its full value: the Hebrew word *khayil* is much stronger than "noble character."[7]

Khayil is a common word in the Old Testament, appearing 242 times (three times referring to a woman [Ruth 3:11; Proverbs 12:4; 31:10] and the rest of the time in reference to soldiers and armies). In most cases, it is translated as "strength" or "might" or "valor" and is used to describe a soldier's willingness to stand firm in battle and not run away. David's "mighty men" were called *khayil* men (2 Samuel 23:15–16). When Boaz chose that word to describe Ruth, he in essence said, "All the people of my town know you are a woman of strength. You don't run away in the face of danger or challenge."

Life for women in the ancient Near East was, for the most part, anything but benevolent. Yet God endowed women with an *ezer* strength to overcome a king's order, a husband's folly, and a culture's presuppositions about women.

Ruth and the Proverbs 31 woman were described as *khayil*. It wasn't that they were merely "virtuous" or "of noble character." They were women of strength. This was part of being an *ezer* woman: the woman who can be a help to the helpless must be a *khayil* woman, standing her ground with strength and determination. We see that in the midwives. We see that in Abigail. We see that in Ruth. This was God's intention in creating a woman to be *ezer kenegdo*. She was made to partner with a man, complementing his strengths with her own strengths. They were made to stand together as a team of equals.

---

7. Here in Ruth 3:11 and also in Proverbs 31, the KJV translates *khayil* as "virtuous," the NIV as "noble character," the NASB as "excellent," the NLT as "virtuous and capable," and the NRSV as "capable" (Proverbs 31:10) or "worthy" (Ruth 3:11). None dared to give the Hebrew word its normal meaning of "strength, valor."

TWO WOMEN PROPHETS IN
A PATRIARCHAL WORLD

Patriarchy, according to the Oxford dictionaries is "a system of government in which the father or eldest male is head of the family, and descent
is reckoned through the male line; also, a system of government in which
men hold the power and women are largely excluded from it."[8] When
we turn to the Bible, we see the beginnings of patriarchy (gender-based
hierarchy) in Genesis 3:16. But throughout the Old Testament, we also
see anomalies to that system. Some of those anomalies show up in the
religious practice of God's people.

Instituting the Necessary Rule of Law

Recall Francis Schaeffer's observation that sin requires hierarchy.
People need some rule of law to curb human evil. As God enabled Moses
to lead the Israelites out of Egypt and on their way to the Promised Land,
they paused at Mount Sinai to receive God's law (Exodus 19). Much of
that law covered the way the people were to relate to one another.

Another major part covered how the people were to relate to their
Creator, the Lord God. What measures would allow them to address
this great God? What kind of intermediaries would they need when
they had done wrong? That part of God's law had to do with the people's
worship for which a cadre of priests would be necessary (Exodus 28–29,
Leviticus 8–9).

To qualify for the priesthood, a person must be male, descended from
the tribe of Levi (Aaron's ancestor), and free from any kind of physical
blemish. Obviously, no woman could be a priest. Nor could any man
who could not trace his ancestry back to Levi, Jacob's third son by Leah.
A man could become a priest only if he fit the template laid down by

---

8. Online at www.oxforddictionaries.com/definition/patriarchy (accessed November 21,
2016).

genealogy and physical fitness. Becoming a priest had nothing to do with the possession of special spiritual gifts, merit, or competence. Priests were "holy" in terms of ritual observance, not in terms of personal goodness and sanctity.

Priests had two tasks: they were in charge of worship (Leviticus 1:7–7:34) and they were to teach the people the law of God (Leviticus 10:11; Deuteronomy 33:10; 2 Chronicles 15:3; Ezekiel 44:16–24).

As we watch some of the priests in action later in the Old Testament and in the New Testament gospels, we see that over time the priesthood became elite, exclusive, and professional—an institution of power, both political and economic. Both the Old Testament prophets and Jesus in the gospels excoriated the priests for their scandalous disregard of God's law (cf. Ezekiel 22:26; Hosea 4:6–9; Zephaniah 3:4; Matthew 23). The priestly team had, with a few stellar exceptions, failed miserably.

An Alternate Team: the Prophets

In the Old Testament, how could a person qualify as a prophet? People became prophets, not from ancestry, but by God's call and empowerment. God had originally given to the priests the task of teaching God's law to the people, but when they failed, a new team was needed for that purpose. In times of apostasy, the priests still carried out formal worship activities, but the task of teaching the word of the Lord to the people shifted to the prophets. A prophet was someone who announced or interpreted God's purposes for us.

At no time in the Old Testament do we find any woman functioning as part of the priestly power structure (just as we do not find any man functioning as priest if he did not descend from Levi and did not have a healthy physical body). We do, however, find women exercising the prophetic ministry of the word. Who were two of these women?

First, meet *Deborah*—*ezer* prophet, judge, and military adviser—in the hill country of Ephraim. The Bible tells us that Israelites came to her from all over the land to settle their disputes (Judges 4:4–5). Deborah was Israel's judge.

The Bible describes Deborah by three roles. First, she was a *prophet*: God had gifted her to speak to men and women to strengthen, comfort, and encourage them. God also gave her knowledge of the future and insight into how to apply it to the people's lives.

Second, she was the *wife* of Lappidoth. She was not a single woman who could give her whole attention to ministry for God and nation. She also had responsibilities at home. But note the order of the sacred text: she was first a prophet and then a wife.

Third, Deborah was Israel's *leader*, called a *judge* at that time. Most judges were mainly military leaders who came to power in times of national crisis. In one sense, they were more generals than judges. But some judges rose to power because they also had wisdom and were able to administer justice in the family, tribe, or nation. Deborah was both a military leader and one who could mete out justice.

In the centuries-long period between Joshua's death and Saul's crowning as Israel's first king, the Israelites lived as a loose confederacy of tribes worshiping the Lord, Israel's God, at the tabernacle in Shiloh. But during those centuries, a pattern repeated itself several times: with no stable central government, the twelve tribes of Israel each did their own thing. Judges 21:25 notes that "in those days Israel had no king; everyone did as they saw fit."

It was a time of anarchy and apostasy. The Israelites repeatedly copied their neighbors' pagan practices—human sacrifice and ritual prostitution—adding these to the worship of the Lord. As a result, one tribe after another would fall to foreign powers and would be enslaved or forced to pay exorbitant tributes. After years of servitude, someone in the tribe would call out to God, begging for deliverance. A judge would rise up to organize a military campaign to throw off the oppressors. Then the tribe would live in peace until the people again wandered from God.

From Judges 4 we learn that Deborah combined the best qualities of the Old Testament judge: she was splendid in military strategy and superb as a judge adjudicating problems the people brought to her.

Jabin, king of Canaan with his capital in Hazor, cruelly oppressed the northern Israelite tribes for twenty years. The situation was bad: people couldn't use the roads, but had to sneak from village to village by hidden paths and clandestine trails. Village life ceased. Farmers threshed grain in secret at night in caves. Life and property were worth nothing. People were hunted down like rabbits. Women were raped. It was a brutal oppression and it had gone on for twenty years.

Jabin didn't oppress all of Israel, but only the tribes in the north. Deborah lived and worked in the south, but as she heard stories of Jabin's cruelty, she moved into action. She called a northerner (Barak of Naphtali) and commissioned him to raise an army to take on Jabin's occupation forces. Deborah said to Barak, "God wants you to raise an army of ten thousand men from the two northern tribes afflicted by this oppression. Then you're to assemble them on the flanks of Mount Tabor above the plain. We both know that Sisera, the commander of Jabin's army, has nine hundred iron chariots and you have none. But you leave them to God, who will enable you to defeat that powerful military force" (Judges 4:6–7, my paraphrase).

Barak's response tells us about his confidence in Deborah's leadership. In essence, he said, "Okay. But only if you're next to me when the battle starts. If you're not with me, I won't do this" (Judges 4:8). Here was a man who wasn't afraid to follow a woman leader when he believed that she spoke the very words of God.

What followed is a familiar story of God's deliverance. With many reasons for fear, Barak and his poorly armed soldiers assembled on Mount Tabor's slopes in full view of Jabin's army down on the plain with vast military might. Then Deborah shouted to Barak, "Go! This is the day the LORD has given Sisera into your hands. Has not the LORD gone ahead of you?" (Judges 4:14). As Barak and his troops started down the mountainside, a powerful storm hit Sisera's army full in the face; the plain turned into a muddy swamp that trapped the chariots and horses; and the Kishon River, normally a trickling stream, flooded and carried many Canaanite soldiers out to sea.

God used *ezer* Deborah to motivate Barak (a "Blessed Alliance"), and God gave supernatural help through nature. Judges 5:31 tells us that "the land had peace" for forty years. God's gift to Israel in an hour of need was wrapped in the mind and heart of an *ezer* woman. Deborah shatters our stereotypes of what a leader must be. She was God's spokeswoman to whom generals and commoners alike listened, a strong leader whose word commanded the strongest in the land.

Ezer women don't thirst for the power that men around them might have. Instead, they use their particular strength only as situations call for it. We see this in *Huldah*, also a prophet, who lived in Jerusalem at a critical time in Israel's history.

Kings David and Solomon had passed on, and the nation had split into two rival groups. Idolatry, Baal worship, ritual prostitution, and human sacrifice had once again invaded the religious worship of the people. The Lord God was merely one god among many or wasn't worshiped at all.

Many kings were evil men, and the nation was corrupt. But in the midst of this, a prince named Josiah was born. His grandfather (Manasseh) and his father (Amon) were evil rulers. The young boy suddenly found himself on Judah's throne, but with one difference: somewhere Josiah had learned to walk in the law of the Lord, following

David's example. Into a totally pagan generation with corrupt rulers came a young boy whose heart was turned toward the Lord.

Eighteen years into his reign, Josiah ordered a total renovation of God's temple in Jerusalem. It had lain in shambles, desecrated by pagan worship, and it would take a lot of work to restore it. In the middle of this restoration process, a workman stumbled on an ancient scroll, the Book of the Law, which no one could understand or interpret. Even Hilkiah, the high priest, could not understand this sacred writing. He reported the find to the king.

When King Josiah heard part of the scroll read to him, he tore his robes and ordered everyone to find out about this book. If what the scroll said was true, his kingdom was in great danger. The king concluded, "Great is the LORD's anger that burns against us because those who have gone before us have not . . . acted in accordance with all that is written there concerning us" (2 Kings 22:13). Josiah was a man of action. He wanted an interpreter for this book, a prophet who could discern its meaning.

At that time, several prophets lived in or near Jerusalem. Jeremiah had been in Jerusalem, receiving prophetic messages from God for at least five years at the time the scroll was found (Jeremiah 1:2). Also Zephaniah was prophesying in or near Jerusalem in the reign of Josiah (Zephaniah 1:1). So does it strike you as strange that in 2 Kings 22:14, the high priest Hilkiah turned to a woman for an explanation of the word of the Lord? They brought in the prophet Huldah, who was also the wife of Shallum, the keeper of the royal wardrobe.

Sometimes we're told that God has to use women to do men's work because no men are available. We can't support that from 2 Kings 22. Though godly male prophets were in the vicinity, God had given a spiritual gift to the woman Huldah and then used her to speak his message to the high priest and to the king.

The fact that the high priest and the king's advisors sought her out tells us that she could be trusted to tell them the true words of God sharply, clearly, and accurately. In their presence, three times she prefaced her prophetic interpretation with the words, "This is what the LORD, the God of Israel, says."

Huldah spoke strong, decisive words, not holding back: God is going to bring disaster on this place and its people. Why? Because they've forsaken the Lord and served idols. But because Josiah has a humble heart and wants to do the right thing, God would delay that punishment until another king ascended to Judah's throne (2 Kings 22:15–20).

Huldah didn't apologize for God's word or refuse to speak because she was a woman and didn't want to offend the men. She simply used her God-given gift of prophecy. We don't hear of her again. She was on and off the stage in one quick but powerful scene. Both the king and the high priest knew she was God's spokesperson. They didn't seek a second opinion, but instituted a sweeping religious reform in Judah.

God called Deborah and Huldah to use their *ezer* strength when men needed what only they could provide. Barak and the oppressed northerners needed Deborah to bring about their deliverance. King Josiah and his court needed Huldah to give them a true understanding of God's intentions for the apostate people.

Complementarians have written that "the God-given sense of responsibility for leadership in a mature man will not generally allow him to flourish long under the personal, directive leadership of a female superior."[9] The actions of General Barak and the high priest and leaders in King Josiah's court show that this assumption is untrue. What does this say about the fragility of a man who can't flourish under the leadership of a woman?

---

9. John Piper and Wayne Grudem, eds., *Recovering Biblical Manhood and Womanhood: A Response to Evangelical Feminism*, 2nd ed. (Wheaton, IL: Crossway, 2006), 52.

Questions for Personal Reflection or Group Discussion

1. Why do you think God would create women as *ezer kenegdo*?
2. Each of these women was blessed by God for the actions she took. How does this shape your concept of a woman as *ezer kenegdo*?
3. How do Deborah and Huldah exemplify what it means to be created as an *ezer kenegdo*?
4. Gender-based hierarchy restricts women in both home and church. As you review the ways in which God raised up female leadership in various periods of Israel's life, what implications do you see for women in the church today?

Chapter Four

JESUS AND WOMEN: THE DIVINE COUNTERPUNCH

Some biblical scholars tend to limit the move from Old to New Testaments to a shift from law to grace (e.g., Romans 3:28: "we maintain that a person is justified by faith apart from the works of the law"). But Jesus inaugurated his public ministry by choosing to read Isaiah 61:1–2 in his hometown synagogue: "The Spirit of the Lord is on me, because he has anointed me to proclaim good news to the poor. He has sent me to proclaim freedom for the prisoners and recovery of sight for the blind, to set the oppressed free, to proclaim the year of the Lord's favor" (Luke 4:18–19). He then startled his audience by remarking, "Today this scripture is fulfilled in your hearing" (4:21).

Furthermore, in his teaching on the mountainside, Jesus was clear that he had not come "to abolish the Law and the Prophets," but instead to fulfill them. He amplified that, saying, "For truly I tell you, until heaven and earth disappear, not the smallest letter, not the least stroke of a pen, will by any means disappear from the Law until everything is accomplished" (Matthew 5:17–18). So if Jesus did not come to abolish the Law, what is "new" in the New Testament?

First-century religious leaders in Israel usually referred to the Old Testament as "the Law and the Prophets." We've already seen in chapter 3 that the priests' task was to teach God's Law to the people, but when the priests ignored that commission, God turned to the prophets to carry it out. What did the prophets frequently face with that task?

The prophet Ezekiel captured the enormity of their task in Ezekiel 22: the *princes* use their power to shed blood and treat their parents with contempt (verses 6–7). They are slanderers who desecrate the Sabbath and commit lewd acts while sleeping with other men's wives. Furthermore, the *priests* do violence to the Law and profane holy things, shutting their eyes to violations of God's Sabbath (verse 26). And the *leaders* of Jerusalem "are like wolves tearing their prey; they shed blood and kill people to make unjust gain" (verse 27). Even the *prophets* tell lies in order to whitewash the deeds of the leaders: "They say, 'This is what the Sovereign LORD says'—when the LORD has not spoken" (verse 28). So much so that *the people* of the land are caught up in this evil spiral: they "practice extortion and commit robbery; they oppress the poor and needy and mistreat the foreigner, denying them justice" (verse 29).

The task given to the Old Testament prophets of God was huge! Often they stood alone against a society so corrupt, so evil in every way, that the situation looked impossible. And eventually the situation did become so impossible that God allowed, first, Assyria, and then Babylon to defeat the Jews and carry them off into exile. Nothing less than a long exile could begin to cure the perverseness of the people.

Half a millennium later, the Jews were back in the land of Israel, now under Roman rule. The exile had cured them of idolatry but had not touched their souls with concern for the poor, the blind, or those imprisoned, if not behind bars, by customs and practices that kept them in their place at the bottom of the stack. When Jesus stood in the Nazareth synagogue that day and read from Isaiah 61, declaring that he had come to bring in that new order, the divine counterpunch had begun. He came to overturn the inequities and social sins still rampant among the nation's leaders. His message was broader than issues of law versus grace. He came to fulfill that law by filling it full of God's loving purpose for every person. Jesus was clear that external religion mocked God if it lacked the interior commitment to love God wholeheartedly and to love others as we love ourselves (Matthew 22:37–39). Jesus' overwhelming message in sermon and parable was about God's unfailing love for everyone and the lengths to which he had gone "to seek and to save the lost" (Luke 19:10).

Don't underestimate Jesus' purpose and work. God entered the human race as a human being to begin the Great Reversal. He died to pay our penalty for our sins, but he also lived and walked the paths of Galilee and Judea to overturn the kinds of hierarchies that destroy lives and hinder God's purposes. God anointed him to proclaim good news to the *poor*, freedom for *prisoners*, and the year of the Lord's favor. In the process, his purpose was to set the *oppressed* free (Luke 4:18–19). His work included challenging all of the hierarchies that kept people down, whether hierarchies of class, of race, or of gender.[1]

SHOW AND TELL:
JESUS AND WOMEN IN THE GOSPELS

Jesus' opposition to all oppressive human hierarchies was explicit in his teachings and implicit in his actions. To see how he viewed hierarchical structures of power and influence, watch him in John 13. In the midst of a final meal with his disciples, Jesus took off his robe, tied a towel around his waist, filled a basin with water, and began washing each disciple's feet. When Peter remonstrated with him, he reminded him and the others at the table that what he was doing was an example of what they should do for others: "Do you understand what I've done for you? . . . Now that I, your Lord and Teacher, have washed your feet, you also should wash one

---

1. Not all hierarchies are evil. As Francis Schaeffer noted, sin requires hierarchy to curb sinful practices. Without some hierarchies, sin would have no confining walls around it (*Genesis in Space and Time* [Downers Grove, IL: InterVarsity, 1972], 93–94).

another's feet . . . Now that you know these things, you will be blessed if you do them" (John 13:12–13, 17).[2]

Or listen to him in Matthew 20. The mother of James and John had asked Jesus to give her two sons the favored seats at his right and left hands when he entered his kingdom (verse 21). This would set up a hierarchy among his followers. When Jesus asked the two men if they were able to "drink the cup" he was about to drink (arrest and crucifixion), they said, "Sure!" When the other disciples were upset when they learned about this little game of one-upmanship, Jesus called them together and in essence said, "It's the Gentiles and their high officials who lord it over those beneath them. But that's not how you are to act. If you want to be great, then serve. If you want to be first, then put yourself in the position of a slave. This is what I've done. I didn't come to be served, but to serve. I'll show that by giving my life as a ransom for many" (verses 25–28, my paraphrase). Jesus had no patience for establishing hierarchies among his followers.

Elsewhere he was clear that "many who are first will be last, and many who are last will be first" (Matthew 19:30). When we hear these words, do we understand that Jesus is landing a strong counterpunch against all harmful hierarchies? Again and again throughout the gospels, we hear him denounce human assumptions about power and dominance. He was consistently clear: leadership is from the bottom, not from the top. We lead as we serve.

JESUS IN ACTION OVERTURNING GENDER-BASED HIERARCHIES

Among the hierarchies Jesus overturned was the gender-based hierarchy dominating life in Israel. He showed his followers a radically different way

---

2. Someone may argue that Jesus' relationship to his followers was hierarchical: they called him "Lord." Yet he modeled servanthood toward them. The issue is not hierarchy per se, but any hierarchy that is oppressive or harmful to those caught within it. Even so, Jesus' teachings in Matthew 20:25–28 show the danger in any hierarchy.

of relating to women. Watch him, for example, in John 4 as he deliberately planned his journey in order to encounter a despised woman in Samaria. He shocked the woman at the town well by speaking to her and then by actually drinking water from her cup. When his followers returned from town with some food, they were astonished that he would talk to such a person (verse 27). But even though the woman was an outcast in her town, her testimony to town leaders was so powerful that they also came out to meet Jesus. Ultimately, at their invitation, Jesus stayed for two more days to teach the people, many of whom became his followers. Jesus empowered a despised woman to become a vehicle for evangelizing that community.

Or think of the shock to his followers when Jesus not only allowed Mary of Bethany to sit at his feet and learn (in the posture typical of rabbinic students), but even encouraged her to do so (Luke 10:38–42). Rabbi Eliezer had declared "If any man gives his daughter a knowledge of the Law, it is as though he taught her lechery" (m. Sotah 3:4).[3] Jose ben Johanan of Jerusalem had taught, "He who talks much with womankind brings evil upon himself and neglects the study of the Law and at the last will inherit Gehenna" (m. Avot 1:5). In the eyes of many Jews, not only was teaching theology to a woman not necessary; it was downright wrong.

In New Testament Judaism as practiced by the teachers of the law and the Pharisees, women were held responsible for the evil in the world. For that reason, they were strictly segregated from the social and religious life of their communities. Religious men considered them inferior and unteachable.[4] But Jesus overturned that false hierarchy.

Jesus had come to fulfill the Law, not to annul it. In Deuteronomy 31:12, the Law stated, "Assemble the people—men, women and children, and the foreigners residing in your towns—so they can listen and learn to

---

3. Cited in Aida Spencer, *Beyond the Curse: Women Called to Ministry* (Nashville: Nelson, 1985), 53. The author then asked, "Why 'lechery'? A woman who knew the law would become active in public thereby indirectly inviting sexual advances."

4. Rabbi Eliezer declared, "There is no wisdom in woman except with the distaff" (b. *Yoma* 33b), cited in ibid., 51.

fear the LORD your God and follow carefully all the words of this law." Women, children, and even foreigners had a right, even an obligation, to listen to and obey God's Law. Any hierarchy impeding this right was against God's purposes. When Jesus encouraged Mary of Bethany to take the role of a disciple, he revealed a lot about his view of women: they are intelligent persons who can understand his teachings as well as men can.

In Luke 10, Mary's sister, Martha, was in the kitchen preparing food, in contrast to Mary, who was sitting at Jesus' feet. In John 11, however, we encounter Jesus talking with Martha when her brother had died. We watch Martha rise to the highest level of faith in all of John's gospel when she said, "I believe that you are the Messiah, the Son of God, who is to come into the world" (verse 27). In this one statement, it's clear she understood three fundamental things about Jesus: (1) he was "Lord"; (2) he was the "Christ" (Messiah); and (3) he was divine (the Son of God), with a divine purpose in the world. John stated that the entire gospel had been written so others may believe "that Jesus is the Messiah, the Son of God, and that by believing you may have life in his name" (20:31). It is the woman Martha who saw most clearly Jesus' purpose and ministry.

Or consider Jesus' shocking statement in Luke 11:27–28: "As Jesus was [teaching], a woman in the crowd called out, 'Blessed is the mother who gave you birth and nursed you.' He replied, 'Blessed rather are those who hear the word of God and obey it.'" In that culture, bearing children (particularly sons) was seen as the fulfillment of a woman's life. The absence of children was considered a great misfortune, a divine punishment for some sin a woman had committed. A fruitful womb was a sign of God's blessing; a barren womb was a sign of God's curse. But Jesus challenged that notion by saying that women's response to God's word matters more than bearing children. New creation by God's word, not procreation by the womb, was the fulfillment of female personhood (as it was for men).

In another event, Jesus was teaching in a house when someone noted that his mother and brothers were outside looking for him. Jesus responded with a question and then a statement: "Who are my mother and my brothers? [Then gesturing to his listeners] Here are my mother and my brothers! Whoever does God's will is my brother and sister and mother" (Mark 3:32–35). Note that Mark here included sisters along with the brothers. Jesus' true "relatives" are those who follow him—both men and women. In God's kingdom values, human families count less than the family of God—those who do God's will.

Even more shocking in his day was Jesus' willingness to redeem prostitutes. Luke narrates a dinner party held by Simon the Pharisee. While they were at the table eating, a woman of the streets came to Simon's house, found where Jesus reclined at the dinner table, came up behind him, and began to pour perfume on his feet (Luke 7:37–38). Of course, Simon was shocked that Jesus would allow such unseemly behavior! In the ensuing conversation, Jesus told one of his little story gems about two debtors and their attitudes toward the moneylender when the debts were forgiven. From that, Jesus drew a parallel between the woman's and Simon's treatment of him as guest in the house. Then turning to the woman, he said, "Your sins are forgiven . . . Your faith has saved you; go in peace" (verses 48, 50). The Pharisees watching the prostitute anoint Jesus saw only a fallen, unredeemable woman; Jesus saw only a repentant sinner whose sins he forgave.

In another conversation with the chief priests and elders in the Jerusalem temple, Jesus shocked them by saying, "The tax collectors and the prostitutes are entering the kingdom of God ahead of you. For John came to you to show you the way of righteousness, and you did not believe him, but the tax collectors and the prostitutes did. And even after you saw this, you did not repent and believe him" (Matthew 21:31–32). Again, Jesus overturned their notions of who could or could not enter God's kingdom.

Just six days before his arrest and crucifixion, Jesus was in Bethany as a dinner guest (John 12:2–3; see also Mark 14:3). As he and his disciples reclined on couches around the table, Mary (yes, the same Mary, Lazarus's sister, who sat at Jesus' feet as his rabbinical student) entered with an alabaster container of priceless ointment. Quietly she circled the room until she stood behind Jesus. Watch her as she snapped off the neck of the container and began pouring the costly ointment, first on Jesus' head and then on his feet.

What was the response of the men gathered at the table? Did they enjoy the fragrance of that precious ointment? No, they insisted her gift to Jesus was a waste of something valuable. Piously they observed that the perfume could have been sold for a year's wages and the money given to the poor (Mark 14:5). But Jesus contradicted their piety, saying, "Leave her alone! Why are you bothering her? She has done a beautiful thing for me! You're concerned about the poor? You can help them whenever you wish. Meanwhile this woman has done something beautiful for me. She anointed my body ahead of time for my burial, though you refuse to believe I'm going to die soon. Listen up! Wherever the Good News is preached anywhere in the world, this woman's story will be told in memory of her" (Mark 14:6–9, my paraphrase). Did you hear the exasperation in Jesus' voice as he rebuked the disciples?

Jesus was clear: he would not let the world forget what Mary had done for him. He approved of her way of displaying her love for him.

Of all the women mentioned in the gospels, Mary Magdalene is mentioned most often (fourteen times).[5] From Luke 8:1–3, we know that Jesus delivered her from the power of seven demons and that she was part of the group of women who traveled with Jesus and the disciples itinerantly all over Galilee and back and forth to Jerusalem in the southern part of Palestine for the national feasts. We also know she was at the cross during Jesus' execution; she was present when Joseph of Arimathea and Nicodemus hastily placed Jesus' body in the tomb; and she was one of the first at the tomb to anoint Jesus' body when the Sabbath ended. We also know she was the first to be commissioned by Jesus as a messenger of his

5. Referred to as "Mary Magdalene": Matthew 27:56, 61; 28:1; Mark 15:40, 47; 16:1, 9; Luke 8:2; 24:10; John 19:25; 20:1, 18. Referred to as simply "Mary": John 20:11, 16.

resurrection: "Go instead to my brothers and tell them …" (John 20:17). This function of "witness to the resurrection" later became a favorite way to designate the apostles (Acts 1:22; 2:32). It was the reward for a loyal female disciple that Jesus entrusted her with the most powerful message: *Go and tell my disciples that I'm no longer dead.* It's not surprising that the church fathers called her "the apostle to the apostles."

Jewish rabbinic law held that the testimony of a hundred women is not equal to that of one man. Yet women were the ones who consistently stayed with Christ through his agony and death on the cross and later were first at the empty tomb. If a woman's testimony was to be discounted, why did Jesus choose to appear first to a woman after his resurrection and send her as his messenger to the male disciples?

JESUS' TEACHINGS TO OVERTURN GENDER-BASED HIERARCHIES

One of the reasons often given for keeping women secluded in Jewish society was that they would not be sexually tempting to men. The hierarchy in that society conferred on men the privileged right of ownership: any woman was fair game for the satisfaction of their lust. But Jesus cut across their legalisms by requiring a radical change of heart that would make it unnatural for a man to want to exploit or degrade a woman.

In the Sermon on the Mount, Jesus redefined responsibility for men's morality: "You have heard that it was said, 'You shall not commit adultery.' But I tell you that anyone who looks at a woman lustfully has already committed adultery with her in his heart" (Matthew 5:27). In fact, Jesus went on to say that his required change in mentality toward women could be so difficult to achieve that it would feel like a self-mutilation. Giving up the myth of male privilege in that society may be as demanding as plucking out an eye or cutting off a hand. It would not be easy! But Jesus was clear that such "mutilation" was better than its alternative: hell (verse 30).

Matthew later recorded a conversation Jesus had with the strict religious group known as the Pharisees. They tried to trip him up by asking, "Is it lawful for a man to divorce his wife for any and every reason?" (Matthew 19:3).[6] In response, Jesus quoted Genesis 2:24, making clear that in marriage, a man and woman are no longer two, but have become one. So whatever God has joined together in marriage, no human being should separate. But the Pharisees pressed the question further: "Why then . . . did Moses command that a man give his wife a certificate of divorce and send her away?" To this, Jesus replied, "Moses permitted you to divorce your wives because your hearts were hard. But it was not this way from the beginning" (verses 7–8).

In that society, only men had the power to initiate a divorce; a woman was at her husband's mercy. To protect her, a "certificate of divorce" gave her a legal right to remarry if she had the opportunity. But Jesus was clear that men who would discard their wives were treating them as disposable items, throwaway playthings to be used for a while and then dismissed. The man who would do that had the heart of an adulterer. By addressing his disapproval of divorce to men, Jesus was clear that they should accept the blame for the practice, make amends, and correct it.

In this conversation, Jesus refused to endorse the fall as a basis for defining marriage. He hopped over the fall to base his definition of marriage squarely in the creation ideal.[7] For him, the bottom line for male/female relationships is Genesis 1 and 2. The fall and its consequences are aberrations, not what God intended. These aberrations were overturned when Jesus came. He made God's creation standards normative for the new community. This overturned the authority structure, the hierarchy that was spawned by the fall.

---

6. That question came out of the differences in teaching about divorce from two revered rabbis. The House of Shammai held that a man may divorce his wife only for a serious transgression, but the House of Hillel allowed divorce for even trivial offenses, such as burning a meal (Babylonian Talmud, tractate Gittin, 90a.).

7. Jesus quoted Genesis 1:26 in Matthew 19:4, and Genesis 2:24 in Matthew 19:5.

CONCLUDING REFLECTIONS
ON WOMEN IN THE GOSPELS

Compared to other literary works from the first century, the gospels have a relatively high number of references to women. What is even more remarkable is that in Jesus' actions, there is not a single case in which a woman is put down, reproached, humiliated, or cast into one of the lewd stereotypes of that day.

Unlike other men, Jesus spoke freely to women in public. He taught theology to women. He had women as disciples or followers.[8] He was clear that women would be active participants in the work of his kingdom. As we watch Jesus move through the gospels, we see him take a firmly countercultural stand on many issues because his mission was to oppose all that violated the will of God. Again and again, we see him base his definition of persons and his directives for male/female relationships in God's creational purposes in Genesis 1 and 2.

As we look at these and other women in the gospels, we note that they are presented positively. No woman is shown resisting his initiative, failing to believe, deserting him, or betraying him. This is in sharp contrast to the way John presented men in his gospel. Among even the Twelve there were evidences of hypocrisy (John 12:4–5), vanity (13:37), fickleness (13:38; 16:31–32), obtuseness (3:10; 16:18), deliberate unbelief (9:24–25), and thorough evil (13:2, 27–30).

Because of their faith, their understanding, and their fidelity, women were often paradigms of discipleship for the men who lacked these qualities. In contrast to first-century religious leaders, Jesus affirmed women as

---

8. Some might ask why Jesus named only men to the Twelve. A brief nuanced response to such a question isn't possible, but recall that Jesus is the culmination of Israel's history and the Old Testament prophecies (e.g., Isaiah, Daniel, various psalms, etc.). He is the vital connecting link between the promises to Abraham for the Jews and the new kingdom he inaugurated that would include the whole world. The Twelve represented the Old Testament tribes descended from Jacob. One might well ask why we hear nothing about ten of the Twelve, once God's story passes from the gospels to Acts and the letters. Their function as "the Twelve" ended as the church was born and spread throughout the known world.

whole persons with both the privilege and responsibility to follow him. Jesus came "to proclaim good news to the poor . . . to proclaim freedom for the prisoners and recovery of sight for the blind, to set the oppressed free" (Luke 4:18). That included women and the gender-based hierarchies dominating their lives. Jesus' actions and teachings delivered a strong counterpunch to the patriarchal ideas rampant in that culture.

Complementarian James Borland, writing about women in the life and teachings of Jesus, asserted that "our Lord placed a high value on women, while He continued to recognize role distinctions for men and women . . . Nowhere is this issue seen more clearly than in Jesus' selection of only men for the role of apostle . . . no woman in Christ's ministry was called, commissioned, or named as an apostle, or even performed in the role of an apostle. These roles and functions Christ reserved for men."[9] We'll hold that statement in abeyance as we move into chapter 5. Why? Because we have biblical evidence to the contrary.

Questions for Personal Reflection or Group Discussion

1. How do Jesus' instructions to his disciples at the Last Supper (John 13:12–17) inform your understanding of true leadership?
2. In what ways do you see Jesus' counterpunch against gender-based hierarchy affecting how men and women are to relate to one another in the home and in the church today?
3. As you look at women's encounters with Jesus in the four gospels, what is the primary takeaway from his actions?
4. What emotions do you experience as you reexamine Jesus' approach to women in the four gospels?

---

9. From Borlund's chapter in John Piper and Wayne Grudem, eds., *Recovering Biblical Manhood and Womanhood: A Response to Evangelical Feminism*, 2nd ed. (Wheaton, IL: Crossway, 2006), 113, 120–21.

Chapter Five

POSITIVE IMAGES
OF WOMEN IN NEW
TESTAMENT CHURCHES

A large group of women traveled with Jesus and his men around Galilee during his earthly ministry. We meet some of them in Luke 8. Jesus was busy, moving from one town to another, preaching the good news of God's kingdom: "The Twelve were with him, and also some women who had been cured of evil spirits and diseases: Mary (called Magdalene) from whom seven demons had come out; Joanna the wife of Chuza, the manager of Herod's household; Susanna; and many others" (Luke 8:2–3). In gratitude to Jesus these women used their financial means to help support the Jesus band. Only three of the "many others" are named here by Luke, but we meet others in that band elsewhere in the gospel accounts. Note that these are women who had experienced healing of some kind and who, in gratitude, now had become a traveling band of caretakers for Jesus and his disciples.

How is it that in that first-century Jewish society these women could travel publicly with a band of men without arousing strong criticism from religious leaders? The text tells us that these were women of means. Look, for example, at Joanna.[1] Her husband, Chuza, held a high position

---

1. See Richard Bauckham, *Gospel Women: Named Women in the Gospels* (Grand Rapids: Eerdmans, 2002), 109–50.

in the court of King Herod Antipas. New Testament scholar Richard Bauckham tells us Chuza was not Jewish, but Nabatean by birth. Herod Antipas's grandmother was Nabatean, and Antipas had married a daughter of the king of Nabatea (perhaps to cement some useful diplomatic ties with the neighbor country on his northern border). For reasons not given us, Antipas chose a Nabatean as manager of his household, but for local political reasons he needed to marry that foreigner to a Jewish woman from a wealthy family. Enter Joanna, who, now married to Chuza, lived with him in Antipas's palace in the new Roman city of Tiberias. She had means to use to support Jesus' ministry.[2]

Joanna, Mary Magdalene, Susanna, and the other women introduce us to the world of first-century benefaction. Throughout the Roman Empire, women benefactors had unusual freedom to move about in their communities. If they had financed some public work, they were not bound by the same constraints under which women in the broader society had to live.[3] Later in this chapter, we will meet other female benefactors who helped sponsor the ministries of the apostles.

As we move from the final chapters of the four gospels into the book of Acts, we see that this band of women disciples—faithful to Jesus at the cross, at his burial, and then at the empty tomb—had been the first to announce Jesus' resurrection to the unbelieving disciples. We meet them again in the upstairs room in Jerusalem after Jesus had ascended to God's throne (Acts 1:14). They were likely part of the 120 assembled for prayer on the day of Pentecost and were participants in announcing the story of Jesus Christ to the throngs of pilgrims on that eventful day.[4]

---

2. She also would have had access to King Antipas, assuring Jesus' freedom of movement during his three years of itinerant ministry in Galilee. It was primarily on the trips south to Judea (outside of Antipas's protection) for the great feasts of the nation that Jesus constantly ran into the buzz-saw harassment of religious leaders out to get him.

3. For an extensive discussion of women benefactors, see Lynn H. Cohick, *Women in the World of the Earliest Christians: Illuminating Ancient Ways of Life* (Grand Rapids: Baker Academic, 2009), 285–320.

4. Pentecost brought to the relatively small city of Jerusalem (normally with a population of around 55,000) throngs of pilgrims, swelling the crowds on city streets to around 180,000.

In the book of Acts, Luke picks up the story of the phenomenal growth of the Christian communities, focusing first on Peter's story and then later on Paul's story. We don't have a written record of the work of the other eleven apostles or of Jesus' female disciples in the Bible, but we can be sure they carried the message of Jesus throughout the known world. We learn from external evidence, for example, that Thomas moved out from Jerusalem, possibly taking the news of Jesus as far east as Kerala state in India. A strong, indigenous Christian church there has survived for two thousand years despite pressures to stamp it out.[5]

OUTSTANDING WOMEN IN THE NEW CHRISTIAN COMMUNITIES

In the book of Acts, Luke invites us to journey with the apostle Paul. We find him on his second missionary journey finishing up work in western Turkey as God called him to move on to northern Greece (Acts 16:8–10). His destination was the Roman city of Philippi in Macedonia.[6] Once there, he looked unsuccessfully for the Jewish synagogue. But a synagogue required a minimum of ten Jewish men for its founding.[7] That Roman city did not have enough Jewish men to form a synagogue, so where was he to find anyone with a heart open to his message? Perhaps

---

These pilgrims came from every part of the known world (see the list in Acts 2:5–11). That week of celebration brought so many people together, an ideal audience for Peter's sermon. A week earlier or a week later, Jerusalem would have shrunk to its normal size. But God's Spirit brought folks from everywhere to hear Peter's message and take it back home with them.

5. Some folks point to the fact that we do not hear of Mary Magdalene, Joanna, or the others in Acts or the letters as evidence of their short ministry to Jesus. But neither do we hear of most of the other apostles by name. We cannot discount their ministries just because Luke or the letter writers did not mention them specifically.

6. Philippi was near a major battleground where, in 42 BC, Antony and Octavian had defeated their foes. They then released some of their veteran soldiers, giving each a square of land and pronouncing the new town a Roman colony, a "miniature Rome" under Roman law and governed by two military officers appointed directly by Rome.

7. Though women weren't counted in the formation of Jewish synagogues, they were vital to the birth and life of new churches.

there would be people at prayer out by the river? He and Silas hastened there on the Sabbath.

The Businesswoman Lydia (Acts 16:11–16, 40)

Once there, they found a group of women who listened to them. One of them was Lydia, a woman from the city of Thyatira. Luke tells us she was a "worshiper of God" with a heart open to Paul's message. Note four things about this woman. First, she was from Thyatira, a town in northern Turkey known for its guilds, particularly the guild for the manufacturing and sale of purple dye. Second, she was a dealer in that expensive dye, requiring significant wealth invested in beginning and maintaining her business. Third, while Thyatira was her hometown, she had a large house in Philippi, probably the site of her business in northern Greece. Fourth, she was a "worshiper of God," sometimes called a "God-fearer."

The Greek and Roman worlds, like most or all of the civilizations preceding them, worshiped pantheons of gods and goddesses. Recall, for example, the Old Testament Canaanite gods like Baal and Ashteroth that attracted God's people away from the Lord God. But some men and women in the Roman Empire didn't buy into the gods popular in their community. Instead, God's Spirit stirred them to question those local deities and consider the idea of a single, all-powerful God. In the process they became God-fearers, somewhere between the "old" religion and an unknown "new." We have some epigraphic evidence that up to 80 percent of all God-fearers in the Roman Empire were women. Many were sympathetic to Judaism and were ready to listen to what the Jew Paul preached.

Lydia was Paul's first convert in Greece, a woman of means who provided the meeting place for the new Christian community in Philippi. Her wealth also gave her influence that would aid in the founding of that new community. But the apostles could not settle down in Philippi; their actions had led to a bit of time in the Philippian prison and the strong desire of the magistrates to get them out of the city. (Read that fascinating story in Acts 16:16–40.)

Prominent Greek Women (Acts 17)

Leaving Philippi, Paul and his companions headed to Thessalonica, which had a synagogue where Paul could preach and reason with debaters. Among his listeners were "a large number of God-fearing Greeks and quite a few prominent women" (Acts 17:4). When some jealous Jews stirred up a riot and the city officials wanted the apostles to leave, the new believers sent Paul and Silas on to the town of Berea. There they had more freedom to preach, and "many of them believed, as did also a number of prominent Greek women and many Greek men" (verse 12).

Notice who was responding to the gospel message: God-fearing Greeks and many prominent Greek women. Here again we see how God used men and women of means in planting new Christian communities.[8] To be sure, these prominent women had the leisure to listen and the education to understand what was preached, which many of the working or enslaved men and women in those towns may have lacked.

From Berea, Paul went to Athens. There he was astonished by the number of idols in that city (Acts 17:16). While he continued to reason with both Jews and God-fearing Greeks in the synagogue, he also took on Epicurean and Stoic philosophers in the marketplace. This led to an invitation to speak to the Areopagus, the earliest aristocratic council of ancient Athens.[9] Its members were curious about Paul's teachings: "You are bringing some strange ideas to our ears, and we would like to know

---

8. As people of influence, in many cases they had homes large enough to serve as a meeting place for believers. Throughout the New Testament letters, we find numerous churches being started and maintained in the homes of women. They used what God had given them to benefit God's kingdom.

9. This council took its name from its meeting place on the low hill northwest of the Acropolis, the "Hill of Ares." In classical times, it functioned as the high Court of Appeal for criminal and civil cases.

what they mean" (verses 19–20). Out of that distinguished encounter with some of the best minds in Athens, the gospel was embraced by several hearers, including a member of the debating group, Dionysius, as well as the woman Damaris.

Richard Bauckham reminds us that whenever we see a person's name in Acts or in the apostolic letters, it's there because that person had distinguished himself or herself in Christian ministry. People weren't named unless they were well-known among the churches for their commitment to Jesus Christ and to the spread of his gospel.[10] For example, the Athenian convert Damaris would not have been named in Acts if she had not become a well-known worker in the churches.

Phoebe, Deacon and Prostatis in the Cenchrean Church (Romans 16:1–2)

The apostle Paul went from Athens to Corinth, a major Greek city sprawling across a narrow land bridge (an isthmus) connecting the Greek peninsula (the Peloponnese) to the mainland in the north. Because sailing around this southern peninsula was frequently treacherous, sailors crossing from Italy's Adriatic Sea to the Greek Saronic Gulf preferred hauling their ships overland across this narrow isthmus rather than risk disaster in that turbulent and treacherous part of the Mediterranean Sea.[11] Thus Corinth was a busy cosmopolitan town controlling the traffic between the seaports on both coasts of this land bridge.

Paul settled down here for more than eighteen months, planting house churches across the city (among them the church in the Corinthian suburb of Cenchreae). And here in Corinth, he met and linked up with Aquila and Priscilla in their tentmaking business (Acts 18:1–3, 11). The couple was from Rome but had settled in Corinth, having been driven out by Claudius's AD 50–51 deportation of all Jews. After the months spent in Corinth produced

---

10. See Bauckham, *Gospel Women*, 211–12.
11. Eventually a canal was dug that linked the two ports.

stable house churches, Paul, Priscilla, and Aquila headed to Ephesus for a long and difficult church-planting sojourn there. Eventually, when Jews were permitted to return to Rome, Priscilla and Aquila headed back home to work with the new Christian community in the capital, Rome.

Toward the end of his third missionary journey, Paul was back in Corinth. He had just written his letter to the Romans and needed a way to get it to the churches in Italy. Scholars assume that Phoebe may have been a businesswoman traveling from Corinth to Rome, who offered to carry the letter to the Roman Christians. We meet Phoebe at the end of that letter, in Romans 16:1–2: "I commend to you our sister Phoebe, a deacon of the church in Cenchreae. I ask you to receive her in the Lord in a way worthy of his people and to give her any help she may need from you, for she has been the benefactor of many people, including me." Note that in introducing her to the Roman Christians, Paul told them two important facts about her: she was a "deacon" in the church in Cenchreae and the "benefactor" of many, including Paul himself.

First, she was a deacon (*diakonos*). While we do not know the particular tasks "deacons" carried out in the New Testament churches, we do know that Paul used that word to describe his own ministry (Ephesians 3:7; Colossians 1:23) and that of four other people: Tychicus (Ephesians 6:21; Colossians 4:7); Epaphras (Colossians 1:7); Timothy (1 Thessalonians 3:2; 1 Timothy 4:6); and Phoebe (Romans 16:1). Whatever Paul and his other coworkers were about, Phoebe must also have been doing, or else Paul would not have introduced her to the Roman Christians as *diakonos*.[12]

Second, she was a "benefactor" (*prostatis*). Translators have had a field day with this Greek word, translating it "a great help" or "a patron of many" or "a succourer of many." But according to the lexicographer Joseph

---

12. Bible translators differ in translating this word *diakonos*. Here the NIV rightly translates it "deacon," but other versions translate it "servant." At times translator bias emerges in this verse. For example, translators of the KJV translated *diakonos* as "minister" when it referred to each of the four men, but translated *diakonos* as "servant" in Romans 16:1 with regard to Phoebe.

Henry Thayer, the first meaning is "a woman set over others."[13] It is the feminine form of a noun designating a leader. Lynn Cohick tells us that "the masculine form (*prostatēs*) is employed by Justin Martyr to denote the person presiding at Communion (*First Apology* 65)."[14] The apostle Paul used cognate terms from the same Greek root in Romans 12:8, where the word is translated "to lead." When it appears in 1 Thessalonians 5:12, it is often translated "are over you; have charge of you." Philip Payne notes that "even Charles Ryrie, who teaches that woman's role in the church is 'not a leading one,' acknowledges that *prostatis* 'includes some kind of leadership.' This term almost always refers to an officially recognized position of authority."[15]

So what was Phoebe's ministry in the church in Cenchreae? We don't know the precise details, but we must be alert to the fact that her role in the church as both deacon and *prostatis* included some form of leadership.

Women as Coworkers with Paul (Romans 16:3–5)

We first met Aquila and Priscilla in Corinth, where they and Paul worked together in both tentmaking and in evangelism. After working for a year and a half there, they went with him to Ephesus to plant churches. Eventually they returned home to Rome. They are the first folks Paul greeted in his letter to the Romans, not surprising because of their close ties over the preceding years: "Greet Priscilla and Aquila, my co-workers in Christ Jesus. They risked their lives for me. Not only I, but all the churches of the Gentiles are grateful to them. Greet also the church that meets at their house" (Romans 16:3–5). Few had labored with Paul more than this couple. He had good reason to call them his coworkers.

13. Joseph Henry Thayer, *A Greek Lexicon of the New Testament* (New York: American Book Co., 1886), 549.

14. Lynn Cohick, "Romans," in *The IVP Women's Bible Commentary*, ed. Catherine Clark Kroeger and Mary J. Evans (Downers Grove, IL: InterVarsity, 2002), 644.

15. Philip B. Payne, *Man and Woman, One in Christ: An Exegetical and Theological Study of Paul's Letters* (Grand Rapids: Zondervan, 2009), 63.

The Greek word translated "co-worker" is *sunergon*. It always desig-nated someone who was prominent in ministry with Paul in the various churches. In Paul's letters, we find him using that word to describe eleven people:

- Philemon (Philemon 1)
- Timothy (1 Thessalonians 3:2)
- Aristarchus, Mary, and Justus (Colossians 4:11)
- Titus (2 Corinthians 8:23)
- Urbanus (Romans 16:9)
- Euodia and Syntyche (Philippians 4:2–3)
- Priscilla and Aquila (Romans 16:3)

Note that four of these eleven coworkers with Paul are women: Mary, Euodia, Syntyche, and Priscilla. But if we turn to Romans 16, there we find that seven of the ten people Paul names as colleagues in ministry are women: Phoebe, Junia, Priscilla, Mary, Tryphena, Tryphosa, and Persis. We don't know in each case precisely how these men and women served with Paul, but we can probably assume that as coworkers they were doing pretty much whatever he was doing in ministry.

Women Who "Work Hard in the Lord" (Romans 16:6, 12)

In the greetings at the end of Romans, the apostle Paul singled out four women (Mary, Tryphena, Tryphosa, and Persis) as those "who worked very hard" (*polla ekopiasen*) or "who work hard in the Lord" (*kopiasas en kurio*). What does that mean? Paul repeatedly used this word to describe his own ministry (1 Corinthians 4:12; Galatians 4:11; Philippians 2:16). And in 1 Corinthians 16:16, he also told the Corinthian Christians to submit to "everyone who joins in the work and labors at it" (*sunergounti kai kopionti*). Those honored in Romans 16 with that title included Mary, Tryphena, Tryphosa, Persis, and Priscilla.

Whatever the nature of their ministry, it was worthy of honor from the Christians in Corinth, who were told to submit to such people.

Junia, a Woman Apostle (Romans 16:7)

Paul then wrote, "Greet Andronicus and Junia, my fellow Jews who have been in prison with me. They are outstanding among the apostles, and they were in Christ before I was." Until recently, translators changed the name of the second person greeted here from Junia to Junias. Why? Was it unthinkable that a woman could have been an apostle?

The early church fathers (John Chrysostom, Origen, Jerome) had no difficulty with that idea. They all assumed this apostle was a woman. Chrysostom wrote, "O how great is the devotion of this woman that she should be even counted worthy of the appellation of apostle!"[16] It was Aegidius of Rome (1245–1316) who first referred to Andronicus and Junia as men, after which churchmen assumed that Junia was male. But when scholars searched first-century Roman name lists for *Junias*, they found nothing. Junia was a common women's name,[17] but the male counterpart to it was Junius.

Complementarians have now, for the most part, conceded that Junia was a woman, but they suggest that the text means she was "admired by or well-known to the apostles," but not prominent among the apostles. However, to support that interpretation, it is necessary to use different Greek prepositions (*para, pros*) instead of the actual text: it uses *en* with the plural, which always has the sense of *within* or *among* the apostles.

Note four facts in Paul's description of this couple: (1) they are fellow Jews; (2) they had been in prison with Paul; (3) they were outstanding among the apostles; and (4) they were "in Christ" before Paul became a believer. Who could fill that bill? Because they were Christians before

---

16. John Chrysostom, *In ep. ad Romanos* 31, 2; translation by E. J. Epp, *Junia: The First Woman Apostle* (Minneapolis: Fortress, 2005), 79.

17. Peter Lampe counts more than 250 recorded instances of the female name Junia in Rome alone (cited in Bauckham, *Gospel Women*, 168).

Paul was converted, Andronicus and Junia were most likely Palestinian Jews who were possibly members of the first Christian churches in Jerusalem. They may well have been involved in later years (with the apostle Peter) in founding the Christian community in Rome.[18]

Junia is important not only because Paul called her an apostle, but also for her link to the gospels. Do you remember the names of the women in Luke 8:3 who were benefactors to the Jesus band? "Mary (called Magdalene) . . . Joanna the wife of Chuza . . . Susanna." It turns out that "Junia" is the Latin translation of the Jewish name "Joanna."

Recall the concluding paragraph of chapter 4: "Complementarian James Borland, writing about women in the life and teachings of Jesus, asserted that 'our Lord placed a high value on women, while He continued to recognize role distinctions for men and women . . . Nowhere is this issue seen more clearly than in Jesus' selection of only men for the role of apostle . . . no woman in Christ's ministry was called, commissioned, or named as an apostle, or even performed in the role of an apostle. These roles and functions Christ reserved for men.'"[19]

Is it possible that the apostle Junia and the Jewish disciple Joanna are one and the same person? If so, this would destroy the central argument for gender-based hierarchy in Borland's statement. Biblical scholar Richard Bauckham devotes ninety-four pages (109–202) in *Gospel Women* to intensive research into the connection between Joanna and Junia. Such solid academic research assures us that one of the female disciples of Jesus named in Luke 8:3 is also the female apostle in Rome (Romans 16:7). As unlikely as this may seem on the surface, recall what Luke tells us about Joanna: she is the wife of Chuza, Herod's business manager. Though she was a Jew, she was also an insider in the Roman palace at Tiberias. Joanna was a bridge between her Jewish roots and her

---

18. See ibid., 181.

19. From Borlund's chapter in John Piper and Wayne Grudem, eds., *Recovering Biblical Manhood and Womanhood: A Response to Evangelical Feminism*, 2nd ed. (Wheaton, IL: Crossway, 2006), 113, 120–21.

Roman connections. That she should end up in Rome as an apostolic emissary for the gospel is entirely plausible.

CONCLUSION

As the apostle Paul crisscrossed the Roman Empire starting new churches, women as well as men were important coworkers with him. The church was born on Pentecost as the Spirit of God came on the followers of Jesus, filling them for ministry. Peter, preaching to thousands that day, quoted the words of the prophet Joel: "I will pour out my Spirit on all people. Your sons and daughters will prophesy, your young men will see visions, your old men will dream dreams. Even on my servants, both men and women, I will pour out my Spirit in those days" (Acts 2:17–18). Something new had happened: women as well as men would exercise the gifts of the Spirit in the new churches. This would become the normative model for most of the early congregations.

But when we read Romans 16 alongside 1 Timothy 2:12, we encounter a problem. In his letter to Timothy, Paul wrote, "I do not permit a woman to teach or to assume authority over a man; she must be quiet." In this chapter, we've seen a parade of God-gifted women in ministry, doing virtually everything the apostle Paul was doing. These women and Paul's letter to Timothy are both part of the data we must consider if we are to listen to the whole testimony of Scripture. How are we to understand what looks like a clear contradiction? Some Christians choose to ignore one set of data and accept only the other set. Others may find this seeming contradiction enough to shatter their confidence in the Bible. So it's important to explore *all* of the biblical material.

If we conclude that Scripture forbids women to be in positions of leadership in the church, then it's wrong if a woman does lead. On the other hand, if the Scriptures do permit a woman to be in positions of leadership in the church and we forbid this, the church is deprived of the spiritual gifts God gave women for its benefit. God's intended workforce is cut in half and his kingdom suffers. This would also be wrong.

Part 2 of this book explores four critical teaching areas in the New Testament to help us see how we are to read and understand all of the relevant biblical texts.

Questions for Personal Reflection or Group Discussion

1. It is clear in Scripture that women were active in ministry with the apostle Paul. How does this shape what we believe about women and church ministry today?

2. A number of prominent women in Philippi, Thessalonica, Berea, and Rome were early converts to Christianity. In what ways did their prominence contribute to the formation and growth of local churches?

3. God-fearers were among the early converts to Christianity. What do you think might have compelled them to set aside their faith in the local pantheon of gods and goddesses and search for a better object of belief?

4. In your opinion, in what ways do the ministries of women in the early churches resemble or differ from the ministries of women in Christian churches today?

PART TWO

Assessing the Theology behind Gender-based Hierarchy

As part 1 moved us through the Bible looking at women of note, we've also seen God allowing or even calling out women to overturn the reigning gender-based hierarchy. It's as if God says, "The whole world is structured hierarchically because of sin, but that is not my purpose for you. The fundamental idea of patriarchy—one person over another in some kind of hierarchy—must be challenged." Why? For Christians, "there is neither Jew nor Gentile, neither slave nor free, nor is there male and female, for you are all one in Christ Jesus" (Galatians 3:28).

This book began with an introduction to hermeneutics, the science of interpretation. From the illustration of Christians defending the practice of slavery in the nineteenth century we see how easy it is to use the Bible to support ideas that are contrary to the fundamental teachings of Scripture. Part 2 of this book will take us deep into biblical rationales we must examine carefully for any fallacies in interpretation. To keep us on track (and away from the pitfalls of using the Bible as the Pharisees did), let's take a few minutes to review some basic rules of interpretation as we search the Bible for the truth or falsehood of gender-based hierarchy.

1. "A text without its context is merely a pretext." It's true we can prove just about anything from an isolated Bible verse when that verse is taken out of its context. So a basic rule of interpretation is that a verse's context is king. It fences in what we can or cannot make that verse mean.

2. We have to listen to the full testimony of Scripture. Take, for example, the book of Job: In the nearly forty chapters of argument between Job and his three "friends," it's easy to conclude that the friends are right and Job is talking nonsense. We can quote them and apply their statements in our lives. But when we get to the end of the book, we discover that God has turned everything upside-down: Job is right, and his three friends were dangerously wrong. Just as the nineteenth-century proponents of slavery ignored clear biblical statements that slave dealers should be put to death (Exodus 21:16) and that Paul saw slave traders as "lawbreakers and rebels, the ungodly and sinful, the unholy and irreligious" (1 Timothy 1:9), so we can turn a blind eye to texts that contradict our assumptions. We must listen to the full testimony of Scripture.

3. Bible verses should be used for their main emphasis, not for some sideline message. It is here that context is crucial. In the following chapters, we will see efforts to make lone verses support ideas that are foreign to the context of those verses and of the larger moral imperatives in Scripture.

4. We must allow the context to lead us in discerning whether a given text is merely *de*scriptive of a given situation or is *pre*scriptive for all people in all places at all times. If we fail to note the difference between what is descriptive and what is prescriptive, we can do great violence to the interpretation and application of Scripture in our individual lives, in our homes, and in our churches.

As noted in chapter 1, Jesus had harsh words for the Pharisees: "You hypocrites! You're so scrupulous that you tithe even the spices in your garden, but you ignore the really big issues throughout the Bible—justice, mercy, and faithfulness" (Matthew 23:23, my paraphrase). Despite their religious show, their actions led to injustice, oppression, and structural violence. Likewise from the nineteenth-century anti-abolitionists' use of Scripture, we must beware of any interpretation that ignores the heart of God's teachings.

With these cautions in mind, part 2 will assess the key assumptions behind gender-based hierarchy in the light of Scripture. Chapter 6 examines the biblical texts used to establish a gender-based hierarchy for home and church. Chapter 7 deals with the concept of authority and its application to men and women in the home and church. Chapter 8 goes behind these teachings to scrutinize the doctrine of the eternal subordination of the Son to the Father. This is a current debate among complementarians, and many do not hold this position. But because some have made it a necessary part of their case for gender-based hierarchy, it is important to include it in this discussion. Chapter 9 dissects the nature of ministry and leadership.

In short, part 2 grapples with the theology supporting gender-based hierarchy: Is it valid and therefore should control our lives, or is it invalid and therefore should be dismantled?

Chapter Six

THE BATTLE OF THE TEXTS: 1 TIMOTHY 2:12 AND 1 CORINTHIANS 14:34–35

The complementarians defending Christian gender-based hierarchy state their case with these three presuppositions:

1. "We are persuaded that the Bible teaches that only men should be pastors and elders. That is, men should bear *primary* responsibility for Christlike leadership and teaching in the church. So it is unbiblical, we believe, and therefore detrimental, for women to assume this role."[1]

2. This gender-based hierarchy for church ministries rests on 1 Corinthians 11:3: "Christ is the authority over every man, man is the authority over woman, and God is the authority over Christ."[2]

3. "We think 1 Timothy 2:8–15 imposes two restrictions on the ministry of women: they are not to teach Christian doctrine to men and they are not to exercise authority directly over men in

---

1. John Piper and Wayne Grudem, eds., *Recovering Biblical Manhood and Womanhood: A Response to Evangelical Feminism*, 2nd ed. (Wheaton, IL: Crossway, 2006), 60–61.
2. From Thomas R. Schreiner's chapter in ibid., 128.

the church. These restrictions are permanent, authoritative for the church in all times and places and circumstances as long as men and women are descended from Adam and Eve."[3]

Three key issues emerge. The first is the establishment of a gender-based hierarchy for Christian ministry. The second is the issue of "authority": women are not to teach men or to exercise authority over men in the church. The third issue is the immutability of these factors for Christians at all times in all places.[4]

The New Testament passage most often used to support the establishment of a gender-based hierarchy for Christian ministry is 1 Timothy 2:12. Some still also use 1 Corinthians 14:34–35. We cannot go any further until we have unpacked these two sections of Scripture because they are basic to all discussions of women's roles in the church.

1 TIMOTHY 2:12

I do not permit a woman to teach or to assume authority over a man; she must be quiet.

What are the issues raised by this verse? What is the apostle Paul prohibiting? Is he limiting women from all teaching—or from only a certain kind of teaching? And is the "assume authority over a man" a separate forbidden role, or did Paul intend it to be understood together with "to teach" so that the combination of the two is what he is not permitting?

---

3. From Douglas Moo's chapter in ibid., 180.

4. These three issues will be addressed sequentially: the first in chapter 6 (key Scripture passages on which these restrictions on women's ministries are based), the second in chapter 7 (the meaning of *kephalē* as "authority over"), and the third in chapters 8–9 (implications drawn from "the eternal subordination of God the Son to God the Father," the nature of ministry, and the nature of leadership among the Pauline churches).

What Is the Broad Context of This Text?

As we learned in chapter 1, "a text without its context is merely a pretext." It's true that people have tried to make a case for virtually anything by taking a single verse out of the Bible to support some idea. So we know we must explore the *context* of 1 Timothy 2:12 to understand how this verse fits the apostle's larger argument. This includes asking why Paul is writing this letter to Timothy in the first place, what his concerns are, and how he expects Timothy to act in light of these concerns.[5]

Earlier, Paul had spent three years in the city of Ephesus (in southwestern Turkey) starting new Christian communities (Acts 19). Those years in Ephesus were probably the most difficult and challenging in Paul's career. Some time later, when passing through that territory, he called the elders of the Ephesian churches to meet with him. He warned them about false teachers coming in like "savage wolves" that could utterly destroy the churches (Acts 20:29).

Now what he had predicted had come to pass. The situation in Ephesus was precarious. To counteract the rampant apostasy there, Paul had sent Timothy to Ephesus to teach sound doctrine (1 Timothy 1:3–4). The main thrust of his letter was how young Timothy should deal with this precarious situation in the Ephesian church. That is the broad context of the letter.

What Is the Immediate Context of This Text?

The more immediate context of 1 Timothy 2:12 is the whole of chapter 2. It begins by urging Timothy and his congregations to pray for everyone (verse 1). Pray for what? First, pray for the secular authorities

---

5. When the Bible is chopped up into chapters and verses (as happened in the sixteenth century), it's easy to forget that Paul wrote this letter without the numeric interruptions in the flow of thought. We cannot understand any particular statement until we've immersed ourselves in the total letter and see the apostle's overarching concerns.

(verse 2). This was a "real-time" prayer request, given the intermittent persecution of Christians happening throughout the Roman Empire.[6]

Paul then asserts that living peaceful and quiet lives "in all godliness and holiness" is linked to any future success in evangelism (1 Timothy 2:3–4). God "wants all people . . . to come to a knowledge of the truth" (verse 4), but in Paul's second letter to Timothy (2 Timothy 3:6–7), we learn that impeding this success are some in the church who are "always learning but never able to come to a knowledge of the truth." So how can all people come to truth? In 1 Timothy 2, Paul lays down four things that need to happen.

First, the Ephesian Christians are to pray for all people everywhere (1 Timothy 2:1–7). Second, he calls on the men to pray "without anger or disputing" (verse 8). The controversies sparked by false teachers (noted in 1 Timothy 1:3 and 6:4–5) had led to angry arguments among the men that would impact the influence of the congregation (and destroy their peaceful and quiet lives). Third, he turns to women in the churches, telling them to follow a lifestyle marked by modest dress and good deeds (2:9–10). Finally, women are ordered to learn in the posture of a genuine disciple (verse 11).

The only imperative verb in this chapter is found in verse 11: let a woman learn ("in quietness and full submission"). In a culture in which some rabbis taught that it was "better to burn the Torah than to teach it to women,"[7] the apostle Paul is clear that women must learn so that they can "come to a knowledge of the truth" (verse 4). In quietness, women are to become part of the entire educational process.[8] As they learn, they are to bring restraint and respect to their learning, affirming their teachers.

The *purpose* of this letter to Timothy is to counteract the heretical teaching going on in the Ephesian church. In 1 Timothy 5:13, Paul

---

6. Some scholars think Paul was already in prison in Rome at the time he wrote this letter.

7. Rabbi Eliezer (ca. AD 90) in *y. Sotah* 3:4, 19a7; cited in Joachim Jeremias, *Jerusalem in the Time of Jesus* (Philadelphia: Fortress, 1969), 373.

8. Paul here uses the Greek word *hēsychia* ("quietness"), not the word *sigē*, meaning "silence" as some translators have put it.

speaks of young widows who "talk nonsense, saying things they ought not to." Then, in his second letter to Timothy, Paul speaks of men who "gain control over gullible women" (2 Timothy 3:6–7). To combat this problem, Paul tells women to "learn in quietness and full submission."

This, then, is the immediate prior context of the 1 Timothy 2:12 text. Timothy faces men who even in their prayers engage in angry disputes, and he faces immodest, shallow women who in ignorance are conveying false teachings that are destroying the community. What measures would he need to take to counteract this assault on the Ephesian communities? First, he restricts the women who are feeding the problem, and then in chapter 3, he turns to restrict overseers to those who are fully eligible to serve as leaders.

Issues in the 1 Timothy 2:12 Text Itself

"I do not permit a woman to teach . . ."

This text is the basis on which complementarians prohibit women from preaching and teaching the Bible and doctrine in church. Thomas Schreiner calls this prohibition "universal" and states, "Women are prohibited from teaching or exercising authority because of the creation order."[9] To test that assumption, we'll take this verse step by step, word by word.

The first question we must ask is whether the Greek verb (*epitrepō*) translated "I do not permit" is a blanket universal prohibition or a prohibition for a particular moment in time. It turns out that every occurrence of this Greek word in the Septuagint (the Greek translation of the Old Testament) refers to a specific situation, not to a universal application.[10] A more faithful translation would be "I am not presently permitting" in this specific case. Philip Payne notes that Paul used the identical grammatical

---

9. From Schreiner's chapter in eds., Andreas J. Köstenberger and Thomas R. Schreiner, *Women in the Church: An Analysis and Application of 1 Timothy 2:9–15*, 2nd ed. (Grand Rapids: Baker, 2005), 101, 120.

10. See John E. Toews, "Women in Church Leadership," in *The Bible and the Church: Essays in Honor of David Ewert*, ed. A. J. Dueck, H. G. Giesbrecht, and V. G. Shillington (Winnepeg, MB, Canada: Mennonite Bretheren Bible College, 1988), 84.

construction four times in 1 Corinthians 7 (vv. 7, 26, 32, 40) and again in Philippians 4:2. In every case, it expressed his current desire and not a universal command.[11] But we also note that the only imperative verb in the passage is that women must *learn*. "I do not permit" is not in the imperative form. The overall purpose of this letter to Timothy is to silence *false* teachers, not all teachers.

The second question we must ask is how this interpretation, if it were universally applied, fits with Paul's commendation of women teaching elsewhere. In his letter to Titus, Paul commands him to encourage older women "to teach what is good" (Titus 2:3). Furthermore, if this were a blanket prohibition, Luke would not likely have commended Priscilla for teaching Apollos (Acts 18:26). Nor would Paul have allowed her—and many other women—to serve as his coworkers.

Both men and women were teaching heretical doctrines in the Ephesian house churches. This so threatened the church that Paul not only prohibited women in Ephesus from assuming authority to teach men without proper authorization, but also limited who qualified for church leadership (1 Timothy 3:1–7). The threat level caused by those who were teaching heresies was such that leadership was confined to those who conformed to stringent restrictions.

The Text Continues

"*. . . or to assume authority over a man*"

Can a tiny, two-letter conjunction like *or* have any significance? In 1 Timothy 2:12, this conjunction joins the two infinitive verbs "to teach" and "to assume authority." It looks as if we have two separate ideas in this verse—the idea of teaching and the idea of exercising authority. But the

---

11. See Philip B. Payne, *Man and Woman, One in Christ* (Grand Rapids: Zondervan, 2009), 320. There he cites the following texts in which the word is clearly contingent, not universal: Matthew 8:21; Mark 5:13; Luke 8:32; 9:59, 61; John 19:38; Acts 21:39, 40; 27:3; 28:16; 1 Corinthians 16:7; Hebrews 6:3. See Payne (320–25) for an extensive discussion of this word.

Greek conjunction (translated "or") doesn't function that way in Paul's letters. He typically used it to join two ideas in some way. For example, we might say, "Don't eat and run," meaning "don't leave right after eating." It doesn't mean "don't eat" and "don't run" as two unrelated activities. The apostle's use of the conjunction *or* creates a single idea out of two different actions.[12] With the two verbs connected as they are in Greek, this is teaching of a particular sort.

So in 1 Timothy 2:12, not every form of teaching is prohibited to women, but rather teaching that is combined with *authentein*—the Greek word translated here "to assume authority over a man." Because *authentein* appears only here in the Bible, we can't compare its context to anything elsewhere in Scripture to help us interpret it. To get at its meaning, we must rely on examples of how this strange Greek word was used outside the Scriptures.

Note that Paul chose that word instead of the word he normally used (*exousiazō*) to denote the exercise of authority. We have to ask why, when he always used the normal Greek word to express the exercise of authority, he chose this strange new verb here if he merely meant "the exercise of authority."[13]

So what did that unusual Greek word mean in the first century?[14] When we join it (with the conjunction *or*) to "to teach," we come up with at least six different meanings:

1. To teach autonomously (to "thrust oneself") independent of authorized doctrine

---

12. See Payne, *Man and Woman*, 344.

13. To express the exercise of authority, Paul normally used *exousiadzō* elsewhere, but he also had other Greek words at his disposal. He could have used *kurieuō* or *katakurieuō* meaning "to lord it over." Or he could have chosen *proistēmi*, meaning "to rule or to manage." Because Paul had other words at his disposal, he need not have chosen a coarse word like *authentein* if his intention was merely to prohibit the exercise of authority.

14. Before and during Paul's era, we have no undisputed case of *authentein* meaning "to exercise authority over." That meaning came later in patristic writings.

2. To teach in a contentious manner
3. To teach in a domineering, despotic, or high-handed manner
4. To teach in such a way that destroys virtue (teaching licentious doctrines and practices)
5. To teach in such a way that murders (the truth)
6. To assume authority to teach a man[15]

The standard Greek lexicon defines this word to mean "to assume a stance of independent authority."[16] This does not prohibit a woman with recognized teaching authority like Priscilla from teaching a man (Acts 18:26). Paul shows his respect for her by greeting her in this very city (Ephesus) in 2 Timothy 4:19. She may have been Paul's and Timothy's best resource to convince deceived women of the truth. Paul's choice of words in 1 Timothy 2:12 prohibits women from independently seizing authority to teach a man.

The Rest of the Text's Context: 1 Timothy 2:13–14

For Adam was formed first, then Eve. And Adam was not the one deceived; it was the woman who was deceived and became a sinner.

Complementarians also use the verses following 1 Timothy 2:12 to argue for women's restriction in both the home and the church. In verses 13 and 14, their argument takes us back to Genesis 1–2 (see chapter 2 in this book). Douglas Moo presented the argument in these words:

For Paul, the man's priority in the order of creation is indicative of the headship that man is to have over woman. The woman's being

---

15. Women like Priscilla would not have been restricted by such a prohibition because they already had recognized teaching authority in the church.

16. Walter Bauer, Frederick W. Danker, William F. Arndt, and F. Wilbur Gingrich, *A Greek-English Lexicon of the New Testament and Other Early Christian Literature*, 3rd ed. (Chicago: University of Chicago Press, 2000), 150.

created after man, as his helper, shows the position of submission that God intended as inherent in the woman's relation to the man, a submission that is violated if a woman teaches doctrine or exercises authority over a man.[17]

Note that Moo's argument rests on his use of the verb "create." As noted in chapter 2, Walter Kaiser rebutted Moo's argument by stating that in 1 Timothy 2:13, the verb is *plassō* = "form," not *ktizō* = "create," and that this verse is about Eve's educational formation, not her creation. Other scholars point out that while *plassō* does mean "form," not "create," it was the Greek word used in Genesis 1 and 2 by the Septuagint translators of the Hebrew Bible into Greek. Thus its use here in 1 Timothy 2:13 does refer to Eve's creation "out of Adam's rib." But that does not automatically validate Moo's statement that "woman's being created after man, as his helper, shows the position of submission that God intended as inherent in the woman's relation to the man, a submission that is violated if a woman teaches doctrine or exercises authority over a man."

Recall the six ways we can understand the use of the strange Greek verb *authentein*. The prohibition in 2:12 is against grasping for unauthorized authority to teach a man in a high-handed or despotic manner. This is disrespectful teaching. Women like Priscilla had recognized teaching authority, and teaching the assembled church would not be disrespectful to men. Chapter 7 will unpack this further in the context of a culture of shame and honor as we find in 1 Corinthians 11:3–7.

While Paul states that Eve's deception caused her to become a sinner, elsewhere Paul is clear that Adam was culpable for the fall (Romans 5:12–19; 1 Corinthians 15:21–22).

First Timothy 2 ends with an enigmatic statement that has puzzled biblical scholars through the ages: "But women will be saved through

---

17. From Douglas Moo's chapter in *Recovering Biblical Manhood and Womanhood*, 190.

childbearing—if they continue in faith, love and holiness with propriety" (verse 15). What does "safety in childbearing" or "childbirth as a means of a woman's salvation" have to do with deception? And how does this verse relate to a woman learning in quietness or not teaching with a domineering spirit? This verse is erroneously translated in several places.

In verse 15, the word *women* should be translated "she," a pronoun referring back to Eve in verses 13–14. Her deception, detailed in Genesis 3:13, is followed by God's curse on the serpent (Genesis 3:15): the offspring of the woman will eventually crush the head of the serpent. We know this passage as the first prediction in the Bible of God the Son's final overthrow of Satan and the effects of the fall.

Verse 15 is also mistranslated by omitting "the" in front of "childbearing." Paul wrote that "she will be saved through *the* childbirth," that is, the birth of Jesus Christ. This is spiritual salvation, not safety in childbirth. First Timothy 2:15 is not about women physically giving birth; it's about Eve and all who would come later whose salvation rests on the promise of our Savior, Jesus Christ.

Some ministers teach that women are saved spiritually through bearing children. But this would exclude all women who are single or are married but barren. And this would mean that all women must rear children in order to be saved, but men do not have this requirement for salvation—a strange requirement not borne out elsewhere in the New Testament. No, it is through Christ the Savior that women experience salvation "if they continue in faith, love and holiness with propriety."

Women as Overseers?

Reading a Bible in which books have been chopped up into chapters and verses can sometimes distance us from the continuing thought of the writers. When we come to the end of 1 Timothy 2, it may feel that Paul has said all he intends to say about women, and chapter 3 moves on to men. Not so. When we eliminate the chapter and verse divisions, we move from women who "continue in faith, love and holiness with propriety" (2:15) to "whoever aspires to be an overseer" (3:1). Does this imply that a woman could be an overseer? But you might say, "Ah, yes, Alice, but immediately after 3:1, Paul is talking about men, so clearly only men could be overseers."

In response, Philip Payne reminds us that "there is a principle in Greek literature that when a generic group of people is addressed, masculine grammatical forms are used . . . This principle is rooted in androcentric Greek culture, just as the androcentric Hebrew culture follows the same principle in using masculine forms when groups include men and women. This is known as the principle of 'prior gender.'"[18] We see this in multiple places in the gospels (Matthew 5:19; 10:22; 16:24; 18:4; 24:12–13, etc.) and in Paul's letters (Romans 2:6; 8:9; 1 Corinthians 2:14; 3:12–15; 5:11; 8:3, etc). When Paul encourages "whoever aspires to be an overseer," this can legitimately include women. In chapter 5, we noted that Phoebe was *prostatis* ("standing before; leading") in the church in Cenchreae, a position not unlike that of an overseer.

1 Corinthians 14:34–35

Women should remain silent in the churches. They are not allowed to speak, but must be in submission, as the law says. If they want to inquire about something, they should ask their own husbands at home; for it is disgraceful for a woman to speak in the church.

Because these two verses are sometimes used to support gender-based hierarchy, they will be discussed here. But this text is so harsh that very few expositors take the two verses at face value. For that reason,

---

18. Philip B. Payne, "Greek Uses Masculine Forms for Generic Reference," unpublished article, 2016 Payne Loving Trust.

evangelical biblical scholars have proposed at least four different ideas about the interpretation of this passage:

1. Some believe these two verses do not belong here in the text, but perhaps elsewhere in the letter.
2. Some believe that Paul did not give women permission to speak in 1 Corinthians 11, but dealt with the basic issue of authority, and here in chapter 14, he silenced women altogether.
3. Some believe that chapter 14 doesn't contradict chapter 11, but gives instructions for another problem, namely, talkative women, women speaking in tongues, or women judging men's prophecies.[19]
4. Some believe these verses cite a false prophecy by a self-proclaimed Corinthian prophet.

We'll take each of these arguments in order.

These Verses Do Not Belong Here in the Text

Verses 34–35 appear in this place in 1 Corinthians 14 only in the ancient Eastern manuscripts. In all early Western manuscripts, the two verses appear after verse 40. For three hundred years, the passage was read in the Latin church as moving from verse 33 directly to verse 36. It was Jerome's Vulgate translation (mid-fourth century) that inserted these verses after verse 33.

The chapter flows more freely without verses 34–35 because the verses don't fit the overall context. The verses also inject word usages that differ from the rest of the chapter. For example, the notion of silence in verses 28 and 30 curtails but doesn't eliminate an otherwise legitimate

---

19. See James B. Hurley, *Man and Woman in Biblical Perspective* (Grand Rapids: Zondervan, 1981), 185.

activity, but in verses 34–35, the silence is absolute. Also, "to speak" here is different from its twenty-one uses in the rest of the chapter. Furthermore, the verses contradict 1 Corinthians 11:4–6, in which women can pray and prophesy in public worship without any reproof from the apostles. Finally, Paul's use of "everyone" (in verses 23–24, 31) and "each of you" (verse 26) includes women in speaking activities.

On the basis of these contradictions, some eminent scholars state that verses 34–35 are an interpolation or a scribal gloss, first added in the margin as a comment by a reader, which was later entered by a scribe into the actual text of the letter. While some scholars dismiss this explanation, other scholars insist it is the only explanation that accounts for all the issues raised by the text. The main evidence for it is contextual rather than textual—the fact that the two verses don't fit the flow of thought in the chapter.

If you're inclined to dismiss this explanation as impossible, note that there are some solid technical and textual reasons for accepting it. Philip Payne reminds us that "many who study the New Testament are unaware that the oldest surviving New Testament manuscripts differ, sometimes significantly, and various passages do not appear in the most reliable texts at all, which has led virtually all biblical scholars to conclude that some passages are interpolations."[20]

Paul Here Silences Women Completely

The church father Origen was aware of the tension between "you can all prophesy" (14:31) and this prohibition, but he concluded, "Even if she speaks marvelous and holy things, 'it is shameful for a woman to speak in church' simply because it comes from the mouth of a woman. For a woman to speak forth in church brings her under shame and the

---

20. Payne, *Man and Woman*, 225. He devotes an entire chapter to this passage (217–67) and uses forty-three pages to support this explanation of 1 Corinthians 14:34–35.

condemnation of the whole church."[21] This view contradicts Paul's statements in 1 Corinthians 11:5–10, in which women are both praying and prophesying in public worship.

Paul Isn't Dealing with All Speaking, but with a Particular Kind of Speaking by Women in the Church

This is perhaps the most frequently used method of interpreting these verses. Some see verses 34–35 as a ban limited to disruptive speech in public worship. This has been the view of most Protestant interpreters before the twentieth century. Because Paul wrote this directive to the church in Corinth and not to other churches, some scholars assume the problem was specific to Corinth and perhaps a few other cities like it. If that is the case (that the problem is local in a specific cultural context), then it does not apply to every conceivable situation we face today.

Most scholars who support gender-based hierarchy limit verses 34–35 to being a prohibition against women discerning or judging prophecies made by men in the assembly. They see the central issue to be the behavior of women who dishonor the role of the men in the congregation. Their focus is on the word *disgraceful* or *shameful*, in which women's judging of men's prophecies compromises the calling of the men to be primary leaders in the church.[22]

Applying the verses to women judging prophecies does ignore the fact that verse 35 doesn't mention prophecies, but links the prohibition to women asking questions out of a desire to learn. This view interprets verses 34–35 as prohibiting only the judging of prophecies, but verse 35 also prohibits women from asking questions out of a desire to learn. So this view permits what verse 35 prohibits.

Some commentators hold that silence is required only of women who

---

21. Cited in Claude Jenkins, "Origen on 1 Corinthians IV," *Journal of Theological Studies* 10 (1909): 40.

22. See Piper and Grudem, eds., *Recovering Biblical Manhood and Womanhood*, 71.

are false teachers, uneducated women, or women who are not prophesying or otherwise contributing to worship.

These Verses Cite a False Prophecy by a Self-proclaimed Corinthian Prophet

Numerous scholars have argued that these verses originated from a group in Corinth who opposed Paul. They say that in verses 34–35, Paul is quoting legalists in the church (e.g., the Cephas party mentioned in 1 Corinthians 1:12). Verses 36–38 then are Paul's response to the legalists, refuting their statement. Throughout this first letter to the Corinthians, the apostle does quote from some Corinthian teachers and then refutes their statements (e.g., in 1 Corinthians 11:20, he states the situation in Corinth, and then in 11:22, he challenges people's behavior). Here, some say, the statement silencing women is not Paul's but came from his opponents.[23]

Other scholars question this way of interpreting 1 Corinthians 14:34–35 by noting that none of the other Corinthian quotations are this long, and the verses are not introduced as a false prophecy. Nevertheless, this is still a legitimate possibility.

On the basis of the wide range of interpretations of this passage of Scripture and the fact that very few scholars accept its harsh strictures without some kind of qualification, these verses cannot serve as "proof" of women's exclusion from ministry.

CONCLUSION

The subject of women and church ministry can feel like a third-rail issue—too dangerous to touch. As we work with even the two passages explored in this chapter, we may be tempted to throw our hands up in

---

23. See Gilbert Bilezikian, *Beyond Sex Roles: What the Bible Says about a Woman's Place in Church and Family*, 3rd ed. (Grand Rapids: Baker, 2006), 110–16.

the air and walk away from the issue. But we can't do that. These passages are in the Bible, and we must deal with them. At the same time, it is becoming increasingly clear that the arguments based on them in defense of gender-based hierarchy do not always stand up to scrutiny.

Questions for Personal Reflection or Group Discussion

1. Why, in your opinion, would biblical scholars insist that "context is king"? What difference would the context of a verse make in how that verse is understood?
2. As you think about the application of 1 Timothy 2:12 to women, what are the main points you derive from a clear understanding of the individual words used by Paul?
3. As you think about 1 Corinthians 14:34–35, which of the four interpretations makes most sense to you? How does this inform how you would apply these verses?
4. In light of this chapter, how would you evaluate the case for a gender-based hierarchy for Christian ministry?

Chapter Seven

THE BATTLE OF THE LEXICONS: WHAT DOES *HEAD* MEAN IN THE NEW TESTAMENT?

Words are important when we want to share ideas. But words also morph in their meaning. For example, the 1611 King James Version translation of 1 Thessalonians 4:15 reads, "We which are alive and remain unto the coming of the Lord shall not prevent them which are asleep." Prevent them from what? Four hundred years ago, the word *prevent* meant "to come before." It did not have the sense of opposing someone or something. But now, in the twenty-first century, the verse is translated, "We who are still alive, who are left until the coming of the Lord, will certainly not precede those who have fallen asleep." Over time, the meaning of the word *prevent* has changed.

One Greek word at the center of much discussion around how men and women relate in the home and the church is the word *kephalē*, translated "head." It's a common word in the New Testament, used seventy-two times. Most of the time, it refers to a person's actual head, but it is also used as a metaphor. A metaphor takes a common word and uses it to explain something totally different. For example, we describe someone as a "night owl." The person isn't really an owl, but the metaphor implies someone who stays up very late at night.

But to complicate things a bit further, metaphors can have different meanings in different contexts. The word *cool* has a basic meaning of something that is not hot, as in physical temperature. But when we use *cool* as a metaphor, it can mean different things. To say "he's cool" can mean he's not hot-tempered but keeps his wits about him with a cool head. Or that a "cool" person is very much in tune with the times. Or that a "cool" idea is a good idea, worth pursuing. Metaphors may have multiple meanings.

Two passages in the New Testament that use *head* as a metaphor in the context of male/female relationships are 1 Corinthians 11:3–12 and Ephesians 5:21–33. Because so much wrangling about this word has gone on in Christian circles, let's examine these two passages.

1 CORINTHIANS 11:3–12

In this passage, we find Paul sometimes using the Greek word translated "head" to refer to a person's actual head and sometimes as a metaphor for something quite different. While we may be clear about the word when it's applied to the topmost part of our physical body, we may be less clear when it's applied to something else.

Furthermore, while the metaphorical use of a word may mean one thing to us today, it may have meant something entirely different in biblical times. And even in biblical times, it could mean different things in different contexts. Because this word is prominent in Paul's letters, and especially in his statements about public worship in 1 Corinthians 11, we must look at it carefully. In 1 Corinthians 11, he uses the word solely as a metaphor in verse 3, as both a literal part of the human body and also as a metaphor in verses 4, 5, and 7, and as only a literal part of the body in verses 10 and 13.

In 1986, Wayne Grudem presented "Does *Kephalē* ('Head') Mean 'Source' or 'Authority Over' in Greek Literature? A Survey of 2,336

Examples" at the Evangelical Theological Society's annual meeting.[1] That title points to the basic issue: Does *head* when used as a metaphor mean "source" (as in "the head of the river") or does it mean "authority over" (as in "he is the head of the business")? In that title, Grudem gives two possible meanings of the word translated "head." While many scholars have accepted one or the other of these two definitions, other scholars advocate for other meanings for this metaphor. Amid the plethora of definitions, Walter Liefeld warned against a "one meaning fits all" approach because there's no one single or dominant meaning for the word, and its sense can change even within a biblical passage.[2]

If so much did not turn on this word for both men and women, we could shrug and move on to other things. But because the word is used to support opposing ideas (evangelical gender-based hierarchy versus evangelical complementary equality), we have to explore it further.

Head (Kephalē) in 1 Corinthians 11:3

I want you to realize that the head of every man is Christ, and the head of the woman is man, and the head of Christ is God.[3]

When contemporary meanings are assigned to *head*, this verse looks like a slam-dunk argument for a gender-based hierarchy. But we must answer some questions before we can make that assumption. The first

---

1. An expanded version of Grudem's work is found in appendix A in John Piper and Wayne Grudem, eds., *Recovering Biblical Manhood and Womanhood: A Response to Evangelical Feminism*, 2nd ed. (Wheaton, IL: Crossway, 2006), 425–68.

2. See Walter L. Liefeld, "Women, Submission and Ministry in 1 Corinthians," in Alvera Mickelsen, *Women, Authority and the Bible* (Downers Grove, IL: InterVarsity, 1986), 134–53.

3. The Common English Bible, the New American Standard Bible, and the New King James Version essentially follow the NIV translation. But other translations present variations on this verse. The New Revised Standard Version puts it this way: "I want you to understand that Christ is the head of every man, and the husband is the head of his wife, and God is the head of Christ"—adding marriage language to the original text. The New Living Translation reads, "There is one thing I want you to know: A man is responsible to Christ, a woman is responsible to her husband, and Christ is responsible to God." In addition to marriage language, this translation introduces "responsibility."

question is this: What was the *first*-century understanding of the Greek word translated "head"?

This word appears as a metaphor twelve times in the New Testament. Three occur here in 1 Corinthians 11:3. The supporters of gender-based hierarchy insist that "authority over" is the undisputed way to translate that word.[4] They are emphatic that verse 3 means that "Christ is the authority [head] over every man, man is the authority [head] over woman, and God is the authority [head] over Christ."[5] But other biblical scholars have challenged this.[6] They assert that translating the word (when used as a metaphor) to mean "chief" or "person of highest rank" exercising authority is rare in Greek literature.[7] In fact, some insist the word never meant "authority over" in the first century but began to have that sense at the end of the second century.[8]

This dispute has been called "the battle of the lexicons." A lexicon is a kind of bilingual dictionary useful to scholars working with Greek and Hebrew texts. The problem is that some lexicons list "source" as

---

4. See Wayne Grudem's appendix A in *Recovering Biblical Manhood and Womanhood*, 427.

5. See Thomas Schreiner's chapter in *Recovering Biblical Manhood and Womanhood*, 128.

6. Stephen Bedele writes, "In normal Greek usage, classical or contemporary, *kephalē* does not signify 'head' in the sense of ruler or chieftain of a community. If *kephalē* had this sense in the writings of St. Paul (it certainly has it nowhere else in the New Testament), we must suppose it to have been acquired as the result of the LXX usage of the word to translate [the Hebrew] *rosh*" ("The Meaning of *Kephalē* in the Pauline Epistles," *Journal of Theological Studies* 5 [October 1954], 211).

7. See Gordon Fee, *The First Epistle to the Corinthians* (Grand Rapids: Eerdmans, 1987), 502, note 42. Fee called Wayne Grudem's work misleading both in its presentation and conclusions: "The number 2,336 in the title is especially so since only a small percentage of these are metaphorical, and these are the only ones that count. Furthermore, Grudem's conclusion that 49 of these mean 'authority over' is especially ungrounded—for several reasons: (1) these 49 include 12 New Testament examples which the author prejudges exegetically to mean 'authority over' when these are the very passages in question; (2) of the 37 that remain, 18 are from Greek translations of the OT, which for reasons outlined below are the exceptions that prove the rule that this is *not* an ordinary meaning for this Greek word ... (3) for most of the remaining 19 there is serious exegetical question as to whether the authors intended a metaphorical sense of 'authority over'; and (4) since he used Philo in his calculations, he seems quite mistaken, in light of the passages from Philo ... to conclude that 'no instances were discovered in which *kephalē* had the meaning 'source, origin.' What Grudem has demonstrated was that the metaphorical usage of 'leader' can be found (it is not at all clear that it ever means 'authority over'), but he is quite wrong to assert that the idea of 'source' or 'origin' is not to be found."

8. See Richard Cervin, "Does *Kephalē* ("Head") Mean "Source" or "Authority Over" in Greek Literature: A Rebuttal," *Trinity Journal*, ns 10 (1989): 85–112.

the meaning of *kephalē*, and others list "authority over." Which lexicon does a person judge to be most authoritative to use?[9] Not all lexicons work directly with the Greek text, and we would do well to choose one that does.

We might sigh over such wrangling about a single word, asking what difference this makes, but we get some help from the apostle Paul's use of *head* in the order of the three pairs in 1 Corinthians 11:3:

1. The head of every man is Christ.
2. The head of the woman is man.
3. The head of Christ is God.

Arguments are usually built in some kind of ascending or descending order. What is the order of the three statements? If we take *kephalē* to mean "authority over," then we have:

1. The authority over every man is Christ.
2. The authority over the woman is man.
3. The authority over Christ is God.

But a *hierarchy of authority* would look like this:

1. God is the head of Christ.
2. Christ is the head of man.
3. Man is the head of woman.

---

9. "Some Greek lexicons give a simplistic translation of *kephalē* by imposing their own modern concept on the term and then engaging in a process of circular definition: '*Kephalē* means ruler in the New Testament because it means ruler in these New Testament passages.' In order to understand properly the meaning of 'head' as used by the apostle Paul, it is helpful to determine its meaning within the language spoken by Paul" (Gilbert Bilezikian, *Beyond Sex Roles: What the Bible Says about a Woman's Place in Church and Family*, 3rd ed. (Grand Rapids: Baker, 2006), 226, n. 13.

However, that's not the order in which Paul wrote the three statements. Throughout all of his letters, the apostle Paul is logical, which should alert us to the fact that perhaps he had a completely different idea in mind when he chose to use *kephalē* to describe these three relationships.

Gilbert Bilezikian notes that a particular kind of nonhierarchical but dependent relationship exists in each of the three pairs, hinging on the way the New Testament churches understood the word *head*. For them, the head was the "provider of life and growth"[10]: Christ was the origin or provider of life and growth for the man (Genesis 1–2); the man was the origin or provider of life and growth for the woman (Genesis 2); and God was the origin or provider of life and growth for the incarnate Christ (John 1:14).

This was in contrast to the Judaizers' use of *head* to mean "authority." Bilezikian writes, "In Corinth the Judaizers used their own traditional version of the concept of headship as a weapon to force women into subordination, as was done in the synagogue . . . Paul shows that all relations of derivation find their origin in God. He was the initial giver of all life. But in chronological sequence, the origin of man was in Christ, the Logos of creation. Second, the origin of woman was man since she was formed from him. Third, the origin of the incarnate Christ was God with the birth of Jesus, the Son of God."[11]

When anyone insists that *kephalē* means "authority over" in 1 Corinthians 11:3, it raises the problem of a subordinate relationship of Christ to God in the Trinity.[12] In chapter 8, we will explore the critical issues this interpretation creates.

But it isn't enough just to work a bit with a single verse as we've

---

10. Bilezikian, *Beyond Sex Roles*, 3rd ed., 105.
11. Ibid., 106.
12. It is important to note that at the time of this writing, vigorous debates on the nature of this subordination are taking place among proponents of gender-based hierarchy. Many insist this subordination is restricted to the incarnation (Jesus' earthly life); others argue for the eternal subordination of the Son to the Father.

done here. Recall that the *context* of a text is vital in determining the sense or meaning of that text. Judith Gundry-Volf reminds us that this verse is part of a larger argument in Paul's first letter to the Christians at Corinth—an argument that begins with 8:1 and continues through the first part of chapter 11.[13] In it, we see Paul dealing with various behavioral problems working against the credibility of the gospel in the wider society. Gundry-Volf makes the point that Paul is dealing with a society based on shame versus honor. Both men and women in Corinth are behaving in ways that dishonor one another, and thus they send the wrong message to outsiders. We get into the specifics in 11:4–7. In those verses, note the emphasis on honor/dishonor and on disgrace or shame.

Head (Kephalē) in 1 Corinthians 11:4–7

Every man who prays or prophesies with his head covered dishonors his head. But every woman who prays or prophesies with her head uncovered dishonors her head—it is the same as having her head shaved. For if a woman does not cover her head, she might as well have her hair cut off; but if it is a disgrace for a woman to have her hair cut off or her head shaved, then she should cover her head.

A man ought not to cover his head, since he is the image and glory of God; but woman is the glory of man.[14]

Before we look at the use of *kephalē* both literally and metaphorically in these verses, note that women were praying and prophesying in public worship of some sort. Does this contradict 1 Timothy 2:12 and 1 Corinthians 14:34–35? How is this public participation in leading worship to be explained?

---

13. See Judith Gundry-Volf, "Gender and Creation in 1 Corinthians 11:2–16: A Study in Paul's Theological Method," in *Evangelium-Schriftauslegung-Kirche*, ed. Jostein Adna, Scott Hafemann, and Otfried Hofius (Göttingen: Vandenhoeck & Ruprecht, 1997), 151–71.

14. Emphasis added.

Some commentators insist this did not take place in a public meeting—but later in 1 Corinthians 14:4, Paul reminded his readers that "the one who prophesies edifies the church." The "church" at that time would have been a house church—a small gathering in a home in which "each of you has a hymn, or a word of instruction, a revelation, a tongue or an interpretation" (14:26). Any open gathering of people, large or small, is "public." Others hold that women were praying and prophesying, but only in congregations of women. Nothing in the text implies this, and the context of the chapter is the whole church.

Still others insist that, different from teaching, prophesying was not "authoritative" preaching. But note that in 1 Corinthians 12:28, Paul lists "first of all apostles, second prophets, third teachers," etc. Whether this list should be considered chronological (the order in which workers are needed to plant and grow a church) or as an order of ministry importance, prophets precede teachers in that list.

Now we turn to the issues raised in 1 Corinthians 11:4–6. It's clear that Paul is using *kephalē* both physically and metaphorically in these verses, playing back and forth with the word. These verses are about *God-honoring behavior in public worship*, not about authority structures. So how do these verses link back to verse 3? Both men and women pray and prophesy in public worship, but a man doing so with his physical head covered dishonors his metaphorical head (Christ); a woman who does so with her physical head uncovered dishonors her metaphorical head (the man). What is this about?

The point is this. If Christ is the man's (metaphorical) "head," then his (physical) head cannot be "covered" in worship: he cannot "cover" Christ (his metaphorical head) in God's presence. If man is woman's (metaphorical) "head," then her (physical) head must be "covered" in worship because she reflects "the glory of man" (verse 7), and man's glory must be "covered" in God's presence.[15]

---

15. I am indebted to Morna D. Hooker for clarifying this complex passage in "Authority on Her Head: An Examination of 1 Cor. XI.10," *New Testament Studies* 10 (1963/64): 410–16.

What is this business of "covering"? Some translations introduce the idea of a veil worn by women. But the word *veil* is never mentioned in the Greek text, and enough is known about first-century customs to assume this does not mean a veil (or a prayer shawl) but long or loose hair. Philip Payne makes a strong argument for it being wild hair in contrast to hair cut short (for men) or hair neatly bound up (for women), as seen in many ancient Greek portraits.[16]

Clearly, Paul is speaking theologically here, but he is also addressing a serious cultural issue, as noted by Judith Gundry-Volf. In the cultural context of shame and honor, what difference does it make when those who lead public worship choose a "wild hairstyle"? It turns out that in Paul's day, a man wearing long, "effeminate" hair sent the signal that he was available for a homosexual relationship. A woman letting her long hair hang loose (instead of bound up in a sometimes elaborate netted hairstyle) advertised her availability for sex outside her marriage. In Payne's words, "it symbolized her repudiation of sexual fidelity to her husband."[17]

Corinth was a lusty city, crammed with pagan temples in which virtually every form of sexual activity was part of worship. In the Dionysian cult, women let their hair down as an essential part of engaging in ecstatic prophesying. Long, loose hair hanging down ignored cultural expectations of propriety and decency. When Christians showed up in church with wild hair and participated in worship, Paul was clear in his teaching that their behavior was shameful. In a culture built on concepts of honor and shame, Christians with wild hair were sending the wrong message to the surrounding culture. Furthermore, doing so would blur the distinction between pagan and Christian worship.

---

16. Payne writes, "First Corinthians 11:7–10 recapitulates 11:4–6, adding theological justification for why men (vv. 7–9) and women (v. 10) ought not to wear hairstyles that repudiate marriage . . . Paul is referring to men who wear effeminate hairstyles and women who let their hair down to symbolize rejection of Christian marital and sexual morality" (*Man and Woman, One in Christ* [Grand Rapids: Zondervan, 2009], 175.

17. Ibid., 169.

In these verses, Paul at no point speaks of "authority." His concern is with the woman being the man's "glory," the one without whom he is incomplete (1 Corinthians 11:7–9). In Genesis 2, man by himself was incomplete, and when he sees the woman, he "glories" in her, bursting into song (Genesis 2:23). She came from man and was created for him to complete him. The point of the passage is not hierarchical gender roles, but worship protocol. In the verses that follow, the message is about origins, not about authority structures.

Head (Kephalē) in 1 Corinthians 11:8–12

> *For man did not come from woman, but woman from man; neither was man created for woman, but woman for man. It is for this reason that a woman ought to have authority over her own head, because of the angels. Nevertheless, in the Lord woman is not independent of man, nor is man independent of woman. For as woman came from man, so also man is born of woman. But everything comes from God.*

Paul makes two important theological points in these verses. In both verses 8–9 and 11–12, he argues for the interdependency of men and women, and in verse 10, for a woman's own "authority." Let's begin with verse 10 and then look at its context about interdependency.

Verse 10 contains the only mention of "authority" in the chapter, and it is the woman's own authority. Here is a synopsis of Morna Hooker's cogent explanation of this verse: In Jewish worship, the man played the active role, but now in Christian worship, woman, in contrast to Jewish custom, takes part in prayer and prophecy in public worship. The only reason she can do this is that a new power has been given to her. In Jewish thought, although Adam and Eve were both given dominion and authority over creation (Genesis 1:27), Jewish exegetes did not give it to

Eve. Yet women in the new Christian churches could now speak to God in prayer and declare his word in prophecy.[18] To do this, women need authority and power from God.[19]

The head covering or proper hair that symbolizes the effacement of man's glory in the presence of God (1 Corinthians 11:7), also serves as the sign of *exousia* (power) given to women. With the glory of man now hidden, women, too, can reflect the glory of God. Far from being a symbol of her subjection to man, her head covering or proper hair is what Paul calls it: authority. In prayer and prophecy, she, like the man, is under the authority of God. The differences in creation remain and are reflected in the differences of appearance in one's relationship to God in worship. But in Christ, "nor is there male or female, for you are all one in Christ Jesus" (Galatians 3:28).[20]

The basic teaching of this passage is the interdependence of men and women: all things originate from God (1 Corinthians 11:12). Whatever implications were drawn in the past from a male/female sequence in creation, such implications are now obsolete in Christ. Man and woman are interdependent because of their reciprocal origins. And both men and women in their hair styles and demeanor must respect the other because of those reciprocal origins. This was the issue in 1 Timothy 2:12–13: a woman grasping for unauthorized authority to teach a man in a high-handed or despotic manner disrespected her origin. But both must "ascribe primacy and rulership to God who alone is the originator of all things."[21]

---

18. Paul defines the content of prophecy later in 1 Corinthians 14:3: "The one who prophesies speaks to people for their strengthening, encouraging and comfort."

19. See Hooker, "Authority on Her Head," 410–16.

20. Philip Payne notes that many Bible versions and interpretations mistranslate *exousian echein* in 1 Corinthians 11:10 as though it meant a sign or symbol of man's authority over woman. "All 103 occurrences of *exousia* ("authority") in the New Testament refer to authority held in one's own hand, whether inherent, assigned or achieved. Likewise, all nine references to *exousia* in 1 Corinthians mean 'to have power of one's own'" (*Man and Woman*, 182).

21. Bilezikian, *Beyond Sex Roles*, 3rd ed., 109.

EPHESIANS 5:21–33

Biblical scholars have identified six household codes in the New Testament letters that give ethical directions to husbands and wives, parents and children, and masters and slaves.[22] What was the overall purpose of the codes? Paul wrote, "Give the people these instructions, so that no one may be open to blame . . . Give the enemy no opportunity for slander" (1 Timothy 5:7, 14); Christians were to behave in such a way that "no one will malign the word of God" (Titus 2:5). Before anything else, the household codes are *missional*. They are embedded in Paul's concern for Christian witness. We are to give no offense to non-Christians around us. This is cultural sensitivity in the service of God's gospel. Because God gave himself to redeem us, we are "to be subject to rulers and authorities, to be obedient, to be ready to do whatever is good, to slander no one, to be peaceable and considerate, and always to be gentle toward everyone" (Titus 3:1–2).

The longest of these codes is found in Ephesians 5:21–6:9, where Paul deals primarily with marriage issues and follows with shorter admonitions to children and fathers and then to slaves and masters. It is also the code most often cited because of its use of *kephalē*.

Earlier, in Ephesians 4:32–5:2, Paul laid the groundwork for this code: "Be kind and compassionate to one another, forgiving each other, just as in Christ God forgave you. Follow God's example, therefore, as dearly loved children, and walk in the way of love, just as Christ loved us and gave himself up for us as a fragrant offering and sacrifice to God."

Because Paul had already told everyone this, he could then say to husbands in Ephesians 5:25, "Love your wives, just as Christ loved the church and gave himself up for her." We follow God's example by following Christ's example, which means giving up our lives for one another.

---

22. These codes are found in Galatians 3:28; Ephesians 5:15–6:9; Colossians 3:25–4:2; 1 Timothy 5:1–22; 6:1–2; Titus 2:1–15; 1 Peter 2:11–3:9. Only two of the six codes include all three pairs of relationships, and only three of the six specifically address the relationship of husbands and wives.

Paul had laid further groundwork in Ephesians 5:15–16: "Be very careful, then, how you live—not as unwise but as wise, making the most of every opportunity, because the days are evil." Being careful includes "submit to one another out of reverence for Christ" (verse 21). Because he had said that to everyone, he could now say to wives, "Submit yourselves to your own husbands as you do to the Lord" (verse 22). As British author Anne Atkins writes, "Before we can hope to be good husbands or wives, we must learn to be good Christians. We must all become self-sacrificing and submissive."[23]

Paul then tells wives, "For the husband is the head of the wife as Christ is the head of the church, his body, of which he is the Savior" (Ephesians 5:23). From this verse a doctrine of headship has been established. But nowhere in the Bible does the word *headship* appear. It's an abstraction implying "authority over" in modern usage. We must avoid our twenty-first-century propensity to import our current word usage into the biblical understanding of key words: for example, creating the word *headship* as a biblical term when, in fact, no such word appears in the Bible. We must be clear about what we can and cannot say about *kephalē*, "head."[24]

The Bible simply states that the husband is "head of the wife" analogous to Christ as head of the church in his role as its Savior (source or provider of life and growth). If we ask what this means, theologian Sarah Sumner responds, "Scripture doesn't tell us definitively. It tells us what it looks like—self-sacrifice. Thus we have a picture, not a definition."[25] The picture is a metaphor to help us understand the climax of the passage, Ephesians 5:31–32: "For this reason a man will leave his father and

---

23. Anne Atkins, *Split Image: Male and Female after God's Likeness* (Grand Rapids: Eerdmans, 1987), 155.
24. *Head*, when understood as meaning "source or provider of life and growth," does not carry the authoritarian freight of the abstract term *headship*.
25. Sarah Sumner, *Men and Women in the Church: Building Consensus on Christian Leadership* (Downers Grove, IL: InterVarsity, 2003), 143.

mother and be united to his wife, and the two will become one flesh. This is a profound mystery—but I am talking about Christ and the church."

How can two become one? The mystery of marriage is that two (head and body) become "one flesh." Sumner writes the following:

> When *head* is defined as "leader" and *body* is defined as "helper," the biblical mystery is lost. What is mysterious about a leader coupled up with his helper? Not very much. Nor is it particularly inspiring. But it is altogether breathtaking to see the biblical picture of body and head joined mysteriously as one . . .
>
> The picture of "one flesh" . . . indicates immediately the organic unity that bonds a husband and wife . . . It is not so disturbing to imagine a leader breaking up with his assistant. But it is utterly disconcerting to imagine a body being amputated physically from its head . . . A body belongs to its head and a head belongs to its body. That's why God hates divorce.[26]

The husband as "head" is analogous to Christ as head of the church and as Savior of the body. Giving himself for the body? That is far from emphasizing rule or authority. Yes, Jesus has authority over the church, but Paul uses the metaphor here to describe Christ's work as head of the body, in terms not of authority structures, but of giving himself for the church. Whatever else this metaphor carries, it is not linked to authority. It is about the "head" dying to his own agenda for the sake of the "body." Gilbert Bilezikian noted, "Whenever Christ is upheld as the model for husbands to follow, it is not his power, his lordship, and his authority that are presented as the traits to emulate, but his humility, his abnegation, and his servant behavior."[27]

Paul goes on with a second argument for husbands: "In the same way,

---

26. Ibid., 167.
27. Bilezikian, *Beyond Sex Roles*, 3rd ed., 128.

husbands ought to love their wives as their own bodies. He who loves his wife loves himself. After all, no one ever hated their own body, but they feed and care for their body, just as Christ does the church" (Ephesians 5:28–29). One flesh. The head lives to serve the body just as the body lives to serve the head. They are inseparable. The way you care for yourself is the way you are to care for your spouse.

According to the Bible, marriage is not about a metaphorical plumber and his female helper; it's about two people joined indissolubly as "one flesh." Paul wasn't kidding when he stepped back from what he had written and said, "This is a profound mystery." We must take it for that.

The Bible's Case for Mutual Authority in Marriage

What about "authority" in marriage? Only one passage in the New Testament explicitly addresses the question of authority in marriage:

> But since sexual immorality is occurring, each man should have sexual relations with his own wife, and each woman with her own husband. The husband should fulfill his marital duty to his wife, and likewise the wife to her husband. The wife does not have authority over her own body but yields it to her husband. In the same way, the husband does not have authority over his own body but yields it to his wife. Do not deprive each other except perhaps by mutual consent and for a time, so that you may devote yourselves to prayer. Then come together again so that Satan will not tempt you because of your lack of self-control.
>
> 1 Corinthians 7:2–5

From this passage we see that the authority in marriage relationships is mutual. The authority or power that a husband has over his wife, she has over him. The relationship is absolutely symmetrical. Philip Payne observes that "the strikingly egalitarian understanding of the dynamics of marital relations expressed in Paul's symmetry through this passage is without parallel in the literature of the ancient world."[28]

A woman can fully trust her husband with her body only if she knows he will treat her body as he would treat his own body—with consideration and care. A husband can fully trust his wife with his body only if he knows she will treat his body with the same consideration and care she gives to her own body. They are one flesh. The sexual oneness in 1 Corinthians 7:4 comes after, not before, the mutual affection of 7:3. The self-giving in lovemaking is mutual because the bodies and spirits of both husband and wife first belong to God and then to one another. Love and trust can grow in such soil. But true intimacy isn't possible to those who come to marriage for purposes of self-fulfillment or merely to ease personal loneliness.

Paul in 1 Corinthians 7:4 says that sex in Christian marriage is a safety valve to keep us from sexual immorality. But it's more. It also enacts the self-giving relationship of Christ and the church, and it embodies what it is to be "one flesh."

CONCLUSION

All the stipulations to husbands and wives in Ephesians 5:21–33 had already been mandated for the whole body of Christ. All people of faith are to have submissive spirits. All people of faith are to love one another with a self-sacrificing love. In virtually every case, the rationale for each stipulation was that Christ had already walked that road, and his followers could safely walk it as well (Ephesians 5:1–2). The example of Jesus Christ giving his life as a ransom for many is the reason that wives submit

---

28. Payne, *Man and Woman*, 106–7.

to their husbands and husbands love their wives in a self-giving manner to the same degree that they love their own bodies.

God's case for marriage has remained unchanged since Eden because bent and broken image bearers can be redeemed and transformed. Marriage is designed to transform us. But God's case for marriage also includes the possibility of our being a daily, living demonstration to a watching world of the relationship of Christ to his bride, the church. Marriage is thus a vehicle through which God speaks to the world around us through our changed lives.

Questions for Personal Reflection or Group Discussion

1. How do you respond to the battle over the first-century meanings of the word *head*?
2. If 1 Corinthians 11:3–12 is actually about issues of shame and honor (rather than about authority structures), why do you think Paul insisted on Christians conforming to cultural expectations about hairstyles at that time?
3. What do you believe Ephesians 5:21–33 teaches about the relationship of husbands and wives?
4. How would you harmonize the teachings in Ephesians 5:21–33 with Paul's insistence in 1 Corinthians 7:4 that authority in Christian marriage is mutual?

Chapter Eight

IS JESUS ETERNALLY SUBORDINATE TO GOD THE FATHER? OR ARE THEY COEQUAL?

In June 2016, *Christianity Today* published an important article titled "Gender and the Trinity: From Proxy War to Civil War," noting that "the latest complementarian debate isn't over women's subordination—but Christ's." The article then explained what is going on and why it matters:

> On June 3, the Alliance of Confessing Evangelicals (ACE) published the first half of a guest post by Liam Goligher, senior minister of Tenth Presbyterian Church in Philadelphia, on its blog . . .
>
> In his two-part blog post, Goligher strongly critiqued well-known theologians Bruce Ware (Southern Baptist Theological Seminary) and Wayne Grudem (Phoenix Seminary) for presenting a "novel view of God; a different God than that affirmed by the church through the ages and taught in Scripture."[1]

---

1. Caleb Lindgren, "Gender and the Trinity: From Proxy War to Civil War," *Christianity*

It is essential to note that many complementarians do *not* accept the proposition that Jesus is *eternally* subordinate to God the Father. Most confine Jesus' subordination to God to his voluntary submission during his earthly ministry and his atoning sacrifice on the cross.

At the same time, because some complementarians base hierarchy for women in the church and home on Christ's eternal subordination to God, we must look at the biblical and theological issues surrounding it.

The discussion in chapter 7 centered on how we should translate the Greek word (*kephalē*) translated "head." But that discussion opened the door to a larger discussion around the same verse in Paul's letter: "I want you to realize that the head of every man is Christ, and the head of the woman is man, and the head of Christ is God" (1 Corinthians 11:3). If someone translates *kephalē* ("head") as "authority over" in the third part of that verse, it raises the question of a hierarchy within the Trinity. God and Christ are both persons within one being in the Trinity (i.e., God the Father and God the Son), but some argue that this text clearly shows a chain of command in their relationship—a chain of command that should be reflected in the way men and women relate to each other. So we must ask, "Is God the Son eternally subordinate to God the Father? Or are they coequal?" From the answers to those questions comes the further question: "In what way would this have any relevance for how men and women relate in the church and home?"

Anglican bishop John Rodgers wrote, "God's ordering of the relations of male and female in the family ultimately reflects and rests upon God's own triune nature . . . An eternal headship and submission are lived out in the divine life of love. God the Father . . . is eternally the Father of the Son . . . The main point . . . is that loving headship and submission are eternal in the life of God."[2]

Today, June 20, 2016, www.christianitytoday.com/ct/2016/june-web-only/gender-trinity-proxy-war-civil-war-eternal-subordination.html (accessed November 21, 2016).

2. John H. Rodgers Jr., *A Report of the Study Concerning the Ordination of Women Undertaken*

In support of that, theologian Wayne Grudem asserted that from the time of the Nicene Creed in AD 325, "the doctrine of the 'eternal generation of the Son' has been taken to imply a *relationship* between the Father and the Son that *eternally* existed and that will always exist—a relationship that includes a subordination in role, but not in essence or being."[3]

He then cited A. H. Strong: "We frankly recognize an eternal subordination of Christ to the Father, but we maintain at the same time that this subordination is a subordination of order, office, and operation, not a subordination of essence."[4] To support this distinction, Grudem elsewhere claimed that "the subjection of the Son to the Father for all eternity, a subjection that never began but always existed and a subjection that will continue in the future, does not nullify the deity of the Son."[5] Note that contemporary teachers like Wayne Grudem insist that the Son is equal with the Father in *being* but subordinate in *role*.

What difference does it make whether or not Jesus is subordinated *eternally* to God in the Trinity? Does it seem arcane and far removed from daily experience? We might ask, "So what?" Yet for Christian men and women, much hangs on the outcome of this discussion because, as those who are created in God's image, we are called in our human relationships to reflect or image in some way the relationships within the Trinity.

GOD IN THREE PERSONS: BLESSED TRINITY

Most nations and ethnic groups in the ancient Near East worshiped a panoply of gods and goddesses specific to various urgencies in life. But

by the Anglican Mission in America (2003), online at www.vulcanhammer.org/island/w.pdf (accessed November 21, 2016).

3. John Piper and Wayne Grudem, eds., *Recovering Biblical Manhood and Womanhood*, 2nd ed. (Wheaton, IL: Crossway, 2006), 457.

4. Ibid.

5. Wayne Grudem, *Countering the Claims of Evangelical Feminism* (Colorado Springs: Multnomah, 2006), 244.

to Abraham and his descendants, God was revealed as one: "Hear, O Israel: the LORD our God, the LORD is one" (Deuteronomy 6:4). The Ten Commandments begin with the statement, "I am the LORD your God, who brought you out of Egypt, out of the land of slavery. You shall have no other gods before me" (Exodus 20:2–3). All of the commandments rest on the uniqueness of the Lord, Israel's one and only God.

Yet in the Bible's first chapter, we see God revealed as the Creator, as the Word, as the agent of creation, and as the Spirit of God "hovering over the waters" (Genesis 1:1–2). The chapter ends with God self-identifying as a plurality: "Let *us* make mankind in our image, in *our* likeness" (Genesis 1:26, emphasis added). As the basis for all that he would write about the earthly ministry of Jesus, the apostle John opened his gospel with a stunning statement: "In the beginning was the Word, and the Word was with God, and the Word was God. He was with God in the beginning. Through him all things were made; without him nothing was made that has been made . . . The Word became flesh and made his dwelling among us. We have seen his glory, the glory of the one and only Son, who came from the Father, full of grace and truth" (John 1:1–3, 14). Jesus, the human being, is the eternal Word that became flesh. This is the incarnation, the story told in the four gospels of the God-man who reveals God the Father to finite human beings.

God in three persons—blessed Trinity.[6] While the word *trinity* isn't found in the Bible, we see the three persons of the Trinity cited together by Jesus in the Great Commission: "Therefore go and make disciples of all nations, baptizing them in the name of the Father and of the Son and of the Holy Spirit, and teaching them to obey everything I have commanded you" (Matthew 28:19–20). In John 16–17, we learn that even as God sent Jesus into the world for our salvation, Jesus would send the Holy Spirit to guide us into all truth.

---

6. A trinity is a tri-unity: three persons united in a single being.

This three-in-oneness of the Godhead shows up in Paul's benediction: "May the grace of the Lord Jesus Christ, and the love of God, and the fellowship of the Holy Spirit be with you all" (2 Corinthians 13:14). Peter referred to it on Pentecost: "God has raised this Jesus to life, and we are all witnesses of it. Exalted to the right hand of God, he has received from the Father the promised Holy Spirit and has poured out what you now see and hear" (Acts 2:32–33).

Theologian Millard Erickson concludes, "Although the doctrine of the Trinity is not expressly asserted in Scripture, particularly the New Testament contains so many suggestions of the deity and unity of the three persons that we can understand why the church formulated the doctrine and conclude that they were right in so doing."[7]

FATHER/SON LANGUAGE IN THE TRINITY

It is the fact that these texts often refer to God as Father and Jesus as Son that has led some theologians to assert a doctrine called "the eternal subordination of the Son to the Father." To assess this idea, we must determine how to understand the relationships within this "three-in-one" deity. Two factors must be kept in mind.

First, using the known to comprehend the unknown. Theologian John Jefferson Davis reminds us that "all biblical and human language about God is *analogical* and not strictly *literal* in nature."[8] An analogy is the use of something we know to help us understand what is unknown. For example, God is spirit by nature (John 4:24), and so is not literally a gendered being, though he reveals himself analogically through gendered human language. Consequently, we use what we know (as gendered human beings) as a way to comprehend what is beyond our ability to

---

7. Millard Erickson, *Christian Theology*, vol. 1 (Grand Rapids: Baker, 1983), 332.

8. John Jefferson Davis, "Incarnation, Trinity, and the Ordination of Women to the Priesthood," *The Deception of Eve and the Ontology of Women* (special edition journal ETS 2010; Christians for Biblical Equality), 11.

know (God as spirit). Recall that an analogy is the use of something known to help us understand what is unknown.

The apostle Paul described God as "the King eternal, immortal, invisible, the only God" (1 Timothy 1:17), and later as "the blessed and only Ruler, the King of kings and Lord of lords, who alone is immortal and who lives in unapproachable light, whom no one has seen or can see" (6:15–16). In contrast, we are temporal rather than eternal, mortal rather than immortal, visible rather than invisible. How can our limited reality help us grasp some part of God's infinite reality?

Jesus used different analogies to help us. In Luke 15, he spoke of God as a shepherd seeking a lost sheep, as a woman searching for a lost coin, and as a father welcoming home an errant son as examples of divine persistence in saving us. In his parables, he used such analogies as a farmer sowing seeds, a woman baking bread, and a fisherman sorting a catch. Analogies—the known—abound in Scripture to help us start with what we know and stretch upward to grasp aspects of God we otherwise could not know.

In the New Testament, the paramount analogy used of God is that of Father and Son. Davis comments that Father-Son "language of the biblical and Trinitarian tradition is rooted in the prayer language of Jesus, who taught his disciples to address God as 'Father.'"[9] Thus, while the Father-Son language is analogical, it cannot be dismissed as mere analogy. God is not less than "Father," but is much more. God's personal qualities and perfections are not less than those of a good human father, but are indeed much greater and more perfect than those of any human father. The analogical nature of this language is reflected in texts like Ephesians 3:14–15: "For this reason I kneel before the Father from whom every family in heaven and on earth derives its name." Strictly speaking, "Father" is a relational term, reflecting God's sustaining, providing, and

---

9. Ibid., 12.

protective nature.[10] This helps us grasp how we are to see ourselves in relationship to God as our loving Father. So when we speak of Jesus as the Son of God, the analogy gives us insight into one aspect of God that we can get hold of with our finite minds.

Second, Jesus in eternity versus Jesus' earthly life. A second factor lies in whether or not Jesus is *eternally* subordinated to the Father, or if his subordination was limited to his earthly life. Evangelical scholars agree that in his incarnation, Jesus voluntarily submitted himself to all the strictures of human flesh, including a constant submission to the Father. Paul captured this in his letter to the Christians in Philippi: "[Jesus], Who being in very nature God, did not consider equality with God something to be used to his own advantage; rather, he made himself nothing by taking the very nature of a servant, being made in human likeness. And being found in appearance as a man, he humbled himself by becoming obedient to death—even death on a cross!" (Philippians 2:6–8).

As finite human beings with no other mode of experience, we struggle to imagine what this meant. If we try to grasp this, we could think of ourselves as persons who descend to becoming ants in order to communicate to the world of ants. We'd set aside all our powers and potential as human beings and take on the risks and limitations of being an ant. This analogy doesn't begin to exhaust what it meant for God to take on human form, but it gives a very faint picture of what it meant for God to become a human being. It forces us to give some thought to the severe limitations Jesus voluntarily took on in the incarnation. He did all this "for us and our salvation" (to quote the Nicene Creed).

Evangelical scholars agree that Jesus submitted his will and his work to God the Father during his earthly ministry. But was this submission only for the period of time between his birth and his ascension to the Father, or is it a submission that always was and always will be—an eternal

---

10. In contrast, Yahweh ("the LORD") seems to be a personal, proper name of God's self-revelation and self-designation.

submission? Again, for men and women, much potentially hangs on the response to this question. Davis helps us sort out the issue

> The historic, orthodox understanding of the Christian doctrine of the Trinity is that in eternity . . . the Son is in all things equal to the Father. In time, during his incarnate, earthly ministry . . . the Son was *voluntarily* subordinate (in function, not essence) to the Father. The historic creeds and the church fathers were insistent that this distinction . . . was crucial for right interpretations of the scriptural texts regarding Christ, and for avoiding the various forms of subordinationism that have arisen in the church.[11]

What prompted this distinction? Early in the fourth century, the Alexandrian elder Arius understood "the Father to be 'the fountainhead of deity,' who alone was 'intrinsically God' (*autotheos*) . . . This led him to depict the Son as different *in being* to the Father. On the basis of his largely Greek understanding of God he concluded that the Son (and the Spirit) must be ontologically subordinated to the Father. For him the Son could only be called God in a secondary sense."[12] In order to substantiate this biblically, Arius had to minimize or completely ignore the texts that teach the full divinity of the Son and the "oneness" of the Father and Son (e.g., John 17:21). Opposing Arius's teaching, the Council of Nicaea (in the Nicene Creed) left no room for the idea that Jesus' *being* was in any way different from that of the Father: "We believe . . . in one Lord, Jesus Christ . . . God from God, Light from Light, true God from true God . . . of the same essence as the Father."

While Arius was condemned as a heretic by the Council of Nicaea in AD 325, some form of subordinationism survived and mutated over

---

11. Davis, "Incarnation," 13.
12. Kevin Giles, *The Trinity and Subordinationism: The Doctrine of God and the Contemporary Gender Debate* (Downers Grove, IL: InterVarsity, 2002), 63.

the centuries that followed. In the nineteenth century, the Princeton theologian Charles Hodge promulgated "the principle of subordination of the Son to the Father and the Spirit to the Father and the Son."[13] Unlike Arius, Hodge held that Father and Son were fully equal in their divine nature. Hodge's successor at Princeton, B. B. Warfield, made clear that it is "thoroughly illegitimate . . . to suggest any subordination for the Son or the Spirit which would in any manner impair that complete identity with the Father in being and that complete equality with the Father in powers."[14] Warfield's insistence on the Son's and Spirit's "complete equality with the Father in powers" (as well as in being) appears to be a corrective to Hodge's implicit hierarchy of God / Son / Spirit.

BEING VERSUS ROLE

Some contemporary teachers of the doctrine of the eternal subordination of the Son to the Father draw a line between *being* (ontology, essence) and *role* (function), as noted in quotes at the beginning of this chapter. In doing so, they avoid the accusation of Arian heresy. But one might ask, given the nature of God, is this even possible? Rebecca Groothuis has argued that if subordination is "permanent, comprehensive and ontologically grounded," then the person must logically be inferior in being.[15] If the Son is subordinate to the Father eternally, his nature/being is in some way inferior to the Father's. Alan Myatt writes, "Millard Erickson . . . notes that if authority and submission are essential and not accidental attributes of the Father and Son, then the essence of the Father and the essence of the Son are different. This 'is equivalent to saying that they are not *homoousious* [of one being] with one another.'"[16]

---

13. Charles Hodge, *Systematic Theology* (New York: Scribner, 1871), 1:460.
14. B. B. Warfield, *Biblical Foundations* (London: Tyndale, 1958), 112.
15. Rebecca Groothuis, *Good News for Women* (Grand Rapids: Baker, 1997), 317.
16. Alan Myatt, "On the Compatibility of Ontological Equality, Hierarchy and Functional Distinctions," *The Deception of Eve and the Ontology of Women*, 24. Opponents might counter

At this point it may be useful to distinguish between two English words often used as synonyms: *submit* versus *subordinate*. An Oxford dictionary distinguishes these terms in this way: *submit* has the sense of "surrender [of oneself] to the control of another."[17] A person who is submissive is "humble, obedient, yielding to power or authority, willing to submit." In contrast, *subordinate* as a noun means "of inferior importance or rank, secondary"; as a verb it means "to make subservient." The first word describes the action of the person submitting; the second word describes the action of another in forcing submission.

When we return to Philippians 2:6–8 above, we find that Jesus "made himself nothing by taking the very nature of a servant" and humbling himself. Jesus was not subordinated by the Father; he voluntarily submitted to all the strictures of becoming a human being. He did this as one "who, being in very nature God, did not consider equality with God something to be used to his own advantage." Jesus Christ is in his very nature *God* and is completely equal with God. How are we to harmonize this clear teaching of Scripture with any notions of the eternal subordination of the Son to the Father? We turn to the biblical rationales given for that doctrine.

JESUS, COETERNAL WITH GOD OR SUBORDINATE TO GOD?

Wayne Grudem has laid out the crux of this doctrine: the Son's obedience to the Father arises from the very nature of his being as Son. "Certainly Scripture speaks of that when it says, for example, that when Christ 'had made purification for sins, he sat down at the right hand of the Majesty

---

by distinguishing between "personal essence" and "divine essence." In that case, Father, Son, and Spirit would be identical in their deity, but distinct in their personhood (God unbegotten, Son begotten, Spirit spiration). This would allow for distinction in their essence that does not deny *homoousios.*

17. *Oxford Illustrated American Dictionary* (Oxford: Oxford University Press, 1998), 827.

on high' (Hebrews 1:3). Jesus is at the right hand, but God the Father is still on the throne."[18] Note Grudem's assumption that because God seated Jesus at his right hand, it is God the Father who is on the throne. But in Revelation 21:5, it is the Lamb—Christ—"who was seated on the throne," and in Revelation 3:21, it is Jesus speaking, who said, "To the one who is victorious, I will give the right to sit with me on my throne." John also saw "a Lamb, looking as if it had been slain, standing at the center of the throne, encircled by the four living creatures and the elders" (Revelation 5:6).

Teachers of the doctrine of eternal subordination also use Hebrews 5:7–8 to validate it: "During the days of Jesus' life on earth, he offered up prayers and petitions with fervent cries and tears to the one who could save him from death, and he was heard because of his reverent submission. Son though he was, he learned obedience from what he suffered and, once made perfect, he became the source of eternal salvation for all who obey him." But the fact that he had to "learn obedience" through suffering points to a new reality. Before his incarnation, he was "with God, and . . . was God" (John 1:2) with no subordination. His subordinate status was limited to his incarnate experience, in which he suffered death for our salvation.

To support the eternal subordination doctrine, the text most often cited is 1 Corinthians 15:28: "When [God] has done this, then the Son himself will be made subject to him who put everything under him, so that God may be all in all." Thomas Schreiner explains it this way: "It is clear that this subjection of the Son to the Father is *after* his earthly ministry, so how anyone can say that there is no hint of a difference of order or role within the Trinity is difficult to see. Whenever Scripture says that God sent the Son into the world (e.g., John 3:17), we see subordination in role: the Father commands and sends; the Son obeys and comes into the world to die for our sins."[19]

---

18. Piper and Grudem, eds., *Recovering Biblical Manhood and Womanhood*, 457.
19. From Schreiner's chapter in *Recovering Biblical Manhood and Womanhood*, 129.

But 1 Corinthians 15:28 is the climax of a thrilling passage detailing Christ's powerful work of securing the kingdom to be handed over to God the Father. Just as death came through a human being (Adam), resurrection also came through a human being (Jesus). Just as all die (because of Adam), so all will be made alive (because of Christ). The purpose of all this? As we say in the Lord's Prayer, "Your kingdom come, your will be done, on earth as it is in heaven." The climax of God's redemptive work will occur when Jesus hands over the kingdom to God "after he has destroyed all dominion, authority and power. For he must reign until he has put all his enemies under his feet. The last enemy to be destroyed is death. For he 'has put everything under his feet'" (1 Corinthians 15:24–25).[20] It is clear that this does not include God himself, who put everything under Christ. When he has done this, then the Son himself will be made subject to him who put everything under him, so that the Godhead may be all in all (15:22–28).

At issue in both 1 Corinthians 11:3 and 15:28 is the article "the" in the Greek text before the word *God* (*ho theos*). This article is omitted in English translations, but in both cases it should read "the God" or "the Godhead." The texts would then read "the head of Christ is the Godhead" and "so that the Godhead may be all in all." Philip Payne notes that "this final statement, 'that God may be all in all,' is more appropriate as an affirmation of the oneness and encompassing authority of the Godhead than as a restricted reference to the Father."[21] In Colossians 2:9, the omitted article in the translations of the Corinthian passages is here captured in "the Deity": "For in Christ all the fullness of the Deity [*theotetos* = Godhead] lives in bodily form, and in Christ you have been brought to fullness. He is the head over every power and authority." Christ is head over every power and authority.

---

20. A reference to Psalm 8:6.
21. Philip B. Payne, *Man and Woman, One in Christ: An Exegetical and Theological Study of Paul's Letters* (Grand Rapids: Zondervan, 2009), 134.

The doctrine of the eternal subordination of the Son to the Father is built on our human understanding of the analogy of a son to a father. A weakness in this analogy lies in the changing relationships of human sons and fathers in the life cycle. When he's a child, a son is decidedly subordinated to his father. But when he reaches adulthood, he and his father may develop a fraternal relationship. And when the father is old, it is he who may need to lean on the son. Applying a human analogy to God has its obvious limitations. At the same time, the analogy enables us to see God near us as a loving father, not distant as "the King eternal, immortal, invisible, the only God" (1 Timothy 1:17). The analogy assures us that we can approach the throne of grace without fear, knowing that our heavenly Father cares for us and will listen to our prayers.

THE TRINITY: ONE NATURE, THREE PERSONS, ONE WILL

John Jefferson Davis helps us grasp this vital aspect of the Trinity[22]:

> The orthodox teaching is that the "subordination" of the Son to the Father is the willing subordination of the *human* will of the incarnate Christ . . . to the *one* undivided will common to Father, Son, and Holy Spirit. There are not three separate wills in the Trinity, but one undivided will common to all three . . .
>
> If there were *three* wills in the godhead, it could make sense to posit an "eternal subordination" of the will of the Son to the will of

---

22. Millard Erickson writes, "The Trinity is a communion of three persons, three centers of consciousness, who exist and always have existed in union with one another and in dependence on one another . . . Each is essential to the life of the others, and to the life of the Trinity. They are bound to one another in love, *agapē* love, which therefore unites them in the closest and most intimate of relationships. This unselfish, *agapē* love makes each more concerned for the other than for himself. There is therefore a mutual submission of each to each of the others and a mutual glorifying of one another. There is complete equality of the three" (*God in Three Persons: A Contemporary Interpretation of the Trinity* [Grand Rapids: Baker, 1995], 331).

the Father, but there is one will common to the three persons, not three. Historic orthodoxy teaches one nature and three persons, but not three wills in the Trinity.[23]

In a synod at Rome in 382, Pope Damasus noted, "Anyone who does not say that there is only one godhead, one might, one majesty, one power, one glory, one lordship, one kingdom, *one will* and one truth of the Father and of the Son and of the Holy Spirit is heretical."[24] We can't project the subordination of the human will of the incarnate Son into the eternal life of the Trinity.

So What? How This Relates
to Men and Women

A doctrine eternally subordinating the Son to the Father serves its proponents as a rationale for gender-based hierarchy. As such, it is often connected to the subordination of women to men in the church and in the home. The title of the 1999 Sydney Anglican Diocesan Doctrine Commission paper highlights this: "The Doctrine of Trinity and Its Bearing on the Relationship of Men and Women." That paper argued that just as God the Father is eternally "the head" of God the Son, so man is permanently "the head" of woman.[25]

Kevin Giles notes that "the contemporary conservative evangelical case for the permanent subordination of women frequently asserts that the Son is *eternally* subordinated to the Father. This 'truth' is taken to be both a rationale for women's permanent subordination to men (i.e., the Trinity reflects the God-given ideal for male-female relationships) and an example of how equality in being/essence/nature/dignity and permanent

---

23. Davis, "Incarnation," 15–16.
24. Karl Rahner, ed., *The Teaching of the Catholic Church as Contained in Her Documents* (Staten Island, NY: Alba House, 1967), 91.
25. Reproduced in full in Giles, *Trinity and Subordinationism*, 122–37.

subordination can both be endorsed without contradiction. Women, we are told, are equal with men in their essential being and dignity, yet they are subordinated to men in the home and the church."[26]

With tongue in cheek, John Jefferson Davis pushes this notion to its logical conclusion: "If the subordination of the Son to the Father in *time* supposedly justifies the subordination of women to men in the earthly church, does the supposed subordination of the Son to the Father in eternity justify the *eternal subordination* of women to men in the heavenly church of the new creation? Are women to be *eternally* second-class citizens in the kingdom of God? Such specious arguments and misunderstandings of Scripture and tradition condemn women to positions of unending subordination, and worse still, *rob God the Son* of his coeternal and coequal glory, majesty, and lordship."[27]

Beyond the illogic of this doctrine lies the deeper challenge to God's creational intention for a "Blessed Alliance"—men and women working together, shoulder to shoulder, in both the family and in the larger tasks of stewarding God's earth. This doctrine of eternal subordination overturns the divine intention in Genesis 1:26–28 and ignores the *ezer* purpose in the woman's creation (Genesis 2:18). She has been given a God-like role of bringing "help" to the man as they work together in their common tasks. She was created in no way as a subordinate, but as an equal with unique gifts needed by the man.

While a gender-based hierarchy has been widely taught in some Christian circles, it rests on a misunderstanding or twisting of crucial texts. In the process, it robs both the family and the church of the shared gifts and unique contributions realized when men and women stand side by side in ministry and daily work.

Millard Erickson makes the point that "the image of God must

---

26. Giles, *Trinity and Subordinationism*, 23.
27. Davis, "Incarnation," 18.

consist in a unity in plurality."[28] When God created humanity in the divine image, that humanity (singular, a unity) was created as male and female (a plurality). As bearers of the divine image, we are called in our relationships to image our relational God. If there were an ongoing subordination in the Trinity, we would be called to reflect that in our human relationships. But if a "Blessed Alliance" is the truth of God's Word, then we must strongly oppose any idea of the Son being *eternally subordinated* to God the Father.

Questions for Personal Reflection or Group Discussion

1. What (if anything) does a chapter on this subject contribute to your understanding of how men and women are to relate to one another in the home and in the church?
2. How can the relational analogy of a parent and child (in this case, father and son) help us think about our relationship to God?
3. As you think about God coming to earth as a human being, what would God have to give up in the process?
4. If we are created in God's image and called to image God in our world, what impact would this doctrine of Jesus' eternal subordination to God the Father have on how *we* image God?

---

28. Erickson, *Christian Theology*, 329.

Chapter Nine

WOMEN, LEADERSHIP, AND THE NATURE OF MINISTRY

In the roughly thirty-five years between Jesus' ascension to the Father and the martyrdoms of Peter and Paul, the gospel spread out from Pentecost in Jerusalem to the north, south, east, and west. We have only snippets of information about the great distances covered as the gospel was carried over the Silk Road to the gates of China or down into the heart of Africa. The book of Acts and the apostolic letters detail only the westward progress of the gospel throughout the Roman Empire. In this book, we must be content with that part of God's story.

Thus far in Part 2, we've evaluated two of the three basic complementarian presuppositions supporting gender-based hierarchy for both church and home:

1. "We are persuaded that the Bible teaches that only men should be pastors and elders. That is, men should bear *primary* responsibility for Christlike leadership and teaching in the church. So it is unbiblical, we believe, and therefore detrimental, for women to

assume this role."[1] This presupposition establishes a gender-based hierarchy for Christian ministry.

2. This gender-based hierarchy for church ministries rests on 1 Corinthians 11:3: "Christ is the authority over every man, man is the authority over woman, and God is the authority over Christ."[2] The issue of "authority" is based on the meaning of *kephalē* when it is translated as "authority over." Women are not to teach men or to exercise authority over men in the church.

These first two presuppositions were addressed in chapters 5–8. Now we come to the third presupposition:

3. "We think 1 Timothy 2:8–15 imposes two restrictions on the ministries of women: they are not to teach Christian doctrine to men and they are not to exercise authority directly over men in the church. These restrictions are permanent, authoritative for the church in all times and places and circumstances as long as men and women are descended from Adam and Eve."[3]

As we continue to explore questions about women and ministry, we must ask if Grudem's statement that it is both "unbiblical" and "detrimental" for women to serve as pastors and elders is in force not only in the first century, but "for all times and places and circumstances." We must examine (1) the nature of ministry and leadership according to Jesus and the apostolic letters, (2) the nature of the New Testament churches as the "family of faith, the household of God," and (3) women's roles in this template then and now.

---

1. John Piper and Wayne Grudem, eds., *Recovering Biblical Manhood and Womanhood*, 2nd ed. (Wheaton, IL: Crossway, 2006), 60–61.
2. From Thomas R. Schreiner's chapter in ibid., 128.
3. From Douglas Moo's chapter in ibid., 180.

The Nature of Ministry in
the New Testament Churches

In his letter to the Romans, Paul linked every form of ministry to gift-edness: "We have different gifts, according to the grace given to each of us. If your gift is prophesying, then prophesy in accordance with your faith. If it is serving [*diakonian*], then serve; if it is teaching, then teach; if it is to encourage, then give encouragement; if it is giving, then give generously; if it is to lead, do it diligently; if it is to show mercy, do it cheerfully" (12:6–8).

Ministry is also tied to giftedness in Paul's first letter to the Corinthians: "God has placed in the church first of all apostles, second prophets, third teachers, then miracles, then gifts of healing, of helping, of guidance, and of different kinds of tongues. Are all apostles? Are all prophets? Are all teachers? Do all work miracles? Do all have gifts of healing? Do all speak in tongues? Do all interpret? Now eagerly desire the greater gifts" (12:28–31).

In Ephesians 4:11–13, Paul speaks of ministers as Christ's gifts to the church: "So Christ himself gave the apostles, the prophets, the evangelists, the pastors and teachers, to equip his people for works of service [*diakonias*], so that the body of Christ may be built up until we all reach unity in the faith and in the knowledge of the Son of God and become mature, attaining to the whole measure of the fullness of Christ."

In summary, "ministry" includes prophesying, serving, teaching, encouraging, giving, leading, and showing mercy; it's about apostles, prophets, teachers, miracle workers, healers, helpers, guides, tongues speakers and interpreters, evangelists, and pastors. Note that elder is not mentioned in any of these lists, and pastor is mentioned only once. The range of ministries is wide, and they depend on specific gifting so that we bring to our ministry both the aptitude and the passion for accomplishing the work God has put into our hands to do.

Wayne Grudem added this condition for ministering women: "There are hundreds of ministries open to men and women . . . The issue here is whether any of the women serving with Paul in ministry fulfilled roles that would be inconsistent with a limitation of the eldership to men. We believe the answer to that is No."[4] In chapter 5, his no became a yes when we considered the many women who worked side by side with Paul in every kind of ministry.

Walter Liefeld notes that, contrary to Jesus' emphasis on ministry as servanthood, some have seen the ministry as "a power base giving an incumbent authority over the church."[5] He wonders whether "one of the main reasons why many Christians feel uneasy about allowing women into the ministry is that they think this would give them power or authority that they think the Bible denies them."[6] Much of the literature denying women leadership roles in the church is a preoccupation with authority issues: Who has authority over whom?

THE NATURE OF LEADERSHIP, ACCORDING TO JESUS

When the mother of James and John asked Jesus to give her two sons positions of power at his right or left hand in the coming kingdom, he decided it was time to give the twelve disciples some solid instruction on the subject: "You know that the rulers of the Gentiles lord it over them, and their high officials exercise authority over them. Not so with you. Instead, whoever wants to become great among you must be your

---

4. Ibid., 68.
5. Walter L. Liefeld, "Women and the Nature of Ministry," *Journal of the Evangelical Theological Society* 30.1 (March 1987): 49.
6. Ibid., 54.

servant, and whoever wants to be first must be your slave—just as the Son of Man did not come to be served but to serve, and to give his life as a ransom for many" (Matthew 20:25–28). This is a very different, definitely upside-down definition of leadership. But Jesus is clear: ministry is not about position and authority; it's about servanthood. We lead as we serve. It is not intended to be a power base. Jesus is our model.

Throughout the gospels, Jesus reminded his followers that the first will be last, and the last, first. Then in the final meal with them before his arrest and crucifixion, he demonstrated what kingdom leadership looks like:

> He got up from the meal, took off his outer clothing, and wrapped a towel around his waist. After that, he poured water into a basin and began to wash his disciples' feet, drying them with the towel that was wrapped around him . . .
>
> When he had finished washing their feet, he put on his clothes and returned to his place. "Do you understand what I have done for you?" he asked them. "You call me 'Teacher' and 'Lord,' and rightly so, for that is what I am. Now that I, your Lord and Teacher, have washed your feet, you also should wash one another's feet. I have set you an example that you should do as I have done for you. Very truly I tell you, no servant is greater than his master, nor is a messenger greater than the one who sent him. Now that you know these things, you will be blessed if you do them."
>
> JOHN 13:4–5, 12–17

Leadership in God's kingdom has nothing to do with authority or power. It has everything to do with Jesus' example of leading through serving. The New Testament gives us a very different vision of ministry leadership from that of the assumptions about authority and rulership by pastors or elders. Through the apostolic letters to various churches, we learn much about leadership in the church.

THE NATURE OF THE
NEW TESTAMENT CHURCHES

It is striking to see how the meaning of certain Scriptures is sometimes obscured by the real differences between first-century house churches and today's church practices, at least in the Western world. The church in New Testament times consisted of multiple small gatherings in private homes, radically different from the huge church structures constructed after Theodosius had made Christianity the religion of the Roman Empire in AD 381. Before the fourth century, members did not sit in rows facing a platform or altar in a large sanctuary; they gathered in the room of a house, sharing their ministry gifts as they celebrated the Lord's Supper together. Already that shows us a radical physical difference between our churches today and the "church" at the time the apostles were writing their letters.

As Paul, Peter, and other apostles crisscrossed the Roman Empire in evangelism and church planting, the dominant image of the new congregations was in the private sphere: the *household* of faith, the *family* of God. The well-defined distinction between public and private in the cultural DNA of the Roman Empire placed men in the public square and women in the private household. If the new house churches were in the private sphere, women's leadership in these new churches could be strong, but often invisible to the wider community. It was possible for these new communities of faith to avoid censure for their women leaders because they were nested in the private sphere.

Think about that metaphor: the church as the *household* of faith, the *family* of God. It is based on Galatians 3:28, in which distinctions between Jews and Gentiles, between slaves and free, and between men and women are erased as all came together as equals in Jesus Christ. Jesus' counterpunch to patriarchy was a radical leveling of accepted social distinctions.

Leadership in These First-century Churches

Because much of the following information about the various churches begun by the apostle Paul has come from Gilbert Bilezikian's book *Community 101*, I want to acknowledge my debt to him here.

Of the thirteen letters written by Paul, nine were sent to churches and four to individuals.[7] We learn a lot from these letters about leadership in these congregations. From the letter to the Romans, for example, we see how Paul dealt with the problems existing in the congregations, despite the leadership in place. This church was known throughout the world for the Roman Christians' faith (1:8). In his letter, Paul speaks of "different gifts," with some having leadership functions (12:6–8). But nowhere in the letter is there any mention of types of roles (e.g., deacon, elder) apart from the reference to Phoebe (*diakonos, prostatis* in 16:1) visiting Rome from Corinth. But we can assume some kind of leadership existed in the Roman churches.

Paul's letter tells us that the Roman Christians had some serious relational problems—a judging spirit (2:1–5), Jewish racial superiority over Gentiles (2:17–24), and a disdain for others in the church who ate food considered unclean or who failed to esteem certain days over others (14:1–23). But Paul didn't refer these matters to the leaders. He bypassed the leadership and told the congregation as a whole to deal with these situations. In fact, the leaders did not even rate a greeting as "office holders" in Rome. Paul was convinced that his readers were "competent to instruct one another" (15:14).

Planting churches in Corinth, Paul had ample opportunity to establish a strong leadership structure there, but neither of his two letters

---

7. Gilbert Bilezikian, *Community 101: Reclaiming the Local Church as Community of Oneness* (Grand Rapids: Zondervan, 1997).

to that congregation mention a functioning leadership structure in the Corinthian church.

The Corinthian church had massive problems. Yet despite divisions, personality conflicts, lawsuits, sacrilegious worship, lifestyle issues, doctrinal challenges, and false teachers claiming to be apostles, Paul's strategy for reforming the Corinthian church was not through elders, deacons, or overseers. He addressed, rebuked, exhorted, and commanded the whole congregation directly. For example, for an important decision in 1 Corinthians 5:4, the whole congregation assembled in the power of the Lord Jesus. From 1 Corinthians 16:15–16, we know that the church had strong leaders, like Stephanas and his household, but Paul did not ask him or others to take matters in hand. Instead, he called on the whole congregation to fix its own problems (see 2 Corinthians 13:11).

The churches in the province of Galatia were impacted by Judaizers—a classic case in which strong leadership could take control of the situation. But the only reference to leaders in Paul's letter to them was a note to pay teachers (Galatians 6:6) and a desire that false teachers would be castrated! (5:12). Paul assumed the Galatian Christians themselves could reject false teachings and reembrace truth (5:7–10).

When Paul wrote to the Ephesians, he devoted the letter almost entirely to the doctrine of the church, describing the place of the church in God's purposes. If an elaborate leadership system were essential, this would have been the perfect place to lay that out. But while Paul did include one of the six New Testament household codes (Ephesians 5:21–6:9) in the letter, there are no parallel instructions for organizing the church apart from the command to all believers to "submit to one another out of reverence for Christ" (5:21). When Paul listed some spiritual gifts (4:11), he made no mention of overseers, bishops, elders, or deacons, though the church probably had them.

Only in the letter to the Philippians do we have even a passing mention of elders and deacons, appearing in Paul's greeting in 1:1: "Paul and

Timothy, servants of Jesus Christ, to all God's holy people in Christ Jesus at Philippi, with the overseers and deacons." But after being acknowledged in the opening sentence of the letter, these leaders fade from view.

Similarly, the letters to the churches in Colossae and in Thessalonica show us congregations challenged to deal with their problems as a body. Whatever leadership structure existed in the early churches, it was inconspicuous, discreet, flexible, and ready to intervene if needed. The leaders were invisible servants.

When we turn to the three pastoral letters (1 and 2 Timothy; Titus), suddenly the presence of overseers, elders, and deacons comes to the fore (1 Timothy 3:1–13; 5:17–22; Titus 1:5–9). No other documents in the New Testament have so much information and so many instructions about these roles as do 1 Timothy and Titus. How are we to understand the exceptional prominence of leadership structures in these churches?

Paul had spent three years planting the church in Ephesus. Now, ten years later, the church was in crisis, and Paul sent Timothy there to deal with it. The Ephesian Christians must learn "how people ought to conduct themselves in God's household" (1 Timothy 3:15). The church had regressed into infancy and had to relearn everything. Instead of praying for them with thanksgiving, Paul had to write Timothy a very hard letter about the Ephesian Christians.

What made that necessary? When we look at Paul's prior experiences in Ephesus, we see it had been his toughest assignment as a church-planting missionary. In Acts 20:19, 31, Paul reminded the Ephesian elders that it had taken three long years "with tears" to start that church. Ephesus was the only site where both Jews and Gentiles opposed him (19:8–9, 23–31). And in 1 Corinthians 15:32, we learn that at Ephesus Paul had fought with wild beasts and had come under great pressure, despairing even for his own life (2 Corinthians 1:8). The Ephesian church had cost Paul blood, sweat, and tears.

Years later, at the end of his third missionary journey, Paul met the

Ephesian elders in Miletus (the seaport for inland Ephesus). He warned the elders in Acts 20:29–30 about a coming disaster—an external onslaught ("savage wolves") and an internal onslaught (homegrown heretics who would split the congregation). From all the evidence, when Paul later wrote to Timothy, this onslaught (both external and internal) had happened. The church was reeling, but was still salvageable (1 Timothy 1:3). This letter contains urgent advice and rigid measures designed to bring the Ephesians back in line.[8]

Now it was necessary to put a professional leader from the outside (Timothy) in charge of the church. Here Timothy in Ephesus and Titus in Crete are the ones who lead the ministry, while the congregants are told to pray to live peaceably (1 Timothy 2:2). Even if they have a spiritual gift for teaching, untrained or disqualified people must learn quietly before aspiring to teach (2:11; 2 Timothy 2:2).

In both Ephesus and Crete, Paul called for a contraction of ministry to isolate and eliminate self-appointed peddlers of subversion. Under the new rules, the unauthorized heretics would be silenced (Titus 1:11). Gilbert Bilezikian writes, "Access to ministry was therefore to be withdrawn from the masses and entrusted to carefully screened individuals, reliable and loyal men with proven teaching and managerial abilities. This model was not new. The eldership was the legacy of the Jewish synagogue, itself derived from the ancient patriarchal system of government. The troops had failed; the Old Guard was called in to take over on the front line."[9]

In Acts 6, when the Jerusalem church needed leadership to deal with discrimination against Greek widows, three criteria distinguished

---

8. Timothy would have to deal with false teachers (1:3–4, 7)—some of whom were handed over to Satan (1:19–20)—and with the hypocritical liars in the congregation (4:1–2). The apostate teachers were especially successful with women (5:13–15; 2 Timothy 3:6–8), infiltrating households and gaining control of spiritually unstable women, some of whom turned away to follow Satan (1 Timothy 5:15) and gossiped about these false teachings. The controversies with these heresies resulted in "envy, strife, malicious talk, evil suspicions and constant friction" (6:4–5). The Christian flock was ravaged and divided.

9. Bilezikian, *Community 101*, 112.

those appointed: (1) they were affirmed by the community, who vouched for their character and reputation; (2) they were known to be full of the Holy Spirit (they had cultivated their spiritual walk and used their spiritual gifts); and (3) they had to be full of wisdom, that is, people of experience and discernment. Apart from the three letters to Timothy and Titus, there is no reference in the New Testament to other specifications to qualify for ministry. Furthermore, leaders were not told to exercise authority over their flocks. People were told to obey them and submit to them, as well they should, but the leaders themselves were accountable (Hebrews 13:17). In fact, their leadership style was to be that of a servant, leading by example rather than by fiat (1 Peter 5:1–4). But when we open the pastoral letters (1 and 2 Timothy; Titus), we see leaders on center stage. They are both prominent and dominant. Ministry in other churches was carried out according to each one's spiritual giftedness, but for churches in crisis, only the leaders were allowed to do ministry.

WOMEN'S ROLES THEN AND NOW

What about the women in Ephesus and Crete? Women who have been part of the problem of heresy in Ephesus must learn in quiet submission (1 Timothy 2:11–12). What happened when Ephesian women "turned away to follow Satan" (1 Timothy 5:15) had happened in Eden when Eve followed the temptation of Satan. But this was not the end of the story. In 1 Timothy 2:11, 15, while the Ephesian women had been deceived, they could now "learn in quietness" and "continue in faith, love and holiness with propriety." They were redeemable for God's purposes.

Gilbert Bilezikian notes "an inverse relation between open congregational participation in ministry on the one hand, and heavy leadership structures that monopolized ministry on the other. Whenever allowance was made for congregational participation in ministry, the leadership structure receded into the background. However, whenever ministry opportunities were denied to the congregation or to segments of it, ministry was assumed by the leadership."[10]

If you read through Paul's first letter to Timothy and note his references to false teachings and controversies, you can begin to feel Paul's alarm for a church headed to destruction. These false teachers were especially successful with women (5:13–15; 2 Timothy 3:6–8) who were "always learning but never able to come to a knowledge of the truth" (2 Timothy 3:7). These women were then "going about from house to house . . . saying things they ought not to" (1 Timothy 5:13). In this crisis, the leadership model was to take ministry away from most members and entrust it to carefully screened individuals.

Bilezikian notes that "the normative model . . . called for structures of ministry that were open, participatory, and based on spiritual gifts. The function of leaders was to equip and support congregation-based ministries . . . Most of the New Testament churches tended to move in that direction. The other model was remedial. It is represented by the ministry structures of the Pastorals, which were highly selective."[11]

So in Paul's letters, we find diversity in how churches were led. It is not "one size fits all"—with a gender-based hierarchical structure in place that is permanent and applies to all people in all places at all times. Today if a church is for any reason "in crisis mode," access to ministry may need to be restricted to those who have a high level of maturity and the spiritual discernment necessary to meet the crisis (rather than feed it). Bilezikian calls this "the religious equivalent of martial law." But for most churches, the New Testament norm for any kind of ministry leadership is based on giftedness, character or reputation, godliness, and wisdom. Hierarchies based on race, economic status, or gender have no place in determining who can or cannot serve as God's ministers in the church.

---

10. Ibid., 91–92.
11. Ibid., 121–22.

CONCLUSION

Complementarians have based their case on three presuppositions: (1) the Bible establishes a gender-based hierarchy for Christian ministry; (2) women are not to teach men or exercise authority over them in the church; and (3) that these two presuppositions are immutable and apply to all Christians at all times in all places. But as we examine the Scriptures, we find that in every case, these presuppositions rest on erroneous ways of using the Bible and crumble in the face of an honest examination of God's Word. Women had freedom to lead in various ways in most of the Pauline churches, assuring us that one size does *not* fit all. What men and women can do in any given church depends on the ability of its congregation to handle their issues appropriately as the body of Christ.

Questions for Personal Reflection or Group Discussion

1. How do Jesus' teachings on leadership affect how you think about leadership in the church?
2. How would you define the nature of ministry in the context of the church?
3. What difference does it make whether a church excludes or includes women in its leadership?
4. As you come to the end of your exploration of biblical teachings about women, what do you think are the most important factors to consider?

PART THREE

Historical Realities
That Still Challenge Women

Parts 1 and 2 of this book have been anchored in the texts of the Bible. In them we have seen how errors in biblical interpretation have led to support for gender-based hierarchy in both the church and the home. Scripture has controlled the first two-thirds of this book.

When we turn to part 3, to see how teachings of gender-based hierarchy have permutated through two thousand years of history, the biblical anchor recedes into the background. Instead, we must rely on the work of dozens of historians, both Christian and secular, who help us dissect the ideas and actions that have had particular consequences (some intended, some unintended) for women in the church and in the home.

In part 3, we ask these kinds of questions:

- What ideas led some early churchmen to designate women as uniquely responsible for sin in the world?
- How did Tertullian's ideas shift the concept of the church as the "family of God" to "The Church" as a powerful entity with hierarchies of clerical and lay leadership?

- How did ideas about sexuality lead Augustine to link human sexuality to original sin, with eventual consequences such as a celibate priesthood?
- How did Luther's ninety-five theses (nailed to Wittenberg's church door) overturn long-established notions of women as "whores" to women as honored wives and mothers?
- How did the secular ideas of the Renaissance and later of the Age of Reason (the Enlightenment) alter the trajectory of theological thought?
- What part did the Industrial Revolution play in the development of the Cult of True Womanhood?

Answers to these and other questions form the spine of part 3.

It has been said that those who refuse to learn from history are doomed to repeat it. Part 3 confronts us with the historical realities that still inform or threaten us in the twenty-first century. What have we learned that will help us engage the world, the flesh, and the devil for Christ and his kingdom? This has been the bottom-line question from the beginning of the Christian era. We wrestle "not against flesh and blood, but against the rulers, against the authorities, against the powers of this dark world and against the spiritual forces of evil in the heavenly realms" (Ephesians 6:12). That is our reality. This is not a child's game. It is war against all that threatens God's vision for men and women working together in a "Blessed Alliance."

Chapter Ten

PATRISTIC AND MEDIEVAL ATTITUDES TOWARD WOMEN

Patriarchy was built into the cultural DNA of the Roman Empire. The counterpunch against it began with Jesus and was carried on by leaders of the early churches, but the wider culture pushed back with a thoroughly misogynistic patriarchy. Its roots lay in the writings of Aristotle (384–322 BC), who was explicit that women were inferior to men. He proposed that a woman was a deformity, a failed male. A woman's role in society was dictated by her flawed anatomy. Citing the Pythagorean Table of Opposites, Aristotle described women as "dark, secret, ever-moving, not self-contained, and lacking its own boundaries" in contrast to men who were "light, honest, good, stable, self-contained and firmly bounded."[1] While Plato promoted equality of opportunity for women, he also made degrading remarks about women. For centuries these notions of female inferiority controlled cultural attitudes and actions throughout the Greco-Roman civilization.

---

1. Quoted in Kayla Huber, "Everybody's a Little Bit Sexist," *Eukaryon* (March 2015), www.lakeforest.edu/live/files/2700-hubereverybodypdf (accessed November 22, 2016).

The Interaction of Culture and Theology

At any time in any place, we are always living and working within some kind of cultural framework. We can work against the ideas and practices of a given culture and try not to be influenced by them, but we are never completely outside them. The first-century Christians lived and worked within the powerful cultural influences of Greco-Roman history, myths, and philosophies.

As churches moved through the second century, women's leadership in them was increasingly limited and denounced. By the end of the second century, writings by pastors and theologians (as well as books on discipline and church order[2]) prohibited women from baptizing or conducting the Lord's Supper.[3] In only a century, the tide had turned from the apostle Paul's praise of women in ministry to a baffling wave of misogynistic rhetoric that increasingly marginalized and humiliated women. What was going on? In what ways could the external society influence the thinking of second-century church leaders?

Cultural Ideas linking Women and Blood

Ancient cultures regarded menstruation with fear and suspicion. How was it that a woman could bleed without dying? This was somehow seen as giving women power that was believed to be evil and ultimately destructive. This cultural idea made women the source of some kind of foul contamination. It was widely believed that sex with a menstruating woman would cause castration. These cultural attitudes passed into Judaism and eventually into Christianity. A bishop of Alexandria (Dionysius the

---

2. For example, manuals like the *Didascalia Apostolorum*, a book on church order written between AD 200–250 from Syria, and the *Apostolic Church Order*, regulating practices in Egypt around AD 300.

3. The fact that these practices were now being prohibited indicates they had previously been going on (i.e., that women had, in fact, been baptizing and leading at the Lord's Table).

Great) was the first Christian leader to urge that restrictions be placed on menstruating women to keep them from the altar, even from entering the church. Increasingly, churchmen feared that a menstruating woman would somehow pollute the worship and sacraments of the church.[4]

GNOSTIC INFLUENCES ON CHURCH FATHERS

What did many people in the second-century Roman Empire think about cosmology? One answer was Gnosticism. This was an expanded philosophical version of Aristotle's contrast between men and women. In the gnostic explanation, human reality was divided into two contradictory or opposing spheres: the sphere of the mind/spirit and the sphere of the body/flesh. The mind and spirit were identified with what was good and virtuous, and the flesh represented all that had to be overcome and conquered. Sometimes this dichotomy then condemned the body and the material world as being hopelessly evil and corrupt.

While Gnosticism had its heyday in the postapostolic period, some of its roots reached back to misogynistic ideas set forth centuries earlier by Aristotle and others. So as church leaders accepted this dichotomy, they increasingly identified women with the body and men with the mind.[5] The result was an association of the female with the flesh, the material world, and the drive to satisfy physical desires. In short, women came to be held responsible for the pull toward evil for men. While church history textbooks describing the patristic period focus on the major theological debates and emerging doctrines of the Christian faith, for Christian women, their sexuality moved to center stage. This strongly influenced the later growth of the ascetic spirit in Christianity.

---

4. It is possible these restrictions came from an interpretation of Leviticus 15:19–33 and not merely from the pagan culture.

5. Here again we see the impact of the wider culture on church leaders, who should have known better. Gnosticism's low view of the body and the physical world was unbiblical and contrary to a Christian worldview.

SHIFTING ATTITUDES ABOUT
CHURCH AND WOMEN

One of the most important theologians spanning the second and third centuries was Tertullian (ca. 155–240). A prolific writer, he led radical changes in both the structure of the church and in attitudes toward women.

First, the structure of the church. The apostolic churches had been structured around ministry according to the gifts of the Holy Spirit, but as the third century opened, organizational models for churches began to shift from an emphasis on ministry to an emphasis on governance. Tertullian used the model of Roman political life to shape the basic features of Christianity: the church should resemble the political structure of the empire.[6] He shifted the church from an egalitarian household model to the church as a legal body. His theological construct followed his interpretation of the interaction within the Trinity.[7] Tertullian thought of the church as similar to Roman society, with distinct classes of people and different levels of honor or authority. Gone was any whiff of egalitarian cooperation. He drew a distinction between clergy and laity, turning the clergy's position from collaborative ministry to a privileged position with legal rights. Ministers became rulers. With this shift, three things happened: the church moved from the private sphere to the public sphere; a pecking order within the clergy was born; and a wall was constructed between clergy and laity.

Second, attitudes toward women. Tertullian is better known for his misogynistic statements about women. When we read his sometimes seething prose, we see that behind his angry denunciations were women

6. Because the church saw itself as Israel's successor, he and other church fathers used the analogy of leadership patterns from the Old Testament, whose leaders were indeed rulers.

7. Karen Jo Torjesen writes, "He used the concept of political monarchical rule, a single individual rule that is administered by the Son and Holy Spirit, who become representatives or deputies of the Father. The unity of the Trinity is a political unity. The notion of Christ as the delegated viceroy of God opened the way to consider the bishop as the delegated viceroy of Christ and gave rise to the notion of a monarchical bishop" (*When Women Were Priests: Women's Leadership in the Early Church and the Scandal of Their Subordination in the Rise of Christianity* [San Francisco: HarperSanFrancisco, 1993], 161–63).

in congregations he knew who were teaching and baptizing. He was clear that "it is not permitted to a woman to speak in church, but neither is it permitted her to teach, nor to baptize, nor to offer, nor to claim for herself a lot in any manly function not to say [in any] sacerdotal office."[8] Karen Jo Torjesen notes that "in his new vision of the church as a political body, the church's ministries had become legal rights to be exercised only by full members of the political body. Since according to the public-versus-private gender ideology, women could not hold office, participate in debate, or exercise any public functions, neither could they do any of these things in the body politic of the church."[9]

But Tertullian didn't limit his distaste for women to those seeking church ministries. One of the classical virtues for womanhood was chastity. To this term he gave a new definition: the Christian woman was responsible not only for her own chastity, but for male chastity as well. She wasn't chaste if in any way she excited a man's imagination sexually. He wrote long treatises on women's apparel and their demeanor. Women were exhorted to forgo any kind of bathing, to cover the body from head to toe in dark shapeless clothing so that no part of the female form could be detected, and to live a life secluded from the public square so that men would not be tempted.

Clement of Alexandria (ca. 150–215) also spoke harshly against certain tendencies he saw mainly in women—such as immodesty and wearing luxurious clothes, fashionable shoes, and jewelry, especially gold ornaments.[10] He attributed the desire to own more clothes than necessary to "the weakness of women." He also spoke disparagingly in sermons about the "diaphanous materials" and dresses of any kind that excite lust by revealing the female figure. He was against women attending church without being entirely covered (including face veils), as well as

---

8. Tertullian, *De virginibus velandis* 9:1.
9. Torjesen, *When Women Were Priests*, 164.
10. Clement of Alexandria, *Paedagogus*, bk. 2, chs. 11–13; cited in Ruth A. Tucker and Walter Liefeld, *Daughters of the Church: Women and Ministry from New Testament Times to the Present* (Grand Rapids: Zondervan, 1987), 96–97.

their wearing short hair rather than long hair bound up.

But that was not enough. A theology of female personhood also emerged. Many church fathers came to believe that from Eve on, women were responsible for sin in the world.[11] How so? Because women can use the promise of pleasure to seduce men away from higher things, they must be kept out of sight where they cannot tempt men. The spiritual well-being of men could be compromised by a woman. Of course, the church fathers agreed that women were redeemed by Christ in the same way men were, but because women were bound to the flesh, they had to be segregated and subordinated.

Most of us have heard Tertullian's statement about Eve, but addressed to women as Eve's descendants, that "*you* are the devil's gateway; *you* are the unsealer of that [forbidden] tree; *you* are the first deserter of the divine law; *you* are she who persuaded him whom the devil was not valiant enough to attack. *You* destroyed so easily God's image, man. On account of *your* desert [i.e., punishment], that is, death—even the Son of God had to die."[12] This made women's responsibility heavy indeed.

THE MOVE TOWARD ASCETICISM

The fact of human sexuality had become women's burden. Not only were they to keep themselves pure, but they were tasked with the responsibility to keep men pure as well. This led directly to the development of the ascetic movement.

A Doctrine of Sex as Inherently Sinful

While the apostle Paul noted that the single life would make ministry easier (1 Corinthians 7:25–35), he also insisted that sex in marriage

---

11. See Barbara J. MacHaffie, *Her Story: Women in Christian Tradition* (Philadelphia: Fortress, 1986), 37.

12. Tertullian, *De cultu feminarum* 1.1, cited in Tucker and Liefeld, 103.

was normal and good (7:2–5) and that neither partner was justified in depriving the other of it. Yet by the third century, although most church fathers did not condemn married life as evil and against God's will, it was clear in their writings that even the marital sexual union was tainted with sin. Some saw Adam's creation in Genesis 2 as a single spiritual being who had no sexual apparatus. Others thought that the man and woman in the garden of Eden had sexual characteristics but did not have sex until they were expelled from the garden. John Chrysostom reconstructed the Edentic ideal in these words: "Adam and Eve remained apart from marriage, leading the sort of life in Paradise they would have led had they been in Heaven, luxuriating in their association with God. Desire for sexual relation . . . was removed from their souls."[13] After the fall, lust took over with two results: original sin was passed on to their children, and the relationship between the man and woman was irreparably damaged. Sex was necessary to produce children, but it had to be controlled by the will, not by passion. At the same time church fathers acknowledged the need for procreation, they also urged devout Christians to avoid marriage and sex completely.

The Virgin Life Became the Way to Honor God

The story of the next thousand years in the life of Western Christianity is a story of ascetic practice. Monasticism and eventually clerical celibacy provided a safe place for that practice, as Christian doctrines about sexuality, sin, and human nature were shaped by basic ideas in the writings of Tertullian and Augustine.

One argument for the virgin life was that it freed men and women to be martyrs without earthly attachments. Another argument was that it gave Christians a head start on the life to come by living as if they already had their nonprocreating spiritual bodies. Some argued that the

---

13. Cited in Elizabeth A. Clark, *Women in the Early Church* (Collegeville, MN: Liturgical, 1983), 122–23.

virgin life restored God's original design for humanity. Others were quite sure that by erasing a person's sexuality, men and women were already participating in their future life in heaven like those of angels.

By the end of the third century, men and women who renounced all comforts of life were flocking to the deserts of North Africa (primarily in and around Egypt), seeking Christian perfection in a solitary and ascetic life. The ancient historian Palladius recorded that twenty thousand women lived in poverty, chastity, and solitude as hermits in the deserts around Egypt.[14] Those numbers may be inflated, but the reality was that many women, struggling under the burden of their castigated sex, chose a hermit's life to focus on pleasing God more fully. Other women became early adopters of life in the new monasteries.

When the Roman emperor Constantine the Great (ca. 274–337) signed the Edict of Milan in 313, stipulating religious toleration and the end of the persecution of Christians, Christians could carry on their witness for Jesus Christ more openly and without fear of martyrdom. The emperor's edict opened the door for Tertullian's desire to see Christianity organized as a legal entity. While congregations had been meeting in private homes and then in some cases in houses converted for full-time congregational use, the way was now paved for the public face of Christianity to be seen in the construction of basilicas. As the church moved from the private sphere to the public sphere, the clergy became a kind of power base, with the bishop who oversaw the Roman congregations (1 Timothy 3:1) emerging more as a ruler than minister. The private "family of faith" had morphed into a legal public entity with growing temporal power.

A Further Theological Development against Women

Few voices in church history have been as influential as that of Augustine (354–430). As a young man, he had lived a dissolute life,

---

14. Cited in MacHaffie, *Her Story*, 46.

and his conversion to Christianity was shaped in part by the popularity of the ascetic movement. Augustine could not separate his conversion from his renunciation of sex. Aristotle had taught that the masculine self was rational and could rule the self (in contrast to the feminine self that was irrational). But sexuality weakened that mastery in a man. Augustine concluded, in the words of one scholar, that "sin was a sexually communicable disease."[15] Original sin was passed on from one generation to the next through the irrational passion that produced the next crop of babies.

For Augustine, though men possessed a sinful sexual nature, they were still rational. But women were limited to only one purpose: procreation. Augustine believed the female body had been created for sexual service. For this reason, the male body reflected the image of God in a way a female body could not.[16] On the basis of this, generations of celibate ascetics believed that renouncing one's sexuality was "the central spiritual discipline in the quest for the knowledge of God. This implied that sexuality could not lead to knowledge of God and that sexuality actually undermined the process of spiritual transformation."[17]

As a result, virginity was the only path to holiness for women. In the process, they had to transcend their sexuality by (1) denying their childbearing ability and (2) making themselves as unattractive as possible. Only when they repudiated their femaleness could they become "honorary" males. Karen Jo Torjesen notes John Chrysostom's praise of the ascetic woman Olympias: "Don't say 'woman,' but 'what a man!' because

---

15. Torjesen, *When Women Were Priests*, 218. Augustine taught that the sinlessness of Jesus stemmed directly from his birth from a virgin. Because Mary was impregnated by the Holy Spirit, no irrational or lustful sexual passion was involved in that conception. Thus original sin was not passed on to Jesus.

16. Torjesen elaborates: "This reasoning underlies the statement in the Vatican declaration on the ordination of women that only the male body can represent Christ, because Christ represents God through the maleness of his body" (*When Women Were Priests*, 223).

17. Ibid.

this is a man, despite her physical appearance."[18] It's sad that a woman could be praised only in terms of masculine qualities.

Ambivalence about Women

The church fathers seemed occupied, even obsessed, with women's sexuality and their resulting moral status. The many negative statements about women throughout the patristic period would fill a book. And yet the fathers achieved a paradoxical ambivalence about women. Historian Elizabeth Clark put it this way:

> The most fitting word with which to describe the Church Fathers' attitude toward women is ambivalence. Women were God's creation, his good gift to men—and the curse of the world. They were weak in both mind and character—and displayed dauntless courage, undertook prodigious feats of scholarship. Vain, deceitful, brimming with lust—they led men to Christ, fled sexual encounter, wavered not at the executioner's threats, adorned themselves with sackcloth and ashes.[19]

Cultural notions about the nature of women (often derived from pagan philosophies) informed and then shaped emerging Christian theology in the patristic period. Thus, patriarchy became embedded in Christian doctrine, and human sexuality was the linchpin tying these together. Reading many of the church fathers leaves one with the odd impression that Christian witness was tightly tied to issues of sexual attraction and behavior. In the process, women were loaded down with responsibility for men's sinful thoughts and actions.

Thus the patristic period provides us with a lens for understanding the development of patriarchy as fundamental to Christian practice.

---

18. Quoted in ibid., 211.
19. Clark, *Women in the Early Church*, 15.

The Fall of Rome Signals the Thousand Years of the Medieval "Dark Ages"

Rome's days were numbered, and by the end of the fifth century, the Ostrogothic Kingdom rose from the ruins of the Western Roman Empire. The thousand-year "Dark Ages" had begun, so called because historians have few records from that long period in which much of the earlier culture was lost. In its heyday, the Roman Empire had provided widespread literacy, law, historical records, and an international language of science and literature. But invading barbaric tribes had no interest in preserving much of Roman culture.

When we enter the medieval period following the fall of Rome (variously dated prior to or around 476), historians tell us that ideas about women fell into one of two extremes. On the one hand, women were constantly painted as evil and inferior, while on the other hand, they were lauded as models of virtue and holiness. The doctrine of Mary as the idealized virgin[20] stood against the image of woman the witch, an idea that led to the horrific misogyny of the witch craze that later swept Europe between the fifteenth and eighteenth centuries.[21]

Throughout the medieval period, the church increasingly became almost completely politicized. By the end of the fourteenth century, rival popes in Avignon and Rome claimed the papal throne, and when a third pope was elected to replace the two popes, causing the "Western schism,"

---

20. Historian Barbara MacHaffie reminds us that while the New Testament provides very little information about Mary, a cluster of ideas and stories about her began to grow in the second century, leading eventually to her veneration during the medieval period (and to the doctrine of an immaculate conception in 1854). The fact that she was a virgin at the time of her conception of Jesus buttressed the growing ideal of virginity and the ascetic lifestyle (*Her Story*, 51–54).

21. Allison P. Coudert notes that "belief in witches and witchcraft has existed in just about every society and every part of the world. But only in Christian Europe and Christian America, where witchcraft was characterized as heresy, did witch beliefs lead to a 'witchcraze' responsible for the death of between 60,000 and 200,000 people . . . The epicenter of this misogyny was Germany, where Lutheranism began, the witchcraft panics were most intense, books about the devil most popular, and executions for witchcraft more numerous" (*The Politics of Gender in Early Modern Europe* [Kirksville, MO: Sixteenth Century Journal, 1989], 61).

each refused to resign, leaving the church with three popes. The papacy was often controlled by corrupt leaders and powerful wealthy families. In addition to these political fights, the necessary funding for huge building programs and the Crusades demanded more and more resources, and the church began selling indulgences to offset these costs.[22]

Attitudes toward women mutated again and again, often making life even more miserable for them. But clergymen also faced difficult choices as the church endeavored to control both men's and women's sexuality.

ENFORCING CELIBACY FOR MALE CLERGY

Beginning with the fourth-century Synod of Elvira up through the various papal decrees in the twelfth century, the church struggled to impose celibacy on the clergy.[23] This push for clergy celibacy grew out of the persistent claim that women's sexuality constantly threatened the spirituality of priests.

Recall that Augustine's doctrine of original sin centered on the issue of sexuality: sin was transmitted through the act of sex. He had argued that the female body had been created for sexual service, and because sex was the possible conveyor of original sin, it had to be renounced. As noted earlier, "generations of celibate ascetics had held the renunciation of sexuality to be the central spiritual discipline in the quest for the knowledge of God."[24] They were certain that giving any expression to their sexuality would keep them from knowing God. Think about that: renouncing sexuality is the *central spiritual discipline* in the quest for the knowledge of God? Our sexuality not only cannot lead us to a knowledge of God; it undermines the process of our spiritual formation?

For centuries in the Middle Ages, many married clerics did not

---

22. Indulgences removed any necessary punishment for temporal sins or time in purgatory.
23. A synod was most often a council bringing together delegated clergy to debate theology; it sometimes served as an ecclesiastical court.
24. Torjesen, *When Women Were Priests*, 223.

believe that. But the church fought back with every kind of weapon: limiting appointment of only celibate clerics to better churches, threatening excommunication to parishioners who attended masses led by married priests, calling such priests "fornicators," and placing before clergy the choice of losing their positions and livelihoods or renouncing their wives.[25]

But enforcing this was not easy. Even while emissaries of the pope preached sermons about the danger of association with women, priests actively opposed the idea of forced celibacy. When an abbot in Pointoise in 1074 tried to impose celibacy on priests in his territory, the clerics "responded by spitting on him, beating him and throwing him out." That same year in Rouen, fistfights broke out in a church, and the person imposing celibacy on priests "was greeted with a hail of stones."[26]

It took more than six centuries to impose celibacy on the clergy. But ultimately the church prevailed, and in 1139 (at the Second Lateran Council), celibacy for all levels of church clerics became a fact. Only single men could be ordained, and Pope Innocent III declared all marriages invalid if they were undertaken after ordination. Women who had been legal wives suddenly were being called concubines, whores, or adulteresses.

Behind clerical celibacy lay the doctrine of woman as a dangerous seductress. The abbot of one monastery wrote these words:

> We and our whole community of canons, recognizing that the wickedness of women is greater than all other wickedness of the world and that there is no anger like that of women, and that the poison of asps and dragons is more curable and less dangerous to men than the familiarity of women, have unanimously decreed for the safety of our souls, no less than for that of our bodies and goods, that we will on no account receive any more sisters to

---

25. Ibid., 226.
26. Ibid., 227.

the increase of our perdition, but will avoid them like poisonous animals.[27]

The Demonizing of Women

Many medieval theologians repeated some of the main ideas about women found in the writings of Greek philosophers and continued by early church fathers. Thomas Aquinas (1225–1274), for example, echoed Aristotle's claim that woman was created as subordinate and inferior to man. Not only was she second in the order of creation, but she had less intellectual capacity and thus less ability to make right moral decisions. Based on the revival of certain Greek ideas, Aquinas added that women were "defective" human beings, the result of an accident to the male sperm, which would always produce another male under normal circumstances.[28]

Throughout most of Europe in the Middle Ages, laws gave husbands the right to beat their wives. A thirteenth-century French law declared, "In a number of cases, men may be excused for the injuries they inflict on their wives, nor should the law intervene. Provided he neither kills nor maims her, it is legal for a man to beat his wife when she wrongs him—for instance, when she is about to surrender her body to another man, when she contradicts or abuses him, or when she refuses, like a decent woman, to obey his reasonable commands. In all these and similar cases, it is the husband's office to be his wife's chastiser."[29]

The right to beat a wife was a tame claim in the light of what was to follow in the later Middle Ages. To combat various heresies, the church had set up courts (the Inquisition) to try anyone guilty of some deviation from accepted doctrine. This began in the twelfth century in France, but

---

27. Cited in ibid., 226.
28. See Thomas Aquinas, *Summa Theologica*, 1.92.1, ad. 1.
29. Cited in Julia O'Faolain and Lauro Martines, eds., *Not in God's Image: Women in History from the Greeks to the Victorians* (New York: Harper, 1973), 175.

soon spread to other jurisdictions. Members of the Dominican Order served as judges.[30]

Drawing on Augustine's theology of the sex drive as the conveyor of original sin, some Inquisitors imagined that sexuality's power came from demons. So female sexuality must, in fact, be a demonic power. Women who consorted with the devil became witches with supernatural powers to lure the innocent into sin. In 1484, Pope Innocent VIII issued a papal bull (*Summis desiderantes affectibus*) to enlist the Inquisition in prosecuting witches.[31] Why? It was believed that witches had given themselves to the devil sexually and had become his instruments for either inflaming sexual desire in some or obstructing it in others.

In 1487, two Dominican Inquisitors, Heinrich Kramer and James Sprenger were empowered by Innocent VIII to create a systematic theology linking female sexuality to the magical powers of witches. They published *Malleus Maleficarum* ("Hammer of Witches"), which quickly became the authoritative catechism on demonology. By 1520, this catechism had gone through fourteen known editions. In it, we learn why women rather than men were more likely to give themselves to witchcraft. While the authors stated that women are more impressionable and have slippery tongues, the main problem lay in the defect resident in the first woman, Eve: she was formed from a "bent rib."

To help us grasp the significance of this, Kramer and Sprenger explain the connection between Eve's bent rib and witchcraft: "Since through this defect [the bent rib] she is an imperfect animal, she always deceives ... And indeed, just as through the first defect of inordinate affections and passions, they [women] search for, brood over, and inflict

---

30. The Inquisition ended after the fourteenth century, but the practice was expanded during the Renaissance, the Reformation, and the Counter-Reformation, until it was finally abandoned early in the nineteenth century.

31. It is important to note that the Inquisitions in the southern countries (Italy, Spain) did not treat those accused of witchcraft severely; it was in the northern countries (Germany, etc.) that the Inquisitions were fierce and most likely to condemn to death those accused of witchcraft.

various vengeances, either by witchcraft, or by some other means. Wherefore it is no wonder that so great a number of witches exist in this sex . . . To conclude, all witchcraft comes from carnal lust, which is in women insatiable."[32]

It was a short step from those assumptions to conclude that any woman was a witch if she deviated in any way from a humble recognition of her inferiority.[33] This generated a fear of women and their power, especially their power to cause men to sin.

What qualified a woman to be considered a witch? For the most part it was enough to be female, single, and beyond childbearing age. The accusation usually included some kind of pact (sometimes sexual intercourse) with the devil, who in turn gave the witch extraordinary powers to torment or trouble others. Women who were accused of witchcraft were usually interrogated with severe torture until they confessed to whatever was assumed, after which in most cases they were burned at the stake.

Historians suggest varying numbers of people in Western Europe and North America who were put to death as witches. Most, however, place the number over a two-century period at sixty thousand to two hundred thousand. The overwhelming majority were women for whom death seemed preferable to the tortures they underwent to get them to "confess." The Belgian physician Johann Wier tells of a poor old woman, who, "already set for burning, was brought to confess that she had caused the long winter and extreme cold and persistent ice of 1575. And there were men of authority who thought this truer than truth itself, although there is nothing more absurd in all nature."[34]

---

32. H. Kramer and J. Sprenger, *Malleus Maleficarum*, trans. by Montague Summers (London: Arrow Books, 1971) 119, 122.

33. A witch was anyone who had made a pact with the devil, giving him or her the power to hurt others through the use of potions and sorceries. Barbara MacHaffie notes that "many people believed that witches were able to fly through the air to attend group orgies where they worshiped the devil, ate the bodies and blood of children (mimicking the Christian Eucharist), and indulged their sexual appetites" (*Her Story*, 55).

34. Cited in O'Faolain and Martines, *Not in God's Image*, 214.

Medieval patriarchy not only subordinated women to men, but ultimately demonized thousands of them as consorts of the devil. While the witch craze had its roots in the Middle Ages, the practice of ferreting out women accused of witchcraft peaked during the Reformation.

THE PROTESTANT REFORMATION: PROS AND CONS

Whistle-blowers may at times be surprised by the results of their efforts to finger practices that are often illegal or at least hurtful to some. Sometimes the whistle-blower is defamed, and the effort to bring to light what is wrong may falter. Other times the effort blows things wide-open and begins a process of renewal.

On October 31 in 1517, a German priest named Martin Luther (1483–1546) nailed ninety-five theses (written in Latin, not German) to the door of All Saints Church in Wittenberg.[35] The theses centered primarily on the sale of indulgences in Germany. Luther, who was also a university professor of theology, wanted to start an academic conversation about this abuse.[36] An indulgence was a kind of papal pardon (replacing genuine contrition) to achieve forgiveness of sins. People could buy these indulgences for themselves or for souls in purgatory. In his office as priest, Luther was startled when parishioners coming to confession presented their indulgences so they would not have to repent. He also was incensed that Tetzel, selling "salvation" with these indulgences, preyed on poor, ignorant peasants. He wanted the pope to know what was being done in his name.

Expecting merely to start a debate at the university about the practice, Luther must have been shocked that within two weeks, copies of

---

35. Some historians dispute this story as fanciful, stating that nothing was nailed to the church door, but that the ninety-five theses were only sent to the requisite academics to begin a debate.

36. While primarily about indulgences, the theses also raised questions about nepotism in the church, usury, and other clerical abuses.

his theses had spread throughout Germany—and within two months, throughout Europe. Friends translated the theses from Latin into German and, with the aid of the newly invented movable-type printing press, widely disseminated them. Five years after Luther's bold move in 1517, his popularity was such that most of the churches in Wittenberg celebrated "Lutheran" services rather than the Mass.

Why did Luther become so popular so quickly? In general, people were unhappy with the corruption and "worldly" workings of the Roman Curia.[37] The effort to reform one corrupt practice ignited a movement that far outstripped Luther's imagination. The Reformation was born as a protest against "selling salvation," but it then attacked far more than the problem of indulgences. What other problem areas did the Reformers think needed to be changed?

The Problem of the Monasteries

The first monasteries were built in the fourth century in the Middle East. The newly created women's monasteries provided a "breath of fresh air" for Christian women weighed down with the strictures placed on them because of their innate inferiority to men. Forced to dress in shapeless, drab apparel and appear in public only when fully veiled, women entering the monasteries found new ways to serve God. When women were barred from ministries in the church, they found ample opportunities for service to the needy in the monastic life.

The medieval Dark Ages were dangerous in many ways for women. Marauding barbaric bands from which there was little or no protection pillaged villages, killed men, and raped women. Women's convents or monasteries, often outside walled cities, were especially vulnerable. While women recognized the potential danger of living in such places, these monasteries provided three important advantages:

---

37. The Curia is the administrative body for the church, carrying out the pope's wishes.

1. They gave women an alternative to forced marriages. Many women had absorbed the negative teachings about female sexuality and were convinced the virgin life was highly preferable to marriage. Women from wealthy families were often forced into an arranged marriage to improve their family's assets. To avoid that inevitable end, young women (sometimes in their early teens) took drastic measures to avoid marriage by seeking the security of a virgin life in a monastery.[38]

2. Many of the medieval monasteries for women provided the only education available to females at that time. Most people could not read or write, but nuns in convents had access to some level of education. Because the movable-type printing press had not yet been invented and books were usually hand-made, one of the nuns' tasks was to copy or illuminate manuscripts.

3. Because of their personal piety or shrewd management of the convent, some nuns rose to positions of privilege equal to those of bishops and noblemen. For example, Lioba (an eighth-century English ascetic) was said to have calmed a storm and healed the sick. She was also skilled in classical philosophy, theology, and canon law. Barbara MacHaffie tells us that bishops, nobles, princes, and even the Emperor Charlemagne honored her.[39]

Women's monasteries continued to offer those opportunities to women throughout the Middle Ages. The women who ruled these monasteries (called abbesses) at times exercised temporal and spiritual power. In countries like England and France, abbesses often headed "double

---

38. There are numerous stories of young women's efforts to escape unwanted marriages. Not all ended well. You can find some of these stories in Julia Kavenagh, *Women of Christianity* (the pioneer 1857 narratives of women's lives in the Christian tradition; repr., Eugene, OR: Wipf & Stock, 2006); Tucker and Liefeld, *Daughters of the Church*; Rosemary Ruether and Eleanor McLaughlin, *Women of Spirit: Female Leadership in the Jewish and Christian Traditions* (New York: Simon & Schuster, 1979); and MacHaffie, *Her Story*.

39. See MacHaffie, *Her Story*, 48.

monasteries" for both men and women. In general, the monasteries were not an official part of the church, and in the later Middle Ages, the church hemmed in and then shut down the double monasteries.

By the sixteenth-century Reformation, however, the existing monasteries had become known for their wealth and elegant lifestyle. They were considered corrupt. Karen Jo Torjesen notes that "the worldly power of prince-bishops and the profligacy of the begging monks overshadowed the genuine spirituality that had birthed the [monastic] movement" a thousand years earlier.[40] So the Reformation began by shutting down all the monasteries in its area.[41]

The Problem of Asceticism versus Godly Marriage

Recall the notion that renouncing sexuality is "the central spiritual discipline in the quest for the knowledge of God."[42] This was the spiritual incentive for male celibacy and female virginity. Born in the fourth century, the ascetic idea of celibacy/virginity had been imposed on the clergy in 1139 after six centuries of opposition to it. Now, four centuries later, the practice was universal—until Martin Luther's Reformation.

Reading Genesis 1:26–28 brought Luther to an "aha!" moment: God commanded the man and woman to be fruitful and multiply! They were designed for sexual union! They should feel joy, not guilt, about their sexuality! A wife was God's gift, and married love was the highest human form of love. In fact, he argued that while celibacy focused only on what was good for the *self*, marriage focused on seeking the *other person's* welfare—a far more godly arrangement.[43] But when Luther and John Calvin argued that marriage was preferable to celibacy, they challenged nearly fifteen centuries of the opposite teaching.

---

40. Torjesen, *When Women Were Priests*, 233.

41. In England, under Cardinal Wolsey, Thomas Cromwell launched the English Reformation by closing twenty-nine monasteries in 1525 (see ibid., 236).

42. Ibid., 223.

43. Luther argued that washing diapers pleased God more than reciting penitential psalms (see ibid., 236).

In lands touched by the Reformation, other clergy followed Luther's example and married. This impacted the status of women: they were no longer evil temptresses but were given respect, security, and even rights as married women. Moreover, women now married to clergy had a new sphere as "ministers' wives." Barbara MacHaffie notes that "the Protestant home became an important center for teaching the gospel and passing on the Christian faith."[44] These women found themselves presiding over households that were centers of cultural and intellectual activity. For example, Luther's wife, Katherine von Bora Luther, "presided over barnyard, fishpond, orchard, a host of servants, children, sick visitors, student boarders, and church leaders in their huge Augustinian cloister with forty rooms on the first floor alone."[45]

No longer were these women denounced as seducers. They had a new status. At the same time, the Reformers were clear that God called men and women to different vocations. By God's will, a woman's world was her home, her children, and her care for a husband whom she obeyed. The Reformation removed the stigma under which women had lived for centuries, but it still retained a basic patriarchal structure: Eve's sin still made women's role a subordinate one. Luther was clear that when his wife took his name and moved into his geographical space, she acknowledged her subordination to him. When he and Calvin shut down the monasteries, they closed the option of the virgin life for women. Now the domestic world of homemaking and motherhood would become the norm for all women.[46]

The Reformers' Demand for Universal Education

One of the far-reaching changes brought about by the Reformation was the insistence on education for both women and men. The new

---

44. MacHaffie, *Her Story*, 63.
45. Ibid.
46. At the same time, the Reformers raised women's new roles to the level of a vocation.

movable-type printing presses made copies of the Bible available, and people needed to know how to read. In the Lutheran lands, civil authorities were tasked with establishing schools for both girls and boys. This echoed the apostle Paul's insistence in 1 Timothy 2:11 that "a woman should learn."

One of Luther's signature points of theology was *sola Scriptura*: the Bible and only the Bible is the basis for both faith and practice. Christians must know how to read so they can order their lives after the teachings of Scripture. Literate women were no longer limited to those in convents who had access to education; every woman was now to be given that possibility so that she could read God's Word for herself.

Conclusion

Martin Luther had hoped merely to reform the Catholic Church. While in some ways he failed in that, his Reformation spawned the Catholic Counter-Reformation, which did bring in a period of revival and reform in the Catholic Church in the sixteenth and seventeenth centuries.

Luther's actions also changed women's lives significantly. While women lost the monastery as a sphere of autonomy and power, they gained in other important ways. Barbara MacHaffie notes that "the theology of the Reformation terminated the second-class status of marriage and the association of women with evil because of their reproductive functions. In some places, it also brought educational opportunities for women . . . and *brought reformed Christians at least to the theoretical threshold of full female participation with the doctrine of the priesthood of all believers.*"[47]

Patriarchy had permutated throughout the Middle Ages, and while women emerged in the Reformation free of past stigma, they still lived within a gender-based hierarchy. What would it take to challenge the fundamental idea of female inferiority?

---

47. MacHaffie, *Her Story*, 73, emphasis added.

Questions for Personal Reflection or Group Discussion

1. Even as cultural ideas helped shape Christian theology in the patristic period, what kind of cultural ideas today may impact Christian beliefs?
2. With the strong emphasis on virginity and celibacy as essential to spiritual formation and the knowledge of God, where in your opinion could the medieval church have missed the boat?
3. Weighing the pros and cons of the Reformation on women's lives, how would you evaluate the most important changes for women that came from that movement?
4. While patriarchy in the Middle Ages was harsh to a degree we find unimaginable today, in what ways can patriarchy be harsh today?

Chapter Eleven

CAN PATRIARCHAL IDEAS SURVIVE THE RENAISSANCE AND THE AGE OF ENLIGHTENMENT?

When we read about the Dark Ages, we're not surprised to find them "dark" for most people, but particularly for women. But when we hear words like *Renaissance* (French for "rebirth") or the *Age of Enlightenment* (casting light to dispel the dark), they may give us hope that, at last, circumstances will change for women. Is it possible that in both religious and secular spheres, the modern Western world did not rid itself entirely of the burden of patriarchy?

The great Roman Empire had effectively split into two parts by the end of the fourth century. As northern tribes nibbled at it, the Western Roman Empire began to disintegrate, falling to the Ostrogothic Kingdom by the end of the fifth century. But the Eastern Roman Empire, based in Constantinople (present-day Istanbul), continued to rule parts of the Middle East for a thousand years until it fell to the Ottoman Turks in 1453. For most of that millennium, it was a powerful cultural, economic, and military force, preserving much of the ancient learning and products of "the glory that was Greece and the grandeur that was Rome."[1]

Both before and after the fall of Constantinople, ancient Greek and Roman cultural artifacts found their way to Italy.[2] Historian Mary Beard writes, "Now educated men and women in Italy had at their command, for example, the great histories written by Greek and Roman authorities in antiquity and were attracted by the difference between these human and secular works and the monkish chronicles which, besides being fragmentary, twisted the story of the past to fit theological conceptions of the universe."[3] A narrative different from the one dominating the Middle Ages emerged with this rebirth of learning, and like dawn, it gradually spread over northern Europe.

PATRIARCHY ENCOUNTERS THE RENAISSANCE

The Renaissance was made possible by several concurrent events. One was a migration of Greek scholars and texts from Constantinople to Italy. That led to a rediscovery of classical Greek philosophy and brought the broad trove of classical learning that had been lost to the West during the Middle Ages. This included all that had made possible the advanced cultures of earlier civilizations.

This rebirth of classical learning also led to scientific pursuits (based increasingly on observation and inductive reasoning) and to new perspectives for art and architecture as seen in the works of the sculptor, painter, and engineer Michelangelo (1475–1564) and of the Venetian architect Palladio (1508–1580).

---

1. Edgar Allen Poe's famous line from his 1845 poem "To Helen."
2. The Italian poet Petrarch is sometimes credited with beginning the Italian Renaissance when he found Cicero's letters.
3. Mary R. Beard, *Woman as a Force in History* (New York: Collier, 1946), 259.

Another major factor was the invention of the movable-type printing press by Johannes Gutenberg around 1440. Almost overnight, works that had taken years to copy by hand could be printed in great quantities and distributed widely.

Chapter 10 examined the effect of the Reformation on women.[4] We now must ask how the Renaissance (spanning the fourteenth to seventeenth centuries) touched women's worlds. Its effect was most obvious in its birthplace, Italy. We're told that Italian women moved quickly into new educational opportunities, winning "the highest honors for their sex in every department of science, art and learning . . . The universities which had been opened to them at the close of the Middle Ages, gladly conferred upon them the doctorate, and eagerly welcomed them to the chairs of some of their most important faculties."[5]

Are you rubbing your eyes, not sure you read that correctly? This is so distant from all that we've known about women's lives in the late Middle Ages that we may doubt its truth. Yet we have a substantial list of such women's names and the honors they received. Mary Beard observes that in nearly every great intellectual center of Italy, women were lecturing on philosophy and literature. Classical schools for both girls and boys opened in Italian cities to broaden educational opportunities beyond the ruling circles.[6]

Did this throw a knockout punch at patriarchy? In his massive study of the Italian Renaissance, nineteenth-century historian Jacob Burckhardt noted, "In order to understand the . . . Renaissance, it is necessary to know that woman was regarded as in a position of perfect equality with man . . . The education of the woman among the higher classes is essentially the same as that of the man . . . The same development of mind and heart that perfected the man was necessary for perfecting woman."[7]

---

4. The Reformation occurred within the period of the Renaissance.

5. H. J. Mozan, quoted in Beard, *Woman as a Force*, 261.

6. See ibid., 262. The schools reached children of the business and professional classes. It is unlikely that poorer children had access to this education.

7. Quoted in ibid., 264.

Giovanni Boccaccio (1313–1375) and other writers wrote glowingly of women's abilities. Would this dawn of a new day of education for women spread north, enveloping all of Western Europe?

The printing press permitted the first mass production of books in history, which altered the structure of society. Information now crossed borders more easily, and because people were learning to read, the monopoly of the few on education was broken. This promoted the growth of a middle class. The printing press also allowed publication in local languages, sidelining Latin as the *lingua franca* (language of the land). Beginning with the Gutenberg Bible in 1455, translations of the Bible proliferated as the printing press made books available on a broad scale.

All of these effects of the Renaissance were in place when Martin Luther nailed his ninety-five theses to the door of a Wittenberg church in 1517. So we cannot look at women's lives in the Renaissance apart from all that the Reformation unleashed throughout Europe.

Though Luther's intention had been merely to reform corrupt practices in the Catholic Church, the refusal of the church to make those changes launched Protestant-Catholic wars throughout northern Europe that continued for more than a century. With those wars (culminating in the Thirty Years War of 1618–1648) came massive devastation and dislocation of whole groups of people as territories changed hands.

Ultimately, attitudes toward women in Italy did not take root in the rest of Europe. Monarchs came and went, and with them came changes for their subjects. For example, after Henry VIII in England had separated from Catholic Rome and launched the Church of England (1531), his daughter Mary, who remained staunchly Catholic, succeeded him to the English throne (1553–1558). She became known as Bloody Mary for her vigorous persecution of Protestants, killing 238 English Reformers. When she died after five years on the throne, her half sister Elizabeth

I came to the throne and reversed the persecutions, reestablishing the Church of England and hounding those who opposed it.[8]

A similar pattern emerged in France. Before Martin Luther had posted his theses in 1517, Marguerite of Navarre (1492–1549), sister of King Francis I, had read a commentary on the apostle Paul's letters about justification by faith. Though she remained a Catholic, she became sympathetic to Reformed theology. She denounced the persecution of the Protestant Huguenots. When John Calvin and William Farel were expelled from Geneva in 1539, Marie Dentiere, the well-known French Protestant Reformer in Geneva, turned to Marguerite for help in increasing scriptural literacy and access among women. Marguerite pled for the reform of the Catholic Church. She was not a Calvinist, but she used her power to protect the Reformers from intolerance as long as possible.

Historian Will Durant described Marguerite in these words: "In Marguerite the Renaissance and the Reformation were for a moment one. Her influence radiated throughout France. Every free spirit looked on her as protectress and ideal . . . Marguerite was the embodiment of charity. She would walk unescorted in the streets of Navarre, allowing any one to approach her and would listen at first hand to the sorrows of the people."[9] Her husband, Henry, king of Navarre, believed in her work, and together they financed the education of needy students and set up a model public works program. Yet because of her mediating position, one monk said she should be "sewn in a sack and thrown into the Seine [River]."[10]

Later, Marguerite's daughter, Queen Jeanne d'Albret (1528–1572), reigned over Navarre (1555–1572) as a convert to Calvinism (1560) and as the spiritual and political leader of the French Huguenot movement. This made her a key player in the French Wars of Religion. Ruth Tucker

---

8. Three centuries earlier, the English had set up the Magna Carta to separate church and state. Twice the pope annulled that historic document, but it was reissued, first in 1216 and then in 1225. So Henry VIII's action had a historical precedent for the separation of church and state.

9. Will Durant, *The Story of Civilization*, vol. 6 (New York: Simon and Schuster, 1953), 501.

10. Ibid., 500.

and Walter Liefeld note that, unlike her mother, Jeanne didn't try to establish an atmosphere of toleration.[11] Instead, she imposed restrictions on Catholics in Navarre that merely intensified the hatred between the two sides. Her young son, Henry, was torn between his parents in a bitter custody battle. His father forced him to study under Catholic tutors, while his mother would not allow him to attend Mass. After her death (1572), Protestants were slaughtered en masse in what is called the St. Bartholomew's Day Massacre.[12] Henry later came to the French throne as Henri IV, and at that point for reasons of political expediency, he converted from Calvinism to Catholicism.

The ongoing religious wars were not the only factor devastating Europeans. The Black Plague (bubonic plague) had already decimated populations between 1340 and 1353, killing between seventy-five million and two hundred million people. Historians estimate that roughly 30 percent to 80 percent of the population of the affected countries died in the plague.

Recall from chapter 10 that it was also in this period of the Renaissance that Pope Innocent VIII issued his papal bull to enlist Inquisitors to prosecute witches (1484). Three years later, the Dominican inquisitors Heinrich Kramer and James Sprenger wrote *Malleus Maleficarum*, which became the authoritative catechism on demonology. As a result, between sixty thousand and two hundred thousand people—mostly women—were deemed witches and were put to death, mainly across northern Europe.

The products of the Renaissance in thought and art, though highly

---

11. See Ruth A. Tucker and Walter Liefeld, *Daughters of the Church* (Grand Rapids: Zondervan, 1987), 188.

12. The massacre began when the French king ordered the assassination of the Huguenot military and political leaders gathered in Paris. The slaughter spread throughout the city and spilled over into the countryside and other urban areas, lasting several weeks. Historians estimate that between five thousand and thirty thousand Huguenots were killed in this massacre as it "printed on Protestant minds the indelible conviction that Catholicism was a bloody and treacherous religion" (H. Chadwick and G. R. Evans, *Atlas of the Christian Church* [London: Macmillan, 1987], 113).

complimentary of women, could not filter down in any meaningful way to populations caught in the maelstrom of constant wars, plagues, and witch hunts. The radical change in women's fortunes through the Renaissance was restricted to upper-class women, primarily in Italy. While the Reformation opened some doors for women, it closed others. Catholic attitudes toward women's inferiority did not change significantly during the Renaissance. Patriarchy survived on most fronts. But what about the coming period of the Enlightenment?

Patriarchy Encounters the Enlightenment

Called the Age of Reason, the Enlightenment has also been named the foundation of modern Western political and intellectual culture. The eighteenth-century philosophers who gave us the Enlightenment wanted to replace age-old ideas, superstitions, and practices with a scientific approach to life. Their goal was to find universally valid principles that could be applied across the board for all religious, social, political, and economic issues. Already in the Renaissance, some authors had begun drifting away from religious theories and focused more on people's humanity and daily lives. Now the Enlightenment, with its confidence in human reason to change society, promoted a secular view of the world.

Most movements come into being as a reaction against an unacceptable status quo. This was true of the Enlightenment. Tired of religious conflicts and the chaos of the previous centuries, the Enlightenment thinkers wanted to turn the page from the domination of all of life by the church and king to a new world led by principles like equality, liberty, and personal responsibility. So they attacked ideas like ecclesiastical authority, dogmatism, social restraints, and intolerance. In France, the central doctrines were individual liberty and religious tolerance, in contrast to absolute monarchy and the dogmas of the Catholic

Church. One goal of Enlightenment scholars was to limit the political power of organized religion and prevent any additional intolerant religious wars.

Enlightenment theologians wanted a nonconfrontational faith without the religious controversies that had torn nations apart in the Reformation and Counter-Reformation. John Locke (1632–1704) decided to do away with all the biblical commentaries and just study the Bible alone. He concluded that the essence of Christianity is a belief in Christ the redeemer.

In addition to questioning religious orthodoxies of the day, the Enlightenment thinkers also emphasized empirical scientific research and political theorizing based on several central tenets. These included the idea that the fundamental capacity of any person is the ability to reason, and that all people are equal in their rationality and as a result should be granted individual liberty and equality before the law. Another tenet insisted on tolerance toward other creeds and ways of life. Furthermore, beliefs should be accepted only on the basis of reason, not on the authority of priests, sacred texts, or tradition.[13]

Politically, John Locke's social contract theory was that the government's authority lies in the consent of the governed. People have natural rights, though when we join with others to form a civil society, we have to give up some of those rights. For example, I have the right to drive a car, but I do not have the right to ignore red lights and compromise the safety of other people. Locke's law was grounded in the idea of mutual security. Because everyone is equal, no one has the right to infringe on another's natural rights.

Does any of this sound familiar? The ideas of Enlightenment theorists like Locke and Thomas Hobbes (1588–1679) shout from the pages of the American Declaration of Independence, with its emphasis on every

---

13. These principal ideas of the Enlightenment philosophers are taken from Ted Honderich, *The Oxford Guide to Philosophy* (Oxford: Oxford University Press, 2005), 252.

person's right to "life, liberty, and the pursuit of happiness." Hobbes insisted on the natural equality of all men and that all legitimate political power must be "representative," based on the consent of the people. These thinkers promoted the separation of church and state. Thomas Jefferson (1743–1826) called for a "wall of separation between church and state" at the federal level and was active in establishing such a "wall" in the state of Virginia. Why? Because everyone has a natural right to the liberty of conscience.

In the light of these core notions, it would seem that women would thrive. However, it is here that a number of the Enlightenment intellectuals were glaringly inconsistent. On the one hand, anything that is a universal right must be universally enjoyed. On the other hand, a number of major Enlightenment thinkers defaulted to patriarchal tradition for women. Jean-Jacques Rousseau (1712–1778) concluded that "women's entire education should be planned in relation to men. To please men, to be useful to them, to win their love and respect . . . these are women's duties in all ages and these are what they should be taught from childhood on."[14] For him, women are made to be subservient and dependent on men. He promoted the severe confinement of women to the home by emphasizing the mother-child bond that had the potential to reduce corruption in society at large. Thus he merely put a new face on the age-old prejudice against women. He prescribed a gendered hierarchy for society at the same time that he trumpeted the universal tenet of equality of all people.

Neither did Immanuel Kant's (1724–1804) views on universal rights and the elimination of social hierarchies extend to women. He insisted that a husband has a "right to possess [his wife] . . . [and] a wife's duty to obey her husband is a demand of natural law as well as a moral obligation."[15]

---

14. Quoted in Julia O'Faolain and Lauro Martines, eds., *Not in God's Image* (New York: Harper, 1973), 247.

15. Jean Bethke Elshtain, "Kant, Politics, and Persons: The Implications of His Moral Philosophy," *Polity* 14.2 (1981): 213.

An article on women in Denis Diderot's (1713–1778) *Encyclopédie* describes women as "weak, timid, shrewd, vicious, vindictive, superficial, and deceitful."[16] The writer believed women are to live a life of intentional obscurity, confined to domestic duties. They are basically inferior and exist to serve their male counterparts.

Of course, not all Enlightenment thinkers excluded women from the basic tenet that all human beings are equal. The Marquis de Condorcet (1743–1794) wrote a tract advocating women's full entrance into the public sphere, including the right to vote and to hold public office.[17] And Olympe de Gouges (1748–1793) pointed to the inconsistency of a gender hierarchy within a supposedly universal egalitarian system: "Liberty and justice consist of restoring all that belongs to others; thus, the only limits on the exercise of the natural rights of woman are perpetual male tyranny; these limits are to be reformed by laws of nature and reason."[18]

Was patriarchy overturned by the Enlightenment? Oddly enough, the notion of universal equality left women out. The idea that freedom, equality, and reason could trump prejudice and hierarchy ended up meaning something for men that it did not mean for their female counterparts.

Patriarchy and Revolution

Just as Martin Luther's bold action in 1517 set off major social change with unintended consequences, so the Enlightenment also led directly to unintended anti-establishment revolutions. Three kinds of revolution occurred during the eighteenth century. The first was the *religious* revolution begun by the First Great Awakening, an evangelical revitalization

---

16. Joseph-Francois-Edouard de Corsembleu Desmahis, "Women (Ethics)," in Denis Diderot and Jean le Rond d'Alembert, *Encyclopédie*.

17. Marie Jean Antoine Nicolas de Caritat, Marquis de Condorcet, "On the Admission of Women to the Rights of Citizenship" (1790).

18. Quoted in Isaac Kramnick, *The Portable Enlightenment Reader* (New York: Penguin, 1995), 612.

movement that swept through England and North America mainly in the 1740s. The second was the *economic* or *technological* revolution called the Industrial Revolution, beginning with James Hargreaves's invention of the spinning jenny in 1764 and James Watts's invention of an efficient steam engine in 1765. The third was the *political* revolution overturning monarchical rule in both France and the United States. The American Revolution (1775–1783) and the French Revolution (1789–1799) were both direct consequences of Enlightenment thinking. Strong, new ideas can bring social change, frequently in unexpected and destabilizing ways. They are, in fact, "revolutionary."

Patriarchy, Women, and Religious Revolution

New religions often begin with a charismatic leader whose power draws in followers and creates a sense of mission for them. At first, structures are loose and evolving. But over time, leaders find it necessary to establish consistent means of governing the new faith. So they add rules touching on roles and statuses. We see this mirrored clearly in Christianity's patristic period. Sociologists call this the "routinization" period of a movement's growth. In time, the movement at some point becomes an institution for which policies are elaborated and limits are placed on followers. The letter of the law overpowers the spirit of the law. The major task for leaders then is to jack up the plausibility of the movement's worldview as a means to control members and block out competing worldviews.

At some point in nearly every new religion, its leaders eventually decide it is necessary to stamp out voices of dissent. We saw it in the Roman Empire when Christians refused to say "Caesar is Lord," and many believers were martyred. We saw it in the Middle Ages as the Inquisition was established to root out heresy in any form. We saw it in the religious wars generated by the Reformation and Counter-Reformation. In England, following Henry VIII's dissent from Rome (establishing the Church of England), his successor on the throne, Bloody Mary, tried to stamp out all protesting voices of dissent from the Catholic Church. Her successor, Elizabeth I, did the reverse, stamping out Catholic voices of dissent. She was followed by James I, who returned the favor by stamping out Elizabeth's efforts to reform the Church of England.

While most religions have begun by offering freedom from fear to its followers,[19] sociologists of religion remind us that as these movements become institutions, walls go up around what is or is not allowed and voices of dissent are silenced. Enlightenment thinkers were divided, with more radical thinkers pushing for democracy and the eradication of religious authority. Other more moderate thinkers wanted to find ways to reform problem areas, but within traditional systems of power and faith.

The religious revolution in the American colonies began with the Great Awakening but continued in the disestablishment of all religion. Recall the Puritans' treatment of dissenters in the Massachusetts Bay Colony. It is ironic that its leaders so soon forgot how they had been treated in England, forcing them to emigrate, first from England to Holland, then from Holland to the New World. Once established in New England, they instituted harsh treatments for dissenters.[20] The justification for this was doctrinal, with the Calvinist doctrine of a limited atonement buttressing conformity. Fear of damnation kept many Puritans from any kind of dissent.

Then came the First Great Awakening a century after the Puritan immigration to the New World. Some date its beginning in New England from Jonathan Edwards's fiery sermon, "Sinners in the Hands of an Angry God," preached first in 1741. This Calvinist Puritan preacher had come to believe that God's grace was open to anyone who believed in Christ and that everyone needed a personal religious experience.

The Great Awakening polarized colonists sharply along religious

---

19. Galatians 5:1: "It is for freedom that Christ has set us free. Stand firm, then, and do not let yourselves be burdened again by a yoke of slavery."

20. Punishments could range from spending time in the stocks to the culture-challenging hanging of Mary Dyer in 1660 when she converted to Quakerism.

lines. Individual churches and whole denominations were split as compelling preaching called people to forsake their "unconverted ministers" and experience the new birth.[21] This emphasis on the experience of conversion dramatically transformed men and women. When a person experienced grace, he or she felt compelled to tell others about it. The Awakening encouraged women to participate more openly in revival and congregational activities. That was the first part of the religious revolution for women.

The second part came as the colonies joined together into the United States as the new nation emerged from war with England and drafted its three founding documents: the Declaration of Independence (1776), the Constitution of the United States (1783), and the Bill of Rights (1791). The First Amendment to the Constitution prohibits making any law that establishes a particular religion, impedes the free exercise of religion, abridges the freedom of speech, infringes on the freedom of the press, or interferes with the right to peaceable assembly.[22] Prior to 1791, nine of the thirteen colonies had an "established" or a "state" religion: citizens in that colony were taxed to support the church's ministries and/or were required to attend religious services regularly.[23] In some cases, "establishment" also allowed for persecuting any dissenters.

As early as 1644, Roger Williams in Rhode Island noted the importance of "a hedge or wall of separation between the garden of the church and the wilderness of the world," a phrase that Thomas Jefferson picked up in 1802.[24] But it wasn't until 1833 that all nine states complied with the First Amendment disestablishing a particular religion to the exclusion of others.

---

21. For example, George Whitefield and Gilbert Tennent; see Jessica M. Parr, *Inventing George Whitefield: Race, Revivalism, and the Making of a Religious Icon* (Jackson: University Press of Mississippi, 2015), 96.

22. This amendment was adopted on December 15, 1791, as one of the ten amendments that constitute the Bill of Rights.

23. Massachusetts and Connecticut were Congregational; the other seven were Church of England: Georgia, Maryland, North Carolina, South Carolina, Florida, Virginia, and New Hampshire.

24. Roger Williams, "Mr. Cotton's Letter," *The Complete Writings of Roger Williams*, vol. 1, ed. Perry Miller (New York: Russell & Russell, 1963), 392.

Historian Ann Douglas writes, "In 1800 only one in fifteen Americans belonged to a religious society."[25] Think about that: only 6 percent of all Americans were members of any kind of religious establishment. And most of those members were women. Clergy found fewer and fewer men in the pews.

This was not a new problem. While men had outnumbered women in the original immigrations, by the end of the seventeenth century, women outnumbered male church members by a ratio of three to two. The New World offered opportunities to people who were willing to work hard, and within a generation, colonial men had become less religious and more attentive to economic opportunity. A century later, when the colonies became the United States, the "skyscraper" had trumped the "steeple" in a country first settled by those who sought religious freedom but now lived out their freedom from religion.

Furthermore, disestablishment cut ministers off from automatic funding from the state so that they were forced to compete with other religious groups for members and money. It became necessary for ministers to change their disdain for women to praise for them. To survive, the clergy joined hands with women to bring men back to God. Because the pews were filled with women, sermons and hymns increasingly stressed Christ's love and God's mercy. As the new nation moved into the nineteenth century, women were made the custodians of religion at a time when religion was sidetracked by economic advantage. Was this a setback for patriarchy? Or was patriarchy being given a new face?

Patriarchy, Women, and the Industrial Revolution

From time immemorial, families have worked together for survival. In most parts of the world, homes were modest, and families with any kind of business in the community used the front room as their work

---

25. Ann Douglas, *The Feminization of American Culture* (New York: Avon, 1977), 23–24.

space, with the family living behind or above it. Colonial wives in America knew the family business and could take it over if the husbands were away or deceased. They had important roles as "deputy husbands," which meant they could shoulder male duties. Colonial papers ran abundant notices that such-and-such a woman would carry on the family business after the loss of her spouse. So women ran ferries, shoed horses, painted houses, and carried on other family businesses without a glitch.

But as the eighteenth century dawned with increased economic opportunities for gaining wealth and status in the growing cities, the "pretty gentlewoman" emerged on stage. No longer part of her husband's external world and with enough money to hire servants for domestic duties, she could concentrate on developing social skills in a beautified home as an ornament to her spouse. It was this woman of whom Mary Wollstonecraft wrote that she "is like a bird in a cage with nothing to do but to preen herself, stalking from perch to perch."[26] Late-eighteenth-century novelists like Jane Austen captured the idle life of many middle- and upper-class women.

Meanwhile the vast majority of women were caught up in other massive social changes ushered in by the Industrial Revolution. Life in the village or on the farm was often precarious, and the lure of wage-paying jobs in the new factories and mills was great. A move to one of the new industrial towns would bring benefits to the family: steady jobs would replace the uncertainty of subsistence living, and mass-produced goods would be cheaper to buy.

But with those advantages came severe damage to the way families had always functioned. Fathers would be absent from the home for twelve to fourteen hours a day, six days a week. Parenting responsibilities that had been shared by both parents in the home now fell exclusively to the mother. Sons who had grown up seeing their father's skills every day no

---

26. Mary Wollstonecraft, *A Vindication of the Rights of Women* (Boston: Thomas and Andrews, 1792).

longer had that model to follow. They could not see his competency and learn from him on the job. They too could get jobs in the factories and mills and earn their own way. Their tie to the family weakened, which enabled them to leave home and make their own way in the wider world.

Many mill owners trapped families by providing mandatory rental units for housing and a factory store for all purchases (often next door to a brothel or a bar). The costs of these usually exceeded one wage, and because that wage could not cover the many new expenses in the town, mothers and children were also forced to become wage-earning factory workers. Children as young as six worked long hours at jobs in the mills for a pittance in pay.

The family solidarity and continuity that had been a normal part of life back in the village or on the farm were shattered by this new life from which most families could not escape.

It's not hard to see the impact on women's lives. In the factories, women were paid half the wage paid to men for the same work and hours. Husbands often squandered their earnings at a nearby brothel or bar. Patriarchy dictated the wage differential, leaving women to struggle to meet expenses from their earnings, often running up endless debts.

The lure of the Industrial Revolution was powerful, and the exodus from farms and villages to the new factory towns became a flood. It's impossible to overstate the profound splitting of the family that took place in its wake. Nothing more cataclysmic has happened to the family since. The invention of steam engines and the factory system destroyed the ancient rhythm of family life. For the first time on a wide scale, work was separated from home.

Patriarchy, Women, and the Political Revolution

The French and American Revolutions were more than wars between opposing armies; they were wars between opposing ideas of government. In the American colonies, it was a war for national independence, with the patriots trying to defeat the British loyalists. This was the first time in documented history that colonists successfully rose up against an imperial power and won.[27]

Americans throughout the colonies were reading and talking about John Locke's ideas—the inalienable rights of man to life, liberty, and the pursuit of happiness and the notion that all men were created equal (ideas that made their way into the American Declaration of Independence in 1776). Behind this was the *contract theory* of government: government is a voluntary agreement between a ruler and the people; when the ruler violates the contract, the people have the right to revolt. Britain's king didn't get that. It was time to declare independence from the English throne.

The war politicized women as well as men, with women starting to "dispute on politics and positively to determine upon [their] liberties." As one woman put it, "Though a female, I was born a patriot and can't help it."[28] In the 1760s and 1770s, women decided not to purchase British goods and organized boycotts (like the Boston Tea Party, in which men and women tossed British tea shipments into the ocean). Groups of women signed public pledges to abstain from drinking tea; instead, they made herbal teas, spun and wove their own cloth, and insisted on "buying American." One observer noted that "at every house Women & Children [are] making Cartridges, running Bullets, making Wallets, baking Biscuit, crying & bemoaning at the same time animating their Husbands & Sons to fight for their Liberties."[29] With men off fighting, women took over running farms and businesses. The war had given women increased opportunities to act politically and aggressively from their role as housewives.

---

27. The American Revolutionary War lasted eight years, stretching from April 1775 (with the battle of Lexington) to September 1783. It's unlikely that the patriots would have won without the intervention of the French against the British. France entered the war on the patriots' side in 1778 to avenge its defeat in 1763 by the British in the Seven Years' War on European soil.

28. Quoted in Sara M. Evans, *Born for Liberty: A History of Women in America* (New York: Free Press, 1989), 48.

29. Ibid., 51.

The problem for women was that when men wrote "all men are created equal," they literally meant only *men* of a certain class. For them, women, slaves, and men without property (along with children and the mentally ill) lacked the capacity for independent and rational judgment for the general good and so were not included in that "equality."

This presented a problem for women. If they were not citizens, how were they to relate to the state? In 1776, Abigail Adams wrote her husband, John, "that the new laws should curb the 'unlimited power' of husbands over wives and threatened that 'if particular care and attention is not paid to the ladies, we are determined to foment a rebellion and will not hold ourselves bound by any laws in which we have no voice, or representation.'"[30] In this, she charged men with a form of tyranny, but her husband simply dismissed her letter with a joke.

With women's political involvement in boycotts, the political theories of equality and human rights, and the emphases of the Great Awakening, the new nation faced the problem of female citizenship. The male leaders' solution was to endow domesticity itself with political meaning in the idea of "republican motherhood."[31] Women had a patriotic duty in their role to rear sons and daughters as moral and virtuous citizens of the new republic. This role was distinct from men's and was deemed essential to the nation's welfare. So republican motherhood directed women's political consciousness back into the home, sentimentalizing domestic duties.

But the most important development for "republican mothers" was the ensuing debate on women's education. Women were now responsible to teach their children, but how could they if they themselves had never been taught? Some historians estimate that roughly 50 percent of all women in the colonies were functionally illiterate (unable to sign their

---

30. Ibid., 56.
31. See Linda Kerber, "The Republican Mother: Women and the Enlightenment—An American Perspective," in *American Quarterly* 28.2 (1976): 187–205. Kerber is thought to be the first to use the term "republican motherhood."

own names).[32] The age-old assumption that women had an inferior nature and capacity was still alive and well.

In 1790, Judith Sargent Murray argued that women's disability was their lack of education. Pointing to signs of reason, imagination, memory, and judgment among women, she wrote, "We can only reason from what we know, and if opportunity of acquiring knowledge hath been denied us, the inferiority of our sex cannot fairly be deduced from thence."[33] She and others argued strenuously that the purpose of educating women was not to make them like men but to enable them to fulfill their domestic function as republican mothers. This worked for the transformation, but not the elimination, of traditional roles.

At the close of the eighteenth century, the earliest academies for girls and women taught only rudimentary skills, but the door was now open for women's education. Women entered the nineteenth century with more influence on churches and with some new educational opportunities. At this point, patriarchy took on a new look, defined by the cult of true womanhood and the doctrine of separate spheres.

CONCLUSION

Through the Renaissance, Reformation, the Age of Enlightenment, and many Revolutions, four hundred years of permutation altered the rhetoric of patriarchy but kept its fundamental assumptions intact. The language about women changed dramatically as the witch, the whore, and the evil temptress were replaced by the "angel in the home" as the nineteenth century began. A newly defined gender understanding was now in place, but women's "elevation" was still thoroughly secondary to men's place in the world.

---

32. This estimate came from the percentage of official documents in colonial court archives on which women had to make a mark of some sort in place of a signature.

33. Judith Sargent Murray, "On the Equality of the Sexes," in *The Massachusetts Magazine* (1790).

Questions for Personal Reflection or Group Discussion

1. Over the four centuries covered in this chapter, what do you see as the most important turning points for women?
2. The century of bloody religious wars was one unintended consequence of the Reformation. Could those wars have been avoided? If so, how?
3. How do you respond to the inconsistency of a gender hierarchy within a supposedly universal egalitarian system? What may have contributed to this inconsistency?
4. Which of the three "revolutions" through which American women passed in the eighteenth century do you think had the most impact on women's lives?

Chapter Twelve

RECYCLING THE CULT OF TRUE WOMANHOOD

Can patriarchy survive the modern world's veneration of womanhood? As cultures moved from seeing women as "the whore" or "the witch" to a new view of them as persons of worth, even as persons superior in some respects to the male sex, it would seem that the battle to eliminate patriarchy was nearing victory. But was it?

THE DOCTRINE OF SEPARATE SPHERES

What makes a man a "man"? Before the Industrial Revolution, men confirmed their manliness in three ways. First, their work required physical strength, skill, and often risk to their lives—factors wives and children saw daily. Second, masculine work historically rested on bloody aggression as the hunter or warrior. Whether hunting for food or at war for security, men knew the camaraderie, terror, pain, and joy of battle from which women were excluded. Third, the patriarchal family structure supported a traditional masculine identity. A man's primary role in the family was as father, not husband, and sons were controlled through promised economic security passed on by the father.[1]

---

1. See Betty A. DeBerg, *Ungodly Women: Gender and the First Wave of American Fundamentalism* (Minneapolis: Fortress, 1990), 15–16.

But when the Industrial Revolution took families from farms and small villages to cities or towns for waged labor, what happened to these three primary signposts of masculinity? The tasks at a desk or machine did not require the skills of a hunter/warrior, and men lost control of sons, who could also now get jobs and become financially independent. The old cultural signposts were gone, and men needed new ones. Historian Barbara Berg noted that in the early nineteenth century, "confused and unsure of themselves, men found a foil for their own ambiguous identities through the specific and stagnant qualities they ascribed to women. Women . . . formed the negative imprint of the desirable male self-portrait. Men may not have known who they were or what characteristics they had, but by insisting that woman possessed all the weak and inferior traits, at least they knew what they were not."[2]

Because men needed new measures of what it was to be a man, the doctrine of separate spheres provided an elaborate philosophy of womanhood. This doctrine states that men and women have totally different natures, a fact that would keep women from jeopardizing this new masculine identity. The press and clergy joined hands to teach that gender difference is God-ordained, *and* we must do everything we can to support a strict separation of women's spheres and men's spheres. Many believed that only men were equipped with the necessary aggressiveness and ruthless competitiveness that business required. Numerous printed sermons, pamphlets, and newspaper articles underscored the dangers women courted if they entered the men's world of commerce or tried to use their brains. Physicians reminded women that any woman who spent time trying to use her mind would irreparably damage her reproductive organs, causing them to shrivel up and become useless.

No, it was obvious that woman's place at all times was by her fireside as "the angel" of the home, "where she is enthroned in more glory than all beside, where she is to adorn the doctrines of God her savior in the bearing,

2. Barbara Berg, *The Remembered Gate* (New York: Oxford University Press, 1978), 109.

bringing forth, training, uplifting those who are committed to her keeping."[3] Nineteenth-century rhetoric made an icon of the home as the haven from the rough world of commerce; it was a man's castle and a woman's domain. No longer the *locus* of work, it became a place of *retreat* from work. In the doctrine of separate spheres, the wife was crowned queen of the home.

A woman's world was circumscribed by the four walls of the home that her husband provided. If she stayed in her place, remaining pious, pure, submissive, and domestic, all would go well. In the man's world, he was a captain of industry or commerce. With astuteness and diligence, he could support his wife and children on a single income. Immigrants coming to America provided a ready supply of cheap labor, and in the nineteenth-century middle-class home, servants cooked, did laundry, kept house, and tended children.

THE CULT OF TRUE WOMANHOOD

Firmly in place by 1835, "the Cult of True Womanhood" developed out of the doctrine of separate spheres. As the primary role of the wife shifted to overseeing the care of children and the home, clergy and politicians urged her to see herself as the moral guardian of the family. She was responsible for the ethical and spiritual character of every family member, as well as for the comfort and tranquility of the home. In that role, she had become her husband's moral superior while remaining his legal and social inferior. Her task was to make the home the one place free from the competitive conflicts and insecurities of an expanding capitalist democracy. As such, the family became a "sanctuary," an "oasis," an "ivory tower," a "moated castle."[4] Sarah Josepha Hale, editor/publisher of the magazine *Godey's Ladies Book*, wrote that the home would "remind the dwellers of this

---

3. M. M'Gee, in the *Weekly Recorder* 80.35 (July 6, 1905); quoted by DeBerg, *Ungodly Women*, 44.

4. Stephanie Coontz, *The Social Origins of Private Life: A History of American Families 1600–1900* (New York: Verso, 1988), 210.

'bank-note world' that there are objects more elevated, more worthy of pursuit than wealth," and they were under the care of women.[5]

Nineteenth-century society was an economic roller-coaster: fortunes were made and lost overnight. Social and economic mobility caused so much instability in society that there had to be a still point in this churning world. Historian Barbara Welter identified that still point: it was the True Woman. To be a True Woman was a fearful obligation, a solemn responsibility. Her attributes were four cardinal virtues: piety, purity, submissiveness, and domesticity. With these four virtues intact, she had happiness and power. If anyone (male or female) were to tamper with the complex of virtues that made up the True Woman, such a person was condemned immediately as the enemy of God, an enemy of civilization, and an enemy of the republic.[6]

Women's Benefits from This New Sense of Worth

If as a True Woman a woman was morally superior to a man, then why should she not take a greater part in running the world? As long as women were deferential to male authority, the Cult of True Womanhood gave them the right to extend morality and religion throughout America. Between 1800 and 1850, thousands of women joined a basketful of female voluntary associations to address problems in their world. They formed missionary societies to bring the Christian faith to large segments of the population in "godless" cities or on the "barbaric" frontier. They started Sunday schools to teach poor children religion and how to read. They distributed Bibles and aided churches in poor sections of major cities. They paid preachers to minister to sailors, and they helped young men go through seminary. Their benevolent associations cared for orphaned children, indigent young women, and widows. They provided

---

5. Quoted in Nancy F. Cott, *The Bonds of Womanhood: "Women's Sphere" in New England 1780–1835* (New Haven, CT: Yale University Press, 1977), 68.

6. See Barbara Welter, *Dimity Convictions: The American Woman in the Nineteenth Century* (Athens: Ohio State University Press, 1976), 21–41.

food, clothing, and occasionally shelter for them. Some groups opened schools, which taught women reading, writing, arithmetic, and religion.

Reform associations emerged, directing attention to creating a Christian America through social change. These women were concerned about peace, temperance, prison reform, and moral reform (by closing brothels and converting prostitutes). Crusading women adopted bold tactics, descending on brothels to pray and talk with prostitutes and working against the double standard by publicly listing names of respected men who frequented such places. Women contributed great sums of money and countless hours to the religious and social welfare of many citizens. They improved living conditions in blighted urban areas and met needs that others ignored.

But something deeper was also happening: through all these efforts, women learned how effective organizations operated. They became experienced leaders through the moral reforms that took them out of their domestic worlds. The voluntary associations enhanced their sense of self-confidence and self-worth. They also benefited from the support of other women, learning from one another and acquiring a sense of solidarity with other women.

The clergy encouraged women to get involved as long as they remained helpers, assisting men by doing their work in modest and quiet ways. But like the sorcerer's apprentice, the clergy turned the living "household broom" into a living, energetic being, and they had no spell to turn her back into a broom. Women's new solidarity and skills encouraged them to crusade against every kind of oppression directed against their sex. Temperance groups spoke out against drunk husbands who victimized their wives. Benevolent societies worked against factory owners who took advantage of female employees. And most important, women became active in the antislavery movement. Noting commonalities between freedom issues for African Americans and Victorian women raised the issue of the status of all women.

The doctrine of separate spheres had separated men's and women's worlds. But as women discovered the power of working with other women, they began using their religious and moral position to create new public work spaces and female solidarity. Early on, by the mid-1820s, sophisticated networks of women were raising funds, building charitable institutions like orphanages, orchestrating revivals, and pursuing courses of action as women outside the purview of men. Armed with their moral mission, solidarity, and their zeal to change the world, women began to critique men based on their religious values.

In the process, by the end of the nineteenth century, the True Woman had evolved into the New Woman. She had a new sense of self as being morally superior to the men who made money aggressively, often ruthlessly in the expanding economic frontiers. That moral superiority pushed her out of the home to reform society to the point that some historians have called the nineteenth century "the century of women" or "the age of association."

At the same time, the Cult of True Womanhood may have led women "two steps forward, one step back." Their world was filled with contradictions. As Sara Evans wrote, "If women were to become experts in their own arena, they needed more education than the women's magazines could provide."[7] Barred from colleges and universities by their sex, they began their own women's colleges: Vassar opened in the 1860s, Smith and Wellesley in the 1870s, and Radcliffe in the 1890s. To staff these new colleges, in many cases, determined women went to Europe to sit in on university courses (courses they could audit but not take for credit) to equip them for serious academic work in the new women's schools. All of this took decades to accomplish while women remained without serious educational options.

In 1833, a Female Anti-Slavery Society was formed in Philadelphia, and by 1837, a national convention of antislavery women met in New

---

7. Sara M. Evans, *Born for Liberty: A History of Women in America* (New York: Free Press, 1989), 139.

York, reflecting the extensive system of female antislavery societies. But when leaders of this movement were barred by their sex from attending an international antislavery convention in London, in 1848, three hundred evangelical men and women gathered in Seneca Falls, New York, to call for equal laws for men and women, citizenship for women, and women's right to vote. But it would take seventy-two years of hard work before women received the right to vote in 1920.

Women's Religious Impact on Theology

The Cult of True Womanhood called for piety as the core of a woman's virtue. The cult insisted that religion belonged to women by divine right. It was a gift of God and of nature. God gave her this so that the flame of her piety would throw its beams into the naughty world of men. Women's purifying, passionless love would bring erring men back to Christ.[8] Think about this against the backdrop of the church fathers fifteen hundred years earlier. For centuries, women had been "the devil's gateway" to corrupt men. Now the tables had turned.

During the period 1800–1850, American Protestantism changed fundamentally: it was "feminized." As the church was sidelined by society, it became more expendable and thus the property of the weaker members of society—women. In the nineteenth century, the skyscraper replaced the steeple as a symbol of the American dream. Politics captured the zeal and time once reserved for religion. As the church became more domesticated, more emotional, softer, more accommodating, women and ministers became allies against this usurper from which they were both excluded. Increasingly, in a political world, women and the church stood out as antipolitical forces.[9] Previously, in the revolutionary eighteenth century, the church had defined human nature in terms of original sin,

---

8. From *The Young Lady's Class Book*, ed. Ebenezer Bailey, 1831; cited in Welter, *Dimity Convictions*, 22.
9. See Ann Douglas, *The Feminization of American Culture* (New York: Avon, 1977), 18–19.

while the state defined it in terms of perfectibility through democracy. The nineteenth century reversed this: the churches moved toward the idea of progress, while the democratic state reverted to a more cynical and realistic view of human nature.[10]

Now in the churches, the new Christ was an exemplar of meekness and humility, the sacrificial victim dominated by love, asking nothing but giving everything and forgiving his enemies. The True Woman played the same role. She was never more feminine than when, on her deathbed, the innocent victim of male lust or greed forgave her cruel father, her profligate husband, or her avaricious landlord. The minister who interpreted this feminized Christ to his congregation spoke in a language women understood.[11]

Nineteenth-century hymns also reflected an increasing stress on Christ's love and God's mercy. Christ is a friend and helper.[12] Because so many things were beyond a woman's control, she had to endure what she could not cure. The natural risks of childbirth, illness, death, and loss of security made "thy will be done" a very special female prayer, because submission was among the highest female virtues. The hymns reinforced this. Womanhood and virtue became synonymous, and her first virtue was piety.[13]

THE VICTORIAN HOME

Many people of faith today have an idealized view of the middle-class Victorian family. For many Christians, Victorian clarity about male and female marital and parental roles has shaped their concept of the Christian home. Yet despite the warm glow of this vision of family life,

---

10. Ibid., 85.

11. Ibid., 88.

12. In contrast to more "theological" hymns in an earlier period, typical of nineteenth-century hymnody were Joseph Scriven's (1820–1886) "What a Friend We Have in Jesus," Louise M. R. Stead's (1850–1917) "'Tis So Sweet to Trust in Jesus," Henry Francis Lyte's (1793–1847) "Abide with Me," and Carolina Sandell Berg's (1832–1903) "Children of the Heavenly Father."

13. See Douglas, *Feminization of American Culture*, 88–89.

the reality in the nineteenth century for both men and women was severe strain within its confines. At the apex of the Victorian era, great numbers rebelled against societal pressures to conform to the doctrine of separate spheres. Thousands of men chose to escape the pressures of nineteenth-century life by migrating to the expanding Western frontiers. Tens of thousands of women refused the roles that middle-class society tried to force on them. Although it was a time when spinsterhood was despised, large numbers of American women chose not to marry rather than to enmesh themselves in the constraints of Victorian marriage patterns. In 1867, Louisa Mae Alcott, author of those family-friendly novels like *Little Women* and *Little Men* and *Jo's Boys*, gave this as her rationale for refusing to marry: "Liberty makes the best husband."

Historian Carl Degler may astonish us with these statistics:

> The highest proportion of women who never married for any period between 1835 and the present [1980] were those born between 1860 and 1880...
>
> Although some women may have felt excluded or deeply unhappy because they could not marry, for others remaining single was a conscious choice and one that promised a richness of experience that marriage did not. For a woman to have a life of her own outside of marriage could be not only unusual but liberating... For many such women marriage appeared to be a straitjacket, rather than an opportunity or an improvement in life and status as it may well have seemed in earlier and different times.
>
> Nowhere did this conflict between women's aspirations and marriage surface more obviously than among those women who were graduating from the new women's colleges and coeducational universities during the last half of the nineteenth century.[14]

---

14. Carl Degler, *At Odds: Women and the Family in America from the Revolution to the Present* (New York: Oxford University Press, 1980), 152, 159–60.

Not only were many Victorian women refusing to marry. In the United States, married women were seeking divorces in unprecedented numbers, causing the divorce rate to soar in the final decades of the Victorian era. The ratio of divorces to marriages had been climbing since the 1840s, but a quarter of a century later, the number of divorces reported throughout the country in 1867 was still under ten thousand. But as Degler reports, "Between 1870 and 1880 the number of divorces had grown one and a half times as fast as the population [at a time when immigration was very high], and that in 1886 the annual number of divorces was over 25,000. A second government report calculated that during the 1890s the number of divorces was climbing at a rate almost three times that of the increase in the population."[15]

What was happening to produce so many divorces in the final decades of the Victorian era? In 1867 women filed two-thirds of all divorce petitions, and that figure later rose to nearly three-fourths of all divorces. The Christian periodical *Watchman* in 1880 puzzled that "the sex that is most interested in the security of the home and maintenance of social purity has taken the lead in the war upon both through our perverted legal machinery."[16] When husbands filed for divorce, in 80 percent of cases, they cited their wife's failure to accept her subordinate role submissively, according to the ideal of the Cult of True Womanhood.

Something was going on in the Victorian home that caused both men and women increasingly to turn their backs on marriage and file for divorce. This widespread exodus from marriage set off alarm bells throughout the Christian press.

In 1886, T. DeWitt Talmage, editor of *Christian Herald and Signs of Our Times*, expressed his concern in these words: "Yonder comes . . . a ship having all the evidence of tempestuous passage: salt watermark reaching to the top of the smokestack . . . bulwarks knocked in . . . main

---

15. Ibid., 166.
16. "Our Divorce Laws," *Watchman* 61 (February 12, 1880): 52.

shaft broken; all the pumps working to keep from sinking. That ship is the institution of Christian marriage."[17]

John Milton Williams, writing in *Bibliotheca Sacra* in 1893, insisted, "Woman has no call to the ballot-box, but she has a sphere of her own, of amazing responsibility and importance. She is the divinely appointed guardian of the home . . . She should more fully realize that her position . . . is the holiest, most responsible, and queenlike assigned to mortals; and dismiss all ambition for anything higher, as there is nothing else here so high for mortals."[18]

Every one of the turn-of-the-century Christian periodicals carried editorials, articles, and sermons on the topic, decrying divorce as "the deadliest foe of the home" and "a monster of iniquity" that "threatens to destroy the American home."[19]

In the twentieth century, the Victorian experience of traditional roles leading to divorce was repeated in contemporary America. The Danvers Statement in 1987, setting out the rationale, purposes, and affirmations of the Council on Biblical Manhood and Womanhood, expressed a similar grave concern about women who forsook "vocational homemaking." This 1987 statement mirrors the nineteenth-century reality of female disaffection with a strict confinement to the domestic role.[20] The 1950s in North America replayed the Victorian doctrine of separate spheres, and the decades following (1960s, 70s, 80s, etc.) saw precisely the same pattern of rising divorce rates and female disaffection with marriage. What goes around comes around: the issues on the front burner at the end of the nineteenth century returned with vigor at the end of the twentieth century.

---

17. T. DeWitt Talmage, "Clandestine Marriage," *Christian Herald and Signs of Our Times* 9.5 (January 28, 1886): 53–54.

18. John Milton Williams, "Woman Suffrage," *Bibliotheca Sacra* 50 (April 1893): 343.

19. See Betty A. DeBerg, *Ungodly Women: Gender and the First Wave of American Fundamentalism* (Minneapolis: Fortress, 1990), 68.

20. See appendix 2 in John Piper and Wayne Grudem, eds., *Recovering Biblical Manhood and Womanhood*, 2nd ed. (Wheaton, IL: Crossway, 2006), 469–71.

The Victorian marriage model was no walk in the park for either men or women. The nineteenth century had shifted marriage from an economic partnership in which both contributed equally to the production of the necessities for family survival to a family in which the husband produced all the income and the wife processed that income as a consumer. This led to increasing animosity between husbands and wives. A persistent theme in diaries, letters, and other historical documents is that men resented being expected to provide their entire life for a wife and their children; women resented having their lives limited to the domestic realm.

Men had several practical reasons to marry. For some, it was the need for the emotional support of a wife. For others, it was the basic need to have daily needs met by someone else—laundry, meals, and an inviting place to come home to at the end of the day. Yet in spite of these reasons to marry, more and more men saw society as "effeminate," and they wanted to escape to the new Western frontiers where a man could be a *man*. It was not unusual for married men to leave home for long periods of time. Wives were often happy to have the men gone on such "travels." Both found Victorian domesticity stifling.

The doctrine of separate spheres pitted the sexes against one another throughout the nineteenth century with growing dissatisfaction. But there is more. Historian Betty DeBerg observed that "the stability of the economic warrior (or breadwinner) depended on keeping women out of the male sphere of business, labor, politics, and government."[21] DeBerg tells us that as the nineteenth century ended, women began working outside the home in far greater numbers in both factories and in new white-collar jobs. She cites these statistics:

Between 1880 and 1910, the proportion of employed women increased from 14.7 percent to 24.8 percent. In the ten years

---

21. DeBerg, *Ungodly Women*, 18.

between 1900 and 1910, the percentage of married women working outside the home more than doubled (from 5 to 11 percent). There was a marked difference in the kinds of employment women sought and held. In 1870, almost 60 percent of all employed women were in domestic service, but by 1920, less than 20 percent were. The greatest increases in the number of working women took place in business and in the professions, the middle-class male empire.[22]

What did this do to a masculine identity centered on keeping women out of the workplace? The first nineteenth-century signpost of masculinity was becoming irrelevant as tens of thousands of women surged into the workforce. The older images of the pure and submissive Victorian woman and her benevolent patriarch began to erode more rapidly.

MASCULINIZING A FEMINIZED CHURCH

Because men were missing from the pews,[23] between 1880 and 1920, clergy and Christian writers cried out for a muscular Christianity.[24] What kind of revitalization would lure men back to the church? One major effort was the Men and Religion Forward Movement to remasculinize Protestant churches.[25] This was an interdenominational revival effort across the country in which more than a million men attended its various events. Organizers spent hundreds of thousands of dollars creating large rallies in seventy-six major cities and more than a thousand small

22. Ibid., 25–26.

23. Historian Leonard Sweet notes "an overwhelming fear of effeminacy and an exaggerated attention to masculinity" in an effort to reassert male authority in the church between 1880 and 1920 (*The Minister's Wife: Her Role in Nineteenth-Century American Evangelicalism* [Philadelphia: Temple University Press, 1983], 227).

24. See Colleen McDannell, *The Christian Home in Victorian America: 1840–1900* (Bloomington: Indiana University Press, 1986), 116.

25. Details of this movement can be found in Gail Bederman, "'The Women Have Had Charge of the Church Work Long Enough': The Men and Religion Forward Movement of 1911–1912 and the Masculinization of Middle-Class Protestantism," *American Quarterly* 41 (Sept. 1989): 455.

towns. Until the Promise Keepers movement in the 1990s, the Men and Religion Forward Movement was the only widespread religious revival in American history that explicitly excluded women.

During the late eighteenth and early nineteen centuries, religion and morality had been coded "female," while politics and business had been coded "male." The "male" sphere of business and politics was in opposition to the "female" spheres of religion and morality. By defining women as the naturally religious sex and men as the naturally productive sex, the Victorian gender system had constructed a society that was thought to be both moral and commercial. Pious women would keep men moral; productive men would provide for wives and children. Together they would form godly homes, the epitome of Christian progress. It would be a moral capitalism allowing men to engage in the free market.

But the Victorian gender definitions failed to provide a satisfying relationship between men and women; it also failed to construct a convincing model of an acceptable capitalism. In short, cultural changes had made feminized religion a problem; the cure would be a healthy dose of masculinity into the churches. The result was dozens of organizations like Boys Brigade and Knights of King Arthur, as well as athletics and quasi-military organizations to attract boys.

To become modern and powerful, the church needed men. Nineteenth-century religion had been emotional, with the heart over the head. For a masculine religion, church work had to be seen as part of the modern world of corporate business, using corporate techniques like bureaucratic organizing and aggressive advertising. The entire Men and Religion Forward Movement was organized like a rationalized corporation for that purpose.[26]

---

26. Though the movement aimed to have three million men join churches, they fell short of that goal. In 1912, fifteen thousand fewer men joined churches than had in 1911. But within five years, Protestants had effectively masculinized their churches, and by the mid-1920s, ministers and theologians celebrated Protestantism's businesslike nature. Churches still had more women than men, but the proportions had shifted so that men felt the churches were masculinized.

RECYCLING THE CULT OF TRUE WOMANHOOD

In the nineteenth century, the existing missionary-sending agencies refused to send women overseas except as wives of missionaries. So at mid-century, women began organizing their own missionary-sending agencies. By the end of the century, more than forty such agencies were raising far more money and sending far more missionaries overseas than were the denominational agencies run by men. As the twentieth century began, one by one, the denominational agencies co-opted the women's agencies so that by mid-twentieth century no women's agencies remained. Promises made for equal representation were set aside, and by the 1940s, women realized too late that they had been locked out.[27]

As women protested their marginalization, it became necessary to put biblical or theological legs under the Cult of True Womanhood. Books began to appear, each laying out arguments for a doctrine of separate spheres. The first of these was John R. Rice's *Bobbed Hair, Bossy Wives, and Women Preachers* (1942). Purporting to set forth the scriptural basis for Christian women's behavior and demeanor and stressing that men and women are different, he wrote, "Man is made in the image of God. God is a masculine God. The masculine pronoun is used of God everywhere in the Bible . . . God is not effeminate. God is not feminine, but masculine. And man is made in the image of God. On the other hand, a woman is not made so much in the image of God, but in the image and as a mate to man . . . Blessed is the woman that remembers this; her glory is being a help to a man, and in submission to her husband or her father."[28]

Despite its questionable use of Scripture, Rice's book became the

---

27. See Dana L. Robert, *American Women in Mission: A Social History of their Thought and Practice* (Macon, GA: Mercer University Press, 1997), for an excellent discussion of this history of women's missionary-sending agencies.

28. John R. Rice, *Bobbed Hair, Bossy Wives, and Women Preachers: Significant Questions for Honest Christian Women Settled by the Word of God* (Wheaton, IL: Sword of the Lord, 1942), 68.

"Bible" on male/female relationships for thousands of Christian couples in the 1940s and 50s.

Then in 1958, Charles Ryrie published *The Place of Women in the Church* (later republished as *The Role of Women in the Church*). In contrast to Rice's untempered rhetoric, Ryrie presented a careful historical review of women's place in early ancient Near East cultures, during Jesus' earthly ministry, and during the first three centuries of church history. Though Ryrie's book did not have the popularity of Rice's book, it presented a scholarly investigation of relevant materials anchored in biblical study. The presupposition guiding his work was clear in his conclusion: "In the inspired writings we have the mind of God concerning the full development of women. And this will mean subordination and honor in the home, silence and helpfulness in the church, according to the teaching and pattern of the New Testament."[29] This gave clear support to the Cult of True Womanhood.

A decade later (1977), George W. Knight III published *The New Testament Teaching on the Role Relationship of Men and Women* (a short response to Paul Jewett's *Man as Male and Female* and to the Letha Scanzoni/Nancy Hardesty book *All We're Meant to Be*). His concluding argument is that both elders in church and husbands in marriage are heads, not because they are inherently superior, but because they have been called by God to their tasks.[30] Note the gradual softening of rhetoric in defense of the Cult of True Womanhood.

Four years later (1981), James Hurley published *Man and Woman in Biblical Perspective*.[31] Hurley argued for a wife's submission in marriage analogous to the obedience of the church to Christ, its head. He argued for male leadership in the church based on Old Testament patriarchal patterns he believed carried over to the church.

---

29. Charles Caldwell Ryrie, *The Place of Women in the Church* (New York: Macmillan, 1958), 146.
30. See George W. Knight III, *The New Testament Teaching on the Role Relationship of Men and Women* (Grand Rapids: Baker, 1977), 59.
31. James B. Hurley, *Man and Woman in Biblical Perspective* (Grand Rapids: Zondervan, 1981).

A decade later (1991), John Piper and Wayne Grudem published the edited volume *Recovering Biblical Manhood and Womanhood: A Response to Evangelical Feminism*.[32] Echoing arguments already articulated by Ryrie, Knight, and Hurley for gender distinctions in the home and church, Piper and Grudem introduced the new nomenclature of *complementarity* that took the sting out of previous terms like *patriarchalism* or *hierarchy*. With no changes in its content but with the addition of a second preface (by J. Ligon Duncan and Randy Stinson), this book was republished in 2006 as the ongoing *magnum opus* in support of the Cult of True Womanhood.

As the new century opened (2001), Robert Saucy and Judith TenElshof edited *Women and Men in Ministry: A Complementary Perspective*.[33] There is much in this book to praise, as it moved the conversation to a more nuanced view of gender difference. But in the end, it defaults to the notion that gender difference means separate spheres for both the home and church. The authors' chapters 9 and 10 underscore the centrality of gender difference in God's plan for humanity. Parts of these chapters echo the core egalitarian argument for "complementarity without hierarchy." Nevertheless, the writers back away from some of the obvious implications of the gender-difference reality and default to the cult.

In 1995, Andreas Köstenberger and Thomas Schreiner published *Women in the Church*, with a second edition published in 2006. Ten years later, they completely revamped the earlier editions, making a third edition available in 2016.[34] This dense book is not an easy read, but the authors' efforts to produce solid scholarship is impressive. Particularly helpful is S. M. Baugh's chapter on first-century Ephesus in light of the

---

32. John Piper and Wayne Grudem, eds., *Recovering Biblical Manhood and Womanhood: A Response to Evangelical Feminism*, 2nd ed. (repr., Wheaton, IL: Crossway, 2006).

33. Robert L. Saucy and Judith K. TenElshof, *Women and Men in Ministry: A Complementary Perspective* (Chicago: Moody, 2001).

34. Andreas J. Köstenberger and Thomas R. Schreiner, *Women in the Church: An Interpretation and Application of 1 Timothy 2:9–15*, 3rd ed. (Wheaton, IL: Crossway, 2016).

apostle Paul's troubles with the Ephesian church. A limitation is that the book focuses exclusively on issues surrounding one primary text (1 Timothy 2:12) rather than providing a more comprehensive discussion of a wider range of issues. While the default is a complementarian understanding of gender roles in the church, the contributors have given much useful background information about Greco-Roman life and culture in the period 60–69 (during which decade they assume Paul wrote his letters to Timothy and Titus).

From John R. Rice to Andreas Köstenberger and Tom Schreiner, these writers moved from harsh to conciliatory in tone and increasing efforts at solid research, but in the end, the conclusion is still the same: important gender distinctions are biblical and must be maintained by means of a doctrine of separate spheres. The recycling of the Cult of True Womanhood has produced appealing arguments for this doctrine, but in the end, patriarchy is still alive and well in these circles.

Questions for Personal Reflection or Group Discussion

1. How did the doctrine of separate spheres help men in their shift from early markers of masculinity to those appropriate to their lives in nineteenth-century businesses?
2. In what ways did the Cult of True Womanhood backfire as a means of shoring up the doctrine of separate spheres?
3. What were some of the advantages of newly available advanced education for women at the end of the nineteenth century?
4. What (if anything) do you see in today's world that attempts to reproduce the doctrine of separate spheres or the Cult of True Womanhood?

Chapter Thirteen

WHERE ARE WE TODAY? RETHINKING WHAT WE'VE BEEN TAUGHT

Throughout this book, the term *complementarian* has been used to describe those who support gender-based hierarchy for the church and home. This is their term, which they chose to define their position. At odds with this is the fact that others who do *not* support gender-based hierarchy for the church and home also use the term *complementarity* self-descriptively. They see important differences between men and women that mandate combining their differences for best results.

This confronts us with contrasting notions about this word. Both hierarchicalists and egalitarians would agree that God created humanity as male and female deliberately, purposefully. But how does God intend that gender difference to play itself out in the home or church? Is this difference so startling that all we can say is that "men are from Mars, women are from Venus"? Are men and women from different planets? In that light, is the only solution that we create separate spheres for each sex, with men in authority? Or is there a more valid way of seeing our complementarity as a call to work together, side by side?

MOVING THE GOALPOSTS

In sports, the expression "moving the goalposts" refers to the efforts of one team to deny the opposing team a legitimate win by moving the goalposts. This expression quickly became a metaphor for any action that changes terms in ways that would give one side an intentional but unfair advantage.

Complementarian Wayne Grudem has proved to be a master at moving the goalposts in his defense of gender-based hierarchy for men and women in both the home and the church. In 1991, he and his coeditor John Piper introduced new nomenclature that moved the goalposts in people's thinking about gender roles. The new name they gave for those who support gender-based hierarchy was "complementarian," and those who opposed gender-based hierarchy were then called "evangelical feminists." Knowing well the fear of and distaste for feminism among many evangelical Christians, he scored well by calling anyone opposed to his hierarchical vision by that name.

In 2002, Grudem once again moved the goalposts by asserting that "this controversy is much bigger than we realize because it touches all of life."[1] Ignoring the egalitarians' use of "complementarity without hierarchy" to define their position,[2] he then painted a terrifying picture of the consequences for anyone who does not agree with his complete playbook:

> Within marriage an egalitarian view tends toward abolishing differences and advocates "mutual submission," which often results in the husband acting as a wimp and the wife as a usurper. Because there is a deep-seated opposition to most authority, the drive toward

---

1. Wayne Grudem, ed., *Biblical Foundations for Manhood and Womanhood* (Wheaton, IL: Crossway, 2002), 60.
2. Egalitarians also use the term *complementarity*, as in the subtitle for the Ronald W. Pierce/Rebecca Merrill Groothuis book, *Discovering Biblical Equality: Complementarity without Hierarchy* (Downers Grove, IL: InterVarsity, 2004).

sameness will often result in children being raised with too little discipline and too little respect for authority . . .

Within sports, this viewpoint that attempts to deny differences would tend to be opposed to competition and think of it as evil rather than good. With respect to crime, the criminal would be seen as a victim to be helped and not punished, and punishment would be long delayed. As far as private property is concerned, because there are tendencies to abolish differences, no one would be allowed to be very rich, and there would be large-scale dependence on the welfare state and on government.[3]

The goalposts have now been moved to include dire economic and political consequences for anyone failing to support gender-based hierarchy. Note how far these statements have taken the discussions that most of us assumed were exclusively about hierarchical arrangements for men and women in the home and church. Grudem absurdly asserts that anyone who does not support gender-based hierarchy also believes there are few or no differences between men and women. This is clearly not true, and a case for complementarity without hierarchy will be made later in this chapter.

At the same time, it would be wrong to imply that Grudem alone is responsible for many women's confusion about their personhood or roles. Carolyn Custis James captured the frustration that many Christian women experience as the metaphorical goalposts are constantly being moved by pastors, theologians, and church officials:

Meanwhile, as the arguing continues, half the church is . . . needing to make choices and to move forward with our lives with amber lights flashing caution at every intersection . . .

To complicate things further, . . . the boundary line for

---

3. Grudem, *Biblical Foundations*, 61, 64.

women's permissible activities gets drawn in multiple places *within the same camp.* Even within a single denomination, churches don't agree on where the line should be drawn for women. Within a single organization what women are allowed to do can change as leaders will, from time to time, tighten or loosen restrictions. What is approved in one location is considered taboo in another. What is biblical one day can be declared unbiblical the next, or vice versa. It's hard to maintain your equilibrium much less make forward progress, when the ground is moving underneath you like that.[4]

This ongoing moving of the goalposts calls us to rethink what we're being taught by complementarians.

God's Goalposts

God set up his goalposts for men and women in Genesis 1:26–28, never to be moved:

> Then God said, "Let us make mankind in our image, in our likeness, so that they may rule over the fish in the sea and the birds in the sky, over the livestock and all the wild animals."
>
> So God created human beings in his own image;
>   in the image of God he created them;
>   male and female he created them.
>
> God blessed them and said to them, "Be fruitful and increase in number; fill the earth and subdue it. Rule over the fish in the sea and the birds in the sky and over every living creature that moves on the ground."

4. Carolyn Custis James, *Half the Church: Recapturing God's Global Vision for Women* (Grand Rapids: Zondervan, 2010), 156.

Two startling realities stand out in that manifesto (often called the creation mandate). The first is that God created humanity in two forms (male and female) and both are bearers of the divine image. The second is that the man and woman together were given two major tasks: populating the new world and subduing the earth. These two realities form the two upright posts in God's goal for us.

God's first goalpost: we bear God's image in our relationship to him. Theologians have wrestled over the centuries with the meaning of God's image in human beings, suggesting this or that human quality as the core of God's image in us. Is it our free will or our conscience or our ability to think or our self-awareness or our ability to make relationships? The reality is that all people bear the divine image, but some of them lack one or more of the static qualities or abilities that theologians have come up with to "define" that image. Thus those abstract definitions of the divine image are inadequate. I prefer to think of image bearing as an activity rather than as my "possession."

N. T. Wright caught this idea in his example of an angled mirror: get the angle right, and you can see things that are otherwise invisible to you. For this reason, many roads with sharp curves or blind corners are equipped with mirrors set at the proper angle so that drivers are alerted to oncoming traffic otherwise unseen. Wright suggests that, like these angled mirrors, our vocation as image bearers is to reflect information about God to folks around us by how we live and act, not just by what we say.[5] Our calling, our purpose, is to image God in a godless world.[6]

That, in short, means a life modeled after Jesus' life and teachings. He came into the world to show us God (John 14:8–9). That revelation of God in Jesus' actions and teachings calls us to live 24/7 in ways counterintuitive to the rules for success in our world. It also turns on its head

---

5. "Being an Image Bearer with N. T. Wright," *Biologos*, video available at biologos.org/resources/audio-visual/nt-wright-on-being-an-image-bearer (accessed November 21, 2016).

6. Every human being images what he or she believes about God, whether a devout believer or an atheist. We show what we really think about God in the way we live.

most of our notions of authority: "Whoever wants to become great among you must be your servant, and whoever wants to be first must be your slave—just as the Son of Man did not come to be served, but to serve, and to give his life as a ransom for many" (Matthew 20:26–28).

God's second goalpost: male and female together form a God-blessed team. Carolyn Custis James calls this "the Blessed Alliance."[7] Genesis 1:26–28 is clear that men and women are expected to work together as a team. As noted elsewhere in this book, God did not say to the woman, "Have babies and build the family," and to the man, "Subdue the earth and rule over it." He gave both commands to both members of the team. So in this text, we see shared parenting and shared stewardship of God's earth—an alliance blessed by God.

Why a team? Why not separate spheres of activity? Does part of imaging God mean that it takes both the man and the woman together to image God fully in this world? Is it that as we combine them, our differences (which are more than physiological) bring different things to the table that God's work needs for the best results?

Unmovable Goalposts: Load-bearing Walls

Carolyn James reminds us that we don't have to be engineers to know that some walls are more important than others. If we tamper with a load-bearing wall, we may end up with a roof falling on our heads:

> God designed the world to stand on two load-bearing walls. The first load-bearing wall is God's relationship with his image bearers. Without this vital relationship, we are cut off from our life supply—homeless, stranded souls in the universe, left to guess at who we are and why we are here. The second load-bearing

---

7. James, *Half the Church*, 135.

wall is the Blessed Alliance between male and female. According to Genesis, male/female relationships aren't simply necessary to perpetuate the human race and make life pleasurable and interesting.

Male/female relationships are *strategic*. God laid out his game plan in Genesis, and the team he assembled to do the job was male and female . . . It would be one thing if God confined this male/female team to home and family and then mapped out the remaining territory into separate spheres for men and women. But he didn't do that. Their mission—*together*—is to rule and subdue the whole earth on his behalf. Men and women together. Our relationships with God and with each other are the load-bearing walls of God's original design.[8]

You don't mess with a load-bearing wall. You don't move God's goalposts.

What Difference Does "Difference" Make for Us as Male and Female? How Does It Relate to Being "Load-bearing Walls"?

We understand our physiological differences. Most of the time, we can see the bodily difference between men and women: beards and busts are markers we recognize. Because we're different physically, we may conclude that a doctrine of separate spheres is our only choice because in real life, men really seem to be from Mars and women from Venus. But some of our differences provide the most potent reasons for working together.

A decade ago, information about the human brain was skimpy, but

---

8. Ibid., 138–39.

with new technologies like PET, DTI, and fMRI,[9] we now know much more about the human brain. It turns out that gender differences in our brains have significant implications for men and women working together as they pool their different modes of thinking for better (joint) decision making.

Iain McGilchrist, a noted British brain scientist, argues that our brains are designed to work back and forth between the right brain (our intuitive and imaginative input) and the left brain (our detail-oriented, analytical input). That is the design, but it is also where gender difference becomes crucial. A 2013 brain connectivity study at the Perelman School of Medicine, University of Pennsylvania, found "striking differences in the neural wiring of men and women that's lending credence to some commonly-held beliefs about their behavior."[10]

It turns out that in men's brains, neural connectivity moves from front to back in each hemisphere, adapting them to tasks involving perception and coordinated actions. Women's brains, in contrast, have more wiring between the right and left hemispheres, making them better at communicating, analyzing, and intuiting. As a result, men, in general, are better at learning and completing a single task at a time (like cycling or figuring out directions). Women, in general, excel at memory and social cognition abilities, making them better multitaskers and group problem solvers.[11] Can you see how pooling these two brain-use modes can make an important difference in decision making?

While men's language functions are specialized in the left hemisphere of the brain, women use both hemispheres for language. With

---

9. PET = positron emission tomography; DTI = diffusion tensor imaging; fMRI = functional magnetic resonance imaging.

10. "Brain Connectivity Study Reveals Striking Differences Between Men and Women," Perelman School of Medicine, University of Pennsylvania (December 2, 2013), http://uphs.upenn.edu/news/News_Releases/2013/12/verma (accessed November 21, 2016).

11. See Michelle Castillo, "Different Brain Wiring in Men, Women Could Explain Gender Differences," December 3, 2013, www.cbsnews.com/news/different-brain-wiring-in-men-women-could-explain-gender-differences (accessed November 21, 2016).

more linking between hemispheres (and thus more input from both sides of the brain), women think more inclusively or bilaterally than men. Whereas men think more linearly, women think more contextually.[12] The problem for women is that to a linear thinker, contextual thinking doesn't look like thinking at all. In reality, it's a complex form of thinking, but it has often been discounted by those who do not think contextually.

Other differences between male and female brains also point to complementary ways in which we need one another. For example, our brains all have both gray matter (where we process information) and white matter (electrical transmitters to other parts of the body). Men's brains have less gray matter and more white matter than women's brains. This allows men to excel at gross motor skills like sports or heavy lifting. With more gray matter, women can process information more quickly. I need my husband's physical strength for everything from opening jars to lifting objects I can't budge. In social settings, he benefits from my ability to pick up on cues more readily.

Women's brainpower has, however, been subjected to ridicule over the centuries. For a long time, brain size was thought to determine intelligence (male brains, on average, are 10 percent larger than female brains). On the basis of that, one mid-nineteenth-century physician, a Dr. Meigs, wrote, "[Woman] has a head almost too small for intellect but just big enough for love."[13] Intelligence tests have since debunked that myth of women's lesser intellectual capacity.

Back to McGilchrist. His research tells us that in the last three centuries (from the Enlightenment onward), only left-brain activity has been valued as "thinking." Right-brain activity (using intuition and imagination) was discounted as not really thinking. McGilchrist writes the following to describe the result of this interpretation:

---

12. These are generalizations, i.e., true in most but not all cases.
13. Charles D. Meigs, MD, *Females and Their Diseases: A Series of Letters to His Class* (Philadelphia: Lea and Blanchard, 1848), 47.

We could expect, for a start, that there would be a *loss of the broader picture, and a substitution of a more narrowly focused, restricted, but detailed, view of the world, making it perhaps difficult to maintain a coherent overview* . . . This in turn would promote the *substitution of information, and information gathering, for knowledge, which comes through experience* . . . One would expect the left hemisphere to keep doing refining experiments on detail, at which it is exceedingly proficient, but to be correspondingly blind to what is not clear or certain, or cannot be brought into focus right in the middle of the visual field. In fact one would expect a sort of *dismissive attitude to anything outside of its limited focus, because the right hemisphere's take on the whole picture would simply not be available to it.*[14]

Not only would it be "nicer" if men and women pooled their approaches to thinking, but the failure to do so sharply reduces what can be seen and understood. Men need women, and women need men, for a full cognitive picture in any situation.

Now think of this in the light of ministry. Completely apart from other differences between men and women, can you see how vital it is that men and women work together, pooling their unique strong points for maximum impact? Whenever we insist on a separation of men's and women's work in the name of "complementarity," we hobble kingdom workers with only half the resources God has given for that purpose. Even more, we take down one of God's load-bearing walls for subduing and stewarding the earth. Men need women, and women need men, to ensure that God's gifts to each are available to both as they work together. Not the least of these gifts lies in the complementary differences between male and female brains.

---

14. Iain McGilchrist, *The Master and His Emissary: The Divided Brain and the Making of the Western World* (New Haven, CT: Yale University Press, 2009), 428–29. Italics are mine.

CONFINEMENT IN SEPARATE
SPHERES CAN CAUSE PAIN

As I complete the writing of this book, I want to highlight this fact: *confinement in separate spheres can cause pain to both men and women.*

When gender is used to make the first cut, whatever gifts and abilities God has given to men and women may end up on a closet shelf. The sense of frustration that the denial of these gifts may generate is one consequence, but even more is the anger or sadness experienced when an intrinsic part of our personhood has been discounted.

Let me get personal. Many years ago, when my husband and I served as missionaries in Europe, I was sitting on our bed one morning reading Matthew 25. When I came to the end of the parable of the bags of gold, I found myself crying. And I prayed, "Lord, will you cut me some slack for not using what you've given me because the powers that be won't let me?" Gender had trumped gifting, and I felt helpless to do anything about it. That is not an uncommon experience for many Christian women.

Gifted women who feel shut down in complementarian churches have three choices: (1) stay put and keep their mouths shut; (2) stay put but make noise about the issue; or (3) leave the church. I've known many women trying to cope with their exclusion from the full use of their God-given gifts to the church. Some have stayed quietly, not knowing what to do with the pain they experienced. Others spoke out but were silenced and sometimes ridiculed. Many left in search of a different venue for the gifts and calling God had on their lives.

An Old Testament scholar who eventually chose to leave both the church and Christianity wrote this:

> While women sit silent, perhaps even unaware that they are dead-
> ening themselves in order to do so, others leave the churches and
> synagogues, cutting off their relation with the biblical God. In both

cases, women who once had powerful feelings about the God of biblical tradition may be denying part of themselves. They may be deadening their religious sensibility altogether, suppressing powerful, conflicting feelings toward God that come to them, perhaps, "in the night, tinged with hatred, with remorse, but most of all with infinite yearning." A woman who swallows her anger and bitterness at God may also cut off her longing for the God who provoked her to anger.[15]

A complementarian reading that paragraph may shake his head and, with a shrug, say, "See? This is what happens when women overstep the line God has drawn for them." But is there a better way to cope with women's fears, frustration, and even anger?

Men can also experience frustration about their confinement into spheres for which they feel they have no aptitude. In a 1996 unpublished study, numerous Christian men struggled to figure out how to be the "head" in the home.[16] One man wrote, "I am not a born leader. I am a follower. So I constantly struggle with playing the part of the leader." Another wrote, "Striving to understand what being 'leader' means and encompasses—the tension resolves as we talk things out" [an egalitarian approach to solving the problem]. Still another wrote, "What does it mean to be the head of the home? I thought at times I had to make tough decisions and even ignore her or overrule her feelings, her beliefs, her decisions, her wishes, never in the sense of the tyrant, but certainly in the sense of not being respectful of her. It caused much friction at times."[17]

---

15. Carol P. Christ, *Laughter of Aphrodite: Reflections on a Journey to the Goddess* (San Francisco: HarperSanFrancisco, 1987), 30. The quotation embedded in this paragraph is from Elie Wiesel's *The Town beyond the Wall*, 190.

16. Alice Mathews, "Prescription and Description: The Gap between the Promise and the Reality in Women's Experience of Hierarchical Marriage," PhD dissertation, University of Denver / Iliff School of Theology, 1996.

17. How then can couples resolve issues between them? It's not a question of taking turns being the head. In most cases, the person with the most invested in the issue or the most skill and experience in the task will take the lead in resolving or handling the matter.

Is this frustration and the tension in marriages caused by a doctrine of separate spheres honoring to God's intention for a couple pledged to one another for life? Is the pain this causes to both men and women something we can ignore?

My Personal Experience

At this writing, I am eighty-six, and my husband, Randall, is ninety. This year, we have celebrated sixty-five years of marriage to one another. We entered marriage as Christians who had just graduated from a Christian college and planned for a life together in Christian ministry. Over the years, God gave us four children and also gave us pastoral ministries in a number of places in North America and as missionaries in Europe for seventeen years.

We entered marriage in 1951. Recall that era: it was the only time in history when the Cult of True Womanhood was implemented in a social setting with a strong middle class. In the nineteenth century, less than 10 percent of the population was either middle- or upper-class. Most people were the working poor. But in the 1950s, the social climate gave the Cult of True Womanhood its best shot at success.

As a True Woman at that time (pious, pure, domestic, and submissive), I was ready to play my part as Randall's helper in the plumber's assistant mode. As he went through seminary, I typed his papers and gave piano lessons to supplement our meager income. As a pastor's wife, I focused on shoring up weak spots I saw in the church ministries, but always staying in the background. My role was the care of our four children and keeping an impeccable parsonage, always ready to welcome my husband's friends as our guests. (My highest accolade during those years was the comment made by the chairman of the church deacon board when he called me "Mrs. America," a title given to a woman who was the epitome of domesticity.)

But along the way, we hit bumps in the road. I assumed Randall would handle balancing the checkbook and any paperwork regarding finances, like income tax returns, etc. It turned out that his strong suit did not lie in that area, but because I come from a good line of engineers and have that DNA, I could unscramble hopelessly messed-up checkbooks and assemble neatly all of the pieces for tax returns, property purchases, etc. But in the 1950s, that wasn't what good married women did. Over time and out of that emerged our mutual realization that tasks should be assigned to one or the other by giftedness, not by gender. It was a good and happy turning point in our married relationship.

Though life has turned out well for the two of us, I've worked with too many devout Christian women for whom the story has been tragically different. Though complementarians have repeatedly moved the goalposts to make gender-based hierarchy seem softer and more palatable for godly women, the system itself reflects not God's original design for his image bearers, but a surrender to the ways of a sinful world. Why ask who's in charge? Does someone have to be in charge? Why not let God be in charge as we humbly work together for his kingdom?

TRUE COMPLEMENTARITY IN THE CHRISTIAN HOME AND CHURCH

God's model begins in Genesis 1: a man and a woman together were blessed by their Creator with a mandate to fill the earth and subdue it. They stood before God with anatomical differences, brain (thinking) differences, and differences in creative potential—and somehow they were to work together as one, together. This is the biblical picture of complementarity.

The difference between a man and a woman is not a call to assign them to separate spheres in life. The purpose in complementarity is to pool the unique resources of each as they work together in a common endeavor. It is a call for "all hands on deck," each bringing to their common task what is needed for success, contributing what would otherwise be lacking. Whether this is pooling brainpower for a more comprehensive grasp of the concept or challenge, or recognizing the opposite sex as a key player in common concerns, it is a call for men and women to stand shoulder to shoulder as comrades in God's kingdom.

In our world, many people think that women want the power men have. Some may, but that is not what this is about. It's not about men having to move over and share their authority with women. Jesus' last words to his followers before his ascension began this way: "*All* authority in heaven and on earth has been given to *me*" (Matthew 28:18, emphasis added). It is Jesus who has authority; we have a commission. Together we work under his authority. This is a radical revaluing of our working relationship within Jesus' kingdom. Ultimately, it's not about authority versus equality; it's about each one bringing to our common tasks what we can contribute.

Conclusion

Most of this book has dealt with biblical material that some think proves gender-based hierarchy for the people of God, the church. But a careful reading of Scripture forces us to rethink what we've been taught. Let me add one more biblical piece to our rethinking.

Madame Blocher-Saillens,[18] a theology professor and pastor of the largest Baptist church in France in the 1930s and 40s, points us to a seldom-noted factor in Genesis 3. When God questioned Adam about eating fruit from the forbidden tree, Adam immediately pointed his finger of blame at both Eve and God: "the woman you put here with me" (verse 12). But when God turned to Eve with the same question, she didn't blame Adam but pointed to the real source of sin, the serpent. When

---

18. The grandmother of renowned theologian Henri Blocher.

God then meted out punishments to the pair, he began with the ultimate source of trouble, the serpent, stating among other punishments, "I will put enmity between you and the woman" (verse 15). Blocher-Saillens makes a strong point that this enmity between Satan and the woman is real and ongoing: *"Satan poursuit lui aussi son plan, la guerre contre la femme, sa plus terrible enemie, continue* [Satan pursues his plan, continuing the war against the woman, his most terrible enemy]."[19]

Is it possible to take seriously this enmity between the devil and half the human race? Or do we dismiss it as irrelevant—or even hilarious? If the enemy of our souls can keep half the Christians in the world holding back the other half from active duty in service to God's kingdom, he has won a great victory.

C. S. Lewis's senior devil, Screwtape, in a letter to his junior devil, Wormwood, wrote, "Our policy, for the moment, is to conceal ourselves."[20] As a result, it's easy to be oblivious to dark forces at loose in the world. Do we really believe that "the devil has gone down to you ... filled with fury, because he knows that his time is short" (Revelation 12:12)? Do we take seriously the apostle John's observation that "the whole world is under the control of the evil one" (1 John 5:19)? In a world shot through with sin, in cultures that automatically default to gender-based hierarchy, do we really believe God's world is under assault by unchecked forces of evil? More to the point, in the light of that reality, do we see how we might innocently become complicit in the devil's warfare against God?

If gender-based hierarchy is allowed to continue destroying lives and disrupting God's work of redeeming a broken world, it plays into Satan's hand. You may respond, *"Oh, please,* it can't be that dramatic!" To think that is to ignore Paul's words to Ephesian Christians when he warned that "our struggle is not against flesh and blood, but against the rulers, against the authorities, against the powers of this dark world and against

19. Mme. Blocher-Saillens, *Liberees par Christ pour Son Service* (Paris: Les Bons Semeurs, n.d.), 10.
20. C. S. Lewis, *The Screwtape Letters* (1942; repr., New York: HarperOne, 2001), 31.

the spiritual forces of evil in the heavenly realms" (6:12). We cannot shrug off church history as if the millions of women's blighted lives didn't matter. The enmity between the serpent and the woman (Genesis 3:15) is an enmity from those powers of this dark world. It is ongoing. It is here. How will we respond to the challenge it presents?

Questions for Personal Reflection or Group Discussion

1. What difference does it make when people move the goalposts having to do with how men and women relate in the church and home?
2. From the brain difference studies, what do you think are possible consequences of failing to pool brain resources in decision making?
3. If it's true that Jesus has "all authority" and commissions us to work together for his kingdom, what difference can that make in how we think about leadership?
4. If the "Blessed Alliance" is one of God's two load-bearing walls in his world, how does this relate to the enmity between Satan and the woman?